P9-CCZ-142

Richard Nixon *A Psychobiography*

Richard Nixon *A Psychobiography*

VAMIK D. VOLKAN

NORMAN ITZKOWITZ

ANDREW W. DOD

COLUMBIA UNIVERSITY PRESS

New York

Columbia University Press
Publishers Since 1893
New York   Chichester, West Sussex
Copyright © 1997 Columbia University Press
All rights reserved
Library of Congress Cataloging-in-Publication Data

Volkan, Vamik D., 1932–
  Richard Nixon : a psychobiography / Vamik D. Volkan, Norman Itzkowitz,
and Andrew W. Dod.
     p.   cm.
  Includes bibliographical references and index.
  ISBN 0-231-10854-0 (alk. paper). — ISBN 0-231-10855-9 (pbk. : alk. paper)
  1. Nixon, Richard M. (Richard Milhous),—1913-   —Psychology.
2. Presidents—United States—Biography. I. Itzkowitz, Norman.
II. Dod, Andrew W., 1965- . III. Title.
E856.V58 1997
973.924'092—dc21   97-3477
                                                                                        CIP

Casebound editions of Columbia University Press books are printed
on permanent and durable acid-free paper.
Printed in the United States of America
c 10 9 8 7 6 5 4 3 2 1

For Elizabeth, Leonore, and Susie

Contents

Foreword by Blema Steinberg ix

Acknowledgments xi

1. Why a Psychoanalytic Biography? 1

PART ONE: *The Life of Richard Nixon* 21

2. Nixon's Parents 23
3. Childhood and Adolescence 32
4. Adulthood 40
5. Nixon as a National Figure 53

PART TWO: *The Mind and Personality of Richard Nixon* 67

6. A Bird's Eye View 69
7. Nixon's Personality: Exaggerated Self-Love
   and Dependency 89

PART THREE: *The Three Faces of Nixon's Personality
   in Policymaking and in Defeat* 107

8. Reflections of Grandiosity 109
9. Reflections of the Peacemaker 118
10. The Final Face: Enemies Everywhere 128

PART FOUR: *Afterword* 141

11. The "Real" Richard Nixon and the Resurrection
    of His Reputation 143

Notes 151

References 169

Index 177

Foreword

Blema S. Steinberg

In their study of Richard Nixon, authors Vamık Volkan, Norman Itzkowitz, and Andrew Dod have made a major scholarly contribution. Although there have been numerous political, historical, and psychological studies of Nixon written to date, this is the first detailed psychoanalytic portrait that has been made of this president, in terms of providing biographical information in conjunction with methodological references. What emerges from the pages of this book is an enhanced understanding of how and why Nixon developed into an excessively self-sufficient, ambitious, and driven man who so desperately needed to be "number one."

From their knowledge of normal child development, the authors have pinpointed specific traumatic events that occurred in Nixon's early life that led to the psychic derailment he experienced as he was growing up. Nixon's undisputed strengths as a political figure, his love of power, his determination, his ability to intellectualize and rationalize, and his refusal to accept defeat are explored within the parameters of the personality structure that formed within him.

Nixon's unconscious need for punishment and the reasons for his behavior—which, as we all know, culminated tragically for both him and the nation in the Watergate crisis that led to his resignation—is skillfully documented from earliest childhood through adolescence and adulthood. The authors provide insight into other unanswered questions about Nixon as well, such as his insistence on retaining the incriminating tapes. The matter of the "smoking gun," which has long puzzled so many observers, can be explained by what psychoanalysts term oral greediness and anal retentiveness on Nixon's part. The collection of tapes appears to have afforded Nixon a certain degree of emotional security—they represented tangible evidence for him that he was both powerful and loved.

The Nixon who emerges from the pages of this book is a truly humanized figure and a rather poignant one. He materializes as a troubled man—a classic example of the type of individual who somatizes and becomes physically ill whenever his grandiosity is not supported sufficiently by those around him. Specifically, Nixon's periodic bouts with sinus trouble and the timing of these occurrences are shown to be linked to anniversary reactions to his parents' deaths; and his development of painful phlebitis occurred at the height of the critical Watergate revelations, when external support for his narcissism was in short supply and at its lowest ebb.

In the realm of domestic and foreign policy, Volkan and his colleagues expose the unconscious determinants of many of Nixon's political decisions. His support of Vietnamization, for instance, was an expression of his emotional need for self-sufficiency and reflected his belief that only he could end the Vietnam war, a belief that underlined his grandiosity.

As a psychoanalyst and a political scientist, I believe that this psychobiographical portrait of Richard Nixon is notable for reasons that go beyond the light it sheds on a public figure who remains an enigma, despite the volume of research that exists on him. Firstly, it enriches the domains of both psychoanalysis and political science: the former, because it provides a powerful riposte to those psychoanalysts who are skeptical that useful analytic insights can ever be derived from any source other than the sanctity of the couch; the latter, because it offers convincing evidence that determinants of political behavior cannot be derived solely from the external environment—that the unconscious needs, fears, and fantasies of political leaders play a significant role. Secondly, this type of profile serves to educate the general reader about the value of conducting leadership studies. More specifically, systematic analysis of irrational leadership behavior can contribute to an ability to understand it and cope with it. In the case of a world leader such as Richard Nixon, the implications of irrational behavior have proved to have a profound impact on the realms of both domestic and foreign policy.

Blema S. Steinberg, Ph.D.
Department of Political Science
McGill University

Acknowledgments

Vamık Volkan, a psychoanalyst who has studied the psychology of international relations for decades, and Norman Itzkowitz, a historian with psychoanalytic training, have collaborated in writing two earlier books, one of which is a psychobiography of Mustafa Kemal Atatürk, the founder of modern Turkey. Their involvement in the present project was initiated by Andrew Dod, who was one of Itzkowitz's students at Princeton University. Dod was the first among us to become curious about the enigma of Nixon. In his attempt to make sense of the contradictory behavior patterns of the 37th President of the United States, he consulted with both Professors Itzkowitz and Volkan. Dod interviewed many prominent individuals who knew Nixon, among them H. R. Haldeman and John Ehrlichman (who was interviewed twice), and the tapes of these interviews were made available to us. The idea of the three of us collaborating on a book slowly emerged.

We wished to focus on Nixon's mind and personality, which would allow us to offer fresh insight into his behavior. We approached our subject as we would approach an individual on a psychoanalyst's couch. Gradually and systematically we collected various data that, on the surface, did not seem to be related. However, we found that the data could be linked together and, in fact, explained by psychoanalytic findings that dealt with the development of the human mind and the organization of one's personality. In writing about an influential leader, an author has to deal with the interferences coming from his or her feelings and perceptions of the individual. In order to neutralize our own biases, our work was done slowly and with much consultation among us. Since this is a study undertaken from a psychoanalytic perspective, it is inherently non-judgmental: it will come out neither "for" nor "against" Nixon.

In writing this book, aside from the interviews Dod conducted with persons close to Nixon, e.g., Roger Ailes, John Ehrlichman, H. R. Haldeman, James Hastings, Richard Helms, Don Oberdorfer, Elliot Richardson, Kenneth Rush, James St. Clair, Richard Schweiker, and General Brent Scowcroft, we relied on printed, televised and archival material, including the famous Nixon tapes. Additional information was provided by the following individuals through their interviews or through their participation in the oral history program at the Richard M. Nixon Project, California State University, Fullerton: Marcelina Arroues, Mr. and Mrs. William Barton, Dorothy Beeson, Jane Milhous Beeson, Sheldon Beeson, Rowe Boyer, Mr. and Mrs. Herman Brannon, Ollie Burdg, Blanche Burum, Irvin Chapman, Ellen Cochran, Hoyt Corbit, Virginia Shaw Critchfield, Ella Furnas, Richard Gauldin, Elizabeth Glover, James Grieves, Yoneko Dobashi Iwatsura, Helen Letts, Wayne Long, Blanche McClure, Lucille Parsons, Cecil Pickering, Mary Elizabeth Rez, Paul Ryan, and Gerald Shaw. Their contributions are greatly appreciated.

We also benefited from speaking about our work to colleagues: Salman Akhtar and Elizabeth W. Marvick, well-known psychoanalyst and political scientist, respectively, reviewed the first draft of our manuscript and provided further insight; Blema Steinberg, a political scientist as well as a psychoanalyst, was kind enough to show us three chapters of her working manuscript for *Shame and Humiliation: Presidential Decision Making on Vietnam*, which was recently published; Evelyn Speedie, former editorial assistant at the University of Virginia's Center for the Study of Mind and Human Interaction, not only helped greatly in editing this book in the initial stages, but also supplied us with new data on Richard Nixon's life. We would like to thank them, as well as Kurt Volkan, Diane P. Moore, and Carole Hamilton, who edited the book's final drafts, and all others who contributed in our quest to complete this project.

Vamık D. Volkan
Norman Itzkowitz
Andrew W. Dod
April 1997

It is not the critic that counts; not the man who points out how the strong man stumbles, or where the doer of deeds could have done them better. The credit belongs to the man who is actually in the arena, whose face is marred by dust and sweat and blood; who strives valiantly; who errs, and comes short again and again, because there is not effort without error and shortcoming; but who does actually strive to do the deeds; who knows the great enthusiasms, the great devotions; who spends himself in a worthy cause, who at the best knows in the end the triumphs of high achievement and who at the worst, if he fails, at least fails while daring greatly so that his place shall never be with those cold and timid souls who know neither victory nor defeat.

—*Theodore Roosevelt, Sorbonne, Paris, April 23, 1910*

Richard Nixon *A Psychobiography*

1

Why a Psychoanalytic Biography?

> It is a wide span from Watergate to psychoanalysis. But
> Richard Nixon closed the gap. His men invaded our
> space and brought Watergate in direct touch with
> the psychoanalysts' terrain. We might as well get some-
> thing out of it. Nothing can be better than an advance
> in knowledge.   —*Psychoanalyst Leo Rangell, 1976*

In March 1994, an eighty-one-year-old Richard Nixon visited Moscow. While there, acting against the wishes of Boris Yeltsin, he met with Russia's ultranationalist Vladimir Zhirinovsky. Bypassing Yeltsin to combat with someone perceived as a tyrannical enemy fit Nixon's personality. The words "battle," "fight," and "warfare" often appear in Nixon's writings, and he has expressed pride in taking risks and fighting battles in attempting to reach his political goals. To meet with the Russian leader was important to Nixon: one Russian source informed us that Zhirinovsky was paid a substantial sum of money to have a "confrontation" with Nixon.[1]

We can only assume that facing Zhirinovsky reminded him of another encounter he had once had in the then-Soviet capital; we certainly were reminded of his famous debate with Nikita Khrushchev. Nixon was a master of holding his own ground when facing "bad" men. On the way back to the United States after his last trip to Russia, Nixon stopped in London, where his friend and biographer, Jonathan Aitken, MP, gave a dinner party in his honor. At the party, Nixon, without notes, spoke for seventy minutes, giving a fluent analysis of his trip to Moscow, as well as of current international events. This is an example of how Nixon acted as the senior statesman of the United States in the last years of his life: in recovering his damaged self-esteem, he had begun to regain respectability in the eyes of the world.

A month later, on April 22, 1994, four days after suffering a stroke, Nixon was dead. At the time, we were finishing the first draft of this book, the writing of which had taken several years. Through our work, we felt that we had come to know him intimately, even though none of us had personally met him. After Nixon suffered the stroke, we (the authors) spoke on the phone and referred to Nixon as if we were expecting him to come out of his deep coma, "resurrecting" himself, as he had "resurrected" himself from his political death. Twenty years earlier, on August 9, 1974, in a nationally televised farewell to the White House staff in the East Room, the disgraced President had referred to Theodore Roosevelt's remarks about the death of his wife: "And when my heart's dearest died, the light went from my life forever." Nixon had "relit" his political "light," but alas, even "omnipotent" men ultimately must die.

Forty-two thousand people turned out at his funeral in Yorba Linda, California, to bid him farewell. President Bill Clinton called on Americans to remember the "totality" of the 37th President. If Nixon could have spoken at his own funeral, we assume that he would not have been able to resist making a remark such as, "for the *first time* in history five presidents of the United States and their five first ladies attended the funeral of a former President." He was a collector of "first times," whether they were great deeds or trivial events.

As Richard Nixon was being buried next to his wife, Pat, who had died a year earlier, the senior author was attending a meeting of the Gorbachev Foundation in Washington, D.C. Another attendee was Daniel Ellsberg, the man who had made the so-called "Pentagon Papers" public, and the man who is often considered to have initiated the process that led to President Nixon's downfall. At dinner Ellsberg told the American, Russian, and Indian participants of the meeting that he had received many calls from the media asking for his thoughts about Nixon's death. He said he had simply told them that the day belonged to the members of Nixon's family. Ellsberg then recalled how a few years ago, while driving around in California with his son, he had decided they should visit the Nixon Library. When they arrived, the main sections of the library were closed, although he was able to visit the gift shop where he decided to buy a recently published book on Nixon. Having written a check for his purchase, the saleslady asked to see his driver's license in order to verify his signature. Flipping through the pages of the book, Ellsberg told the woman that his name appeared in it many times. He joked that it was all right to have been forgotten; after all, twenty years had passed since he had been in the public eye.

Although we cannot say much about Daniel Ellsberg's current or future renown, we can say we believe Nixon will rank among the most remembered and talked about of Presidents. The reason is this: in spite of all that has been written about our 37th president—before and after his death—he remains an enigma. *The Washington Post* staff writer David Van Drehle, having interviewed many diplomats and scholars the day after the president's death, wrote in regard to Nixon's place in history: "Something about Nixon—the polarizing quality, the complexity of motives, the mystery of the motives—makes it unlikely the debate will be settled any time soon."[2]

Richard Nixon and his Secretary of State, Henry Kissinger, believed in "realism" more than "idealism" in politics and therefore attempted to make decisions and take actions according to rational political analysis.[3] Yet, some of Nixon's decisions and actions cannot be explained by rational thinking. For example, few political events epitomize irrational behavior as completely as the ill-conceived Watergate affair that toppled the Nixon White House. Even today scholars and investigative journalists continue to dig deep into extensive files, and talk show hosts continue to interview the convicted co-conspirators, in hope of understanding one of the most trivial but devastating decisions in the history of American politics. Early in 1996, a controversial Oliver Stone film called *Nixon* and a television movie on him have sparked renewed public interest and debate about Nixon and Watergate.

The fascination with Watergate has not abated since that day in 1974 when Nixon staunchly waved farewell to a scornful public. From that day until the time of his death, he attempted to substitute action and statesmanship for an explanation as to why he felt it necessary, in an election that for all intents and purposes had already been won, to act in connivance with a petty cover-up scheme. Just as he instructed his staff to "stonewall" the Senate Watergate committee back in the 1970s, Nixon exhibited a resolute determination to personally "stonewall" history for all eternity. Since some of his predecessors had organized successful cover-ups he seemed to think that he had simply repeated what others had done; this served as a justification for his involvement in the Watergate incident. He wrote: "The irony of this whole situation is that we are being accused of playing a foul game during the election and so forth, whereas what we have done as compared with previous administrations is hardly worth mentioning."[4] He once said that by the year 2024, fifty years after he left the White House, Watergate would be recalled only as a "footnote."

Throughout his campaign for rehabilitation, he encouraged the notion that the obstruction of justice and other offenses of his presidency were the final point in a direct line that ran from Lincoln's suspension of habeas corpus and FDR's circumvention of neutrality laws to the abuse of the Internal Revenue Service by Kennedy and Johnson. Like Lincoln, Nixon argued, he had to operate under "civil war" conditions. He even sent friends copies of Paul Johnson's *Modern Times*, which described Watergate as a "media putsch."[5]

The "exact truth" about Watergate may elude us forever, because it was an irrational act within a sea of seemingly rational patterns. Nixon and the others implicated in Watergate were obviously involved in conscious planning and decisionmaking, but the whole affair must also be considered an attempt to solve some unseen personal problems at the unconscious level. Thus, a complete analysis of the affair must also include Nixon's "psychic truth." In other words, we assume that multiple factors are interwoven with the President's involvement in Watergate and that some of them, without his being conscious of them, were attempts to gratify certain demands coming from deep inside himself. Thus, the wish or the need to break into the Democratic Headquarters was due mainly to a "reality" constructed mostly by the unconscious demands of Nixon's internal world.

A Psychoanalytic Perspective

This study is based on the premise that a psychoanalytic perspective can augment our potential to understand the seemingly irrational behavior exhibited during a given event. Such an approach helps us to assign meaning to unconscious motivations. Thus, we can seek out the unseen forces that led to Watergate by psychoanalytically examining Nixon's mind and meshing our findings with what is publicly known about his external sphere. Watergate, while perhaps a trivial affair in itself, had a historical impact that elevated its significance; it demonstrates how the internal world of a political figure can intrude into his conscious world, intermingling with external factors, i.e., political and economic, to affect a historical process.

If we adopt the premise that decisions and actions are multidetermined—that they have multiple conscious and unconscious meanings—then by exploring the "psychic truth" associated with Watergate, as traced through the subjective experiences of Richard Nixon, we can attain a higher level of comprehension. Everyone has feelings, wishes, fantasies, perceptions, and thoughts—some unconscious—that form an inner reality that may or may not reflect external reality as observed by others. On occasion, any person may feel compelled to act according to an internal "psychic truth," even when this may lead to an irrational occurrence. By delving into the unconscious layers of meaning behind Watergate, we can arrive at a more comprehensive story of one man's world of politics; we can learn something valuable about the nature of his leadership as well.

Individuals seek leadership positions for various conscious and unconscious reasons. A psychoanalytic developmental study (from childhood on) of a particular leader may resolve critical questions about that person's leadership and leadership in general, help to determine leadership criteria, and illuminate factors that lead to seemingly irrational acts.

Clearly, anyone who attains the exalted office of President brings along "baggage from the past." As we will explain later, Nixon pursued lofty aspirations while laboring under repeated setbacks. Overtly, he considered his actions rational, but covertly, many of them were, in fact, irrational. Many of his actions (for example, the "secret" bombing of Cambodia as well as his combative speech in May 1970 announcing another attack on Cambodia) to a great extent were based on unconscious motivations that contrasted sharply with the overt, strategic thinking that he displayed in other areas. He seemed to have had an unusual sense of entitlement that served him well in his historical achievements and he had a form of exaggerated self-love (narcissism) that directed him to be the leader of the world's most powerful nation. At the same time, however, he was also often dependent, miserly, envious, hungry for adulation, and sometimes trivial in matters that supported his sense of self-justification and well-being. Furthermore, while he usually campaigned well and had many followers, he also seemed to fear intimacy. We will show that Nixon lacked an internal cohesion, which brought about his downfall.

It is not our intention to offer a minutely detailed political biography. We are not going to review Nixon's achievements and failures in the political arena as such, for these facets of his life have been covered extensively elsewhere. For example, Ambrose's three massive biographical volumes provide a thorough detailed account of his early life, his political career, and his career as an international statesman.[6] Rather, we will use selected examples of his activities to demonstrate how his "psychic truth" was regulated by repeating overt and covert behaviors that affected the decisions he made and the actions he took. We will try to interpret the meaning behind these decisions and actions by analyzing the patterns we found in them. Using a psychoanalytic approach we will etch a sharper portrait of the peaks of Richard Nixon's career, and illuminate more fully the valleys. By looking at Nixon through a psychoanalytic lens, we feel that we have succeeded in providing a deeper and broader understanding of the elements that drove Nixon to his vaunted victories as well as to his disastrous defeats.

Before turning our attention fully to Richard Nixon, some background information about the psychoanalytic method will help the reader who is unfamiliar with this kind of investigation. First, we explain our concept of a "psychoanalytic biography" and then we summarize some essential findings on the development of the mind and personality.

Psychoanalytic Biography

The application of psychoanalytic findings and theories to biographical studies is hardly revolutionary, nor is it a clear-cut process. It is quite possible to take more than one approach when writing a psychoanalytic biography.[7]

Early psychoanalytic writings pertaining to biographies primarily sought to clarify the artist's inner motivations for creative work. At first, such writings focused on an interpretation of the symbols used in the artist's works of art. However, soon after psychoanalysis began to establish itself, psychoanalytic biography based on an interpretation of symbols became questionable. The reason for this is that symbols often have more than one meaning, and are less universal than Sigmund Freud assumed.[8] Advances in psychoanalysis have led to a shift in focus from symbols to the subject's actual life story and the open and hidden meanings of his experiences with his environment. In the 1960s Erik Erikson introduced his concept of the psychosocial stages of development, with the adolescent crisis of identity as a central notion.[9] He studied the psychology specific to every level of life and stated that in considering an individual's relationship with his society, we should focus on the years of adolescence during which time the individual expands his horizon from family and neighbors to a wider social existence. With Erikson's work, the character of psychoanalytic biography changed drastically.[10] Under this new stratagem, psychobiographies reflected the thinking that, "While the life space of the infant and child is restricted to the family, the historical situation is significant in the life of a young adult."[11] Subsequently, attention has also begun to be paid to mid-life crises.

In spite of all these advances, however, difficulties in the psychoanalytic approach to biography have persisted. Critics of psychoanalysis charge that what we observe on the surface is placed in the context of unconscious forces (they are called drives or instincts in psychoanalysis), which thereby distorts the surface picture. This accusation of reductionism should have been dispelled by Erikson's model, which included rigorous historical scholarship, but it was not.[12] Reductionism was still considered a most pernicious pitfall of psychoanalytic biography. Avner Falk argues, however, that reductionism should not be equated with the "nothing but" fallacy. He adds, moreover, that reductionism "is a legitimate scientific method because, in truth, all science is reductionist."[13]

Regardless of these viewpoints, it is important to remember that psychoanalysis can be a useful and profound tool of investigation above and beyond the context of discovering and rediscovering that individuals share similar unconscious drives or traverse similar psychosexual and other developmental ladders. Psychoanalysis demonstrates that individuals have their own unique ways of dealing with the demands of their inner world, as influenced by external events and the mental images of these events. It further shows the scope of the nearly endless creative abilities of the human mind. Thus, the approach to psychoanalytic biography that we have adopted in this book involves an examination of our subject's *total life*, and the interaction between his inner and outer worlds throughout the individual's life, beginning in childhood.[14] Following the model established by Volkan's and Itzkowitz's biography of Mustafa Kemal Atatürk we are taking a *developmental approach* in our psychoanalytic biography of Nixon.[15]

Our method should satisfy those critics who fear reductionism, who perceive psychoanalysis as a method that forces us to find *one* causal factor, one germ, in the development of an adult's mind. To those who ask questions such as: why would one person with a certain childhood history, i.e. repeated childhood losses, grow up to become a leader while another person with a similar childhood history grow up to become a carpenter? we would answer that each child's (mostly unconscious) "interpretation" of even very similar events will differ and each experience will "settle in" to their respective minds differently. Furthermore, there is a constant dialogue between one's inner and outer worlds which, like physical appearance, will differ in every person. One's level of intelligence, education, social circumstance, and expected or unexpected opportunities find echoes in the individual's inner world. In turn internal motivations shape the perception of external events, sometimes initiating or modifying thinking and actions in life. This confluence of factors explains why a good psychobiography must take a developmental approach and investigate the subject's entire life.

Perhaps then it goes without saying that the amount of available data will have an effect on the sophistication of the biographer's final product. In our efforts to understand the inner world of one whom we have not known as a patient on the psychoanalytic couch, it is inevitable that we will encounter difficulties. But before we describe those difficulties and begin our analysis of Nixon's mind, let us describe the specific psychoanalytic concepts that are necessary for understanding the mind of a patient on the couch. In writing a psychoanalytic biography, all of the following concepts need to be considered.

Mental Conflicts: At various times during psychoanalysis a patient—an analysand—tells his version of his childhood and adulthood history. He reports repeated behavioral patterns that in themselves connect his childhood experiences and adult reactions with events that consciously and unconsciously remind him of "dangerous" situations that were present earlier in his life. The danger comes from conflicts in the evolution of a sense of self—his attempt to find identity—as well as from the clash between unconscious, unacceptable needs and wishes and prohibitions against them.

Conflicts are normal in the dynamics of life; the life process includes conflicts. Every creature in the world clashes with its environment in its efforts to preserve its own existence. But for a human being, who possesses a highly complicated mind—which evolves slowly—conflicts do not simply originate from external environmental pressures. Human beings also must contend with an internal environment, some aspects of which, such as a death wish for a family member or friend, clash with other aspects of this same world, such as one's conscience. When our internal world interacts with external reality, our perceptions, fantasies, and feelings influence how we "interpret" what happens in the external world. We must deal with conflicts within our internal world as well as those which arise from our interactions with our external environment. When a child solves his conflicts without damaging the integrity of his psyche, his mind grows, since he has gained strength by his new ability to deal with things that previously had troubled him.

Unresolved conflicts are sensed as unpleasant feelings, that is, anxiety. The individual with these unpleasant feelings must resort to defensive mental measures to deal with them. This may include pushing those conflicts into the shadows of the mind (repression); staying away from relationships or events which are reminders of childhood dangers (avoidance); flexing muscles in the face of danger (counterphobia), and so on. The different mental mechanisms used may remain "foreign" to the individual, or he may absorb them into his developing personality and "own" them. Events that are perceived, fantasized, and experienced internally as being so dangerous that they cannot be absorbed by the individual's existing adaptations, and thus cannot be resolved, become classified as traumatic.

There are internal threats and conflicts present in every childhood. The human infant is helpless and dependent for a long time after birth and cannot survive without a mother or a mother-substitute. Children naturally perceive the threat and/or the reality of losing the mother and/or her love as dangerous. Later, this fear is accompanied by a related, perceived threat to body parts; that is, the child feels that he will lose body parts, as punishment, because of unacceptable impulses or desires. Anxiety is therefore induced. As the child grows older, his internal world expands, and he "takes in" what he believes to be his parents' and his society's attitudes, values, and inhibitions, making them his own. At the same time, he identifies with the idealized image of his parents that he has formed. He fears loss of self-esteem if he fails to live up to this ideal image, so he may preempt or "second-guess" his "internal parents" by punishing himself for his impulses and desires to commit acts that might be considered unacceptable.[16]

The "dangerous" events to which we allude here lie on a spectrum that ranges from the biological loss of life to psychological loss of self-respect. As an adult, an individual going through psychoanalysis may still utilize certain specific, adaptive or maladaptive mental operations whenever events occurring in adulthood unconsciously remind him of dangerous childhood events. Once this individual's repression is lifted through the help of the analyst, and he no longer hides from his awareness of images, memories, and feelings of his childhood, his recollection of his childhood history may change as the psychoanalysis progresses.

By way of illustration, let us consider the example of a man consumed by the image of a harsh father in childhood. The man may, in time, come to realize that because of early competition with his father and expectations of punishment, he had, in his own mind, overemphasized the harsh side of his father. He may have perceived his father as dangerous, while this may not actually have been so. Through psychoanalysis this individual explores his conscious and unconscious fantasies. This may lead him to change or modify his perception of his childhood father or other father-substitutes to the point where he is able to react differently to the father, or his substitute, in his present environment. In a similar way, a man who begins his analysis by insisting that his mother was an angel may later allow himself to admit some of her shortcomings and understand the reasons for his idealization of her in the first place, enabling him to overcome the defensive perception that caused him to do so. An individual's own history changes in accordance with changes in his internal world.

Transference Neurosis: The psychoanalytic process is much more complicated than simply telling one's history and finding connections between lifetime events. It involves more direct expressions of unconscious content and examination of previously unconscious conflicts and traumatic events. For example, dreams—which are a biologically determined phenomenon—have contents with hidden meanings. Psychoanalysts are trained to make use of dreams in the course of analysis, but the understanding of an analysand's mind is augmented even further by the development and resolution of what is called *transference neurosis*.[17]

Transference refers to the unconscious displacement of impulses, feelings, thoughts, behavior, and even part of oneself—and the mental defenses against them—from relations with significant people experienced in childhood (such as the mother or father) to other people or objects in adulthood relationships. In psychoanalysis, the patient displaces feelings and perceptions from childhood relationships onto the analyst, who nurtures the transference in order to develop it more fully. The analysand initiates stories with his analyst that symbolize past events, conscious and unconscious fantasies, feelings, and expectations, along with all the anxieties and defenses that pertain to them. As these stories take center stage, with their accompanying emotions in the psychoanalytic sessions (which are conducted from four to five times a week in order to create the necessary intensity to sustain the stories) we say that the individual in analysis is developing a transference neurosis.

Transference neurosis is the heart of the clinical psychoanalytic process. Through it the analysand experientially "re-lives" the mental organization of his childhood. When the transference neurosis is understood through the analyst's interpretations, and is resolved, the analysand can develop more adaptive ways of handling situations that were previously perceived as dangerous. It is through this examination of the transference and the experience of the transference neurosis that an analyst can, with certainty, procure a full history of an analysand's inner world, that is, his "psychic truth."[18]

Countertransference: This concept refers to the stimulation of some reaction on the part of the analyst during the treatment of a patient. This reaction may come about in response to an analysand's transference, or it may be caused by the analyst experiencing the analysand as someone from his own past, and unconsciously acting accordingly. The analyst's ability to notice countertransference reactions in himself is what keeps the analytic work on track. Every psychoanalyst's training includes his own personal analysis and many years of supervised work in order to facilitate his utilization of countertransference in adaptive ways. In writing a psychobiography such as this one, countertransference is a highly significant factor because the writer may unconsciously base his perceptions of the subject on elements from his own childhood background. Thus, it is important to tame one's countertransference.[19]

Substitutes for Transference Neurosis: In writing a psychoanalytic biography of a subject who has not been a patient on the couch, the most crucial task is to examine one's own countertransference and find substitutes for transference neurosis.[20]

Although it is not possible to achieve the same level of revelation in psychoanalytic psychobiography as in clinical psychoanalysis, we can obtain valuable information by focusing on a public figure's transferences in other areas. We can identify *repeating* ways in which he relates to others, to events, and to himself. For example, in the course of their research for the abovementioned psychobiography of Atatürk, Volkan and Itzkowitz interviewed many individuals who knew the Turkish leader personally. They found that an unusual number of those interviewed reported how Atatürk gave them a type of oral examination when they first met him. Once the writers picked up on this pattern they used it to tease out the meaning of this ritual in Atatürk's life.[21] The style an artist adopts in a series of paintings or the recurring themes that appear in a writer's novels may provide similar insight into the unconscious aspects of the mind of the artist or writer, irrespective of the artistic merits of the specific work in question. In describing Richard Nixon, for instance, we will note his repeated insistence on claiming "historical firsts," whether they heralded important events or trivial ones.

Personality: As an individual grows and the mind evolves, he develops a personality. Everyone has a personality; the term refers to observable, customary, and—under average expectable circumstances—repeating patterns of an individual's day-to-day behavior. This pattern is stable and it does not cause concern for the individual.

Personality is an umbrella term that includes what is commonly known as character, temperament, moral standing, and humanness. An individual's personality "absorbs" the effects of the dangerous situations of his developmental years as well as mental defenses against them. Thus, by wearing our personality, or our habitual way of being, as if it were armor, we escape from feeling anxiety engendered by psychological conflicts and traumas. Personality also absorbs the influence of the individual's biologically determined forces and potentials.

Our personality helps us to maintain a stable reciprocal relationship between ourselves and our environment. It also helps to determine the harmony within our inner emotional life and interpersonal relationships.[22] A personality, however, can be chronically maladaptive, that is, a constant source of conflict in relating to others and in maintaining one's own self-esteem. In spite of this, even the maladaptive personality generally is accepted and not questioned by the individual himself.

A political leader's mental *symptoms*—e.g., repetitious disturbing thoughts, sexual deviations, phobias, depressions—may not be known to a psychobiographer unless the subject or those close to the subject have reported them. Symptoms of a mental nature are felt as "alien" and disturbing for the individual. Most likely, he chooses not to inform the public about their existence. But, a political leader's personality is not hidden. The most readily observable aspects of his inner world come to light because so much of political behavior is public. Personalities, therefore, can be observed, but a mental symptom, such as an unwelcome thought, cannot.

In order to understand President Nixon's personality better, it is necessary to review briefly the typical events that affect the developing person and thus are "absorbed" into the personality. To do so we must examine some key elements of childhood development.

The Development of Mind and Personality

Environmental circumstances, including broken homes, abuse or love from parents, and level of wealth, help to shape any developing child's inner world, but the early environment alone does not explain the total nature of an individual's personality. A child is not a thoroughly helpless partner who reacts passively to external events and assimilates their effect. Instead, children respond to their environment according to their given biological and psychological capabilities, with their perceptions and understanding of events, which are colored by their own personal fantasies about these events. Each child absorbs experiences with his environment, and these internalized experiences become the building blocks of his developing personality. Psychologically, the first crucial environment experienced by the child centers around the mother.

The Mother-Child Relationship

If the human infant is to develop in an uncomplicated way, he must be assured of much more than just physical fulfillment from the mother. In the same way that he depends on his mother (or her substitute) for all his physical requirements, he must also receive "good-enough mothering" for his emotional needs.[23] If the mother repeatedly fails to respond to cues furnished by the baby concerning his needs, her ministrations will be misguided or out of phase, and the infant's normal course of development will suffer. Thus, we must pay close attention to the significance of the mother-child relationship. All the people, other than the mother or her substitute, surrounding the child—the father, siblings, etc.—are experienced, emotionally speaking, within the confines of the dyadic mother-child relationship until the child approaches three or four years of age (the oedipal stage). Then the child becomes truly involved in triadic and, later on in life, multiple relationships.

Infants are not mindless creatures capable of only biological functions. Researchers now know that infants and very young children possess a heightened level of innate abilities[24] and that they can sense, in primitive ways, boundaries that separate them from the primary caregiver. But, for practical purposes, until the child finds his individuality he goes through a phase in which he is one member of a psychological unit—the child-mother unit. This phase is known as the *symbiotic* phase. In other words, in the minds of very young infants, the boundaries separating them from the mother or primary caregiver remain permeable or blurred—at first to a greater extent, and later on, less so—until the child slowly matures and finds his own individuality, at about three years of age.[25]

Self-identify

The mother-child relationship is the foundation from which the child's developing mind and personality is based. As such, it has a profound effect on the process of establishing a self-identity, a process which cannot be completed overnight. It involves various factors, such as the potential of the genes with which the child has been biologically endowed as well as the child's family and cultural environment. All of these factors go through the "channel" of the mother-child relationship and become the construction blocks from which the developing child can build an identity and personality. Once various life experiences combine with the child's biologically determined potential, the child's initial unformed mental world can begin to organize itself step-by-step. Then the child gradually becomes able to differentiate between the various aspects of himself—e.g., his pleasurable self, painful self, angry self, etc. He must integrate these different nuclei in order to achieve a cohesive sense of self. In normal development, after initial confusion, the infant progresses from viewing the world as black or white, either "bad" (unpleasant and dangerous) or "good" (pleasurable and safe)—to seeing greys (achieving integration where "good" and "bad" images intertwine realistically).

The process during which the child develops an integrated sense of self and the foundation of his personality is vulnerable to many types of intrusions. For example, some children who encounter disturbances in the mother-child relationship during the first years of life often become prematurely independent; they have an exaggerated self-reliance and feel that they are above all others, while in fact, in a hidden way, they remain psychologically dependent on their caregivers. This may signal the beginning of what psychoanalysts call a *narcissistic* personality, which is characterized as a defensive exaggerated self-reliance and expansion of one's sense of self while covertly holding onto a dependent and "hungry" self.[26] Other children may begin to lay the foundations of other personality types. Some lay the foundation of an *obsessional personality*, in which exaggerated attempts to control one's unacceptable impulses are absorbed. As the child develops, many factors influence the shaping of his personality. Events and available mental reactions from one phase of the developmental ladder combine with events and available mental reactions from another phase to crystallize how the person will habitually behave.

The Oedipus Complex

Although we have focused thus far on the mother-child interaction as the springboard for the beginning of the organization of the child's personality, we cannot avoid referring to the importance of other relationships in the child's immediate environment that further help him to individuate. As we have noted previously, intrapsychically speaking, the child initially interprets others in his environment within the framework of a dyadic relationship. In the course of the child's development, however, his mind is influenced by his father, grandparents, siblings, teachers, and others, in their own right. In writing a psychoanalytic biography we need to address the nature of our subject's triadic and multiple relationships, along with the overriding influence wielded by the initial twosome. We need to keep a continuum in mind.

In psychoanalysis, we examine the early father-child relationship mainly within the framework of what is known as the Oedipus complex. For the purpose of this Nixon psychobiography, our focus will be on the male child's Oedipus complex only. The male child deals with oedipal issues from the ages of three or three and one-half to five or five and one-half years. During this time, in the child's mind, the father enters the scene as an increasingly distinct actor who modifies the dual mother-child relationship, making it a triadic father-mother-child relationship. During the oedipal period the child unconsciously aspires to reach a "sexual" union with the mother. The child's conscious perception of this endeavor will depend on his ability to control his impulses and cognitive capacities. Some male children may actually express the wish to marry their mothers, and they may say that they want their fathers to disappear. One would need to look very closely, with a trained eye, to determine in any specific situation the real emotional impact of the Oedipus complex on a particular male child.

The unconscious wish for union with the mother creates what is known as the threat of "castration," where male children have fantasies— often expressed in hidden forms—about being castrated or mutilated by their fathers in retaliation for involvement with the mother. During the oedipal period the father is the child's greatest rival, but we know that fathers generally do not go around castrating or mutilating their male offspring. Of course, in some cases, some fathers may do so symbolically due to their own unresolved oedipal complexes and/or other psychic problems. (Some may actually threaten their children with castration or other bodily harm.) It is important to bear in mind that although the threat of castration is a fantasy of childhood, it can have an emotional impact as though the possibility really exists.

Resolution of the Oedipus complex can be difficult if the environment keeps the son from taming this fearful fantasy. For example, if the father dies when his son is at the oedipal age, and if there is no substitute father figure available to the child, the fantasy may persist. If, on the other hand, the father is alive but is in reality harsh and punitive, his image will do little to help the son resolve the oedipal passage adaptively by identifying with a "good" father.

In a normal situation the Oedipus complex is resolved when, after struggling with his father, the boy comes to identify with him at last. This development is referred to as *identification with the aggressor*.[27] During identification the child becomes more like his rival, and instead of fighting with him he joins him, becoming like his father, a man. This internal joining paradoxically causes the child to separate himself from his intense involvement in the preceding family drama. At this point the child becomes more independent. When a boy succeeds in negotiating the Oedipus complex he turns a corner, establishing himself as an individual who will feel comfortable with his manhood. When he is unsuccessful he will, as an adult, include and maintain certain unconscious maneuvers in his personality in order to deal with the continuing influence of the complex. For example, he may develop a pattern of doing something self-destructive whenever he is at the peak of success. It is as if by indulging in self-destructive behavior the individual says to his father's image—which is now located within his own mind[28] "Look Dad! I castrated myself. You don't need to hurt me!" Sigmund Freud emphasized the male child's inability to accept success if he was not psychologically prepared to surpass his father.[29] According to this scenario, the son with oedipal problems always fears that the father will punish him, so he does the next worse thing—he punishes himself.

After the Oedipal Period

Classical psychoanalysis tells us that the foundation of a man's psychic organization is laid down and completed by the time he passes through the oedipal period and adaptively or maladaptively resolves the oedipus complex. However, life continues. Modern psychoanalysts, such as Erik Erikson, have stated that every phase of life—from infancy to old age—has its own psychology.[30] Most important here is that the early foundations of a person's psychic organization influence him for the rest of his life. It is not our intent here to review the psychology of each stage of the life cycle, but to outline those that affect personality.

The period between the oedipal years and puberty is called the *latency years*. During this time a child normally channels his energy into education and the acquisition of new skills. Sexual and aggressive drives are held in abeyance while considerable ego development takes place. In other words, the child develops new functions to help him cope with life. As the child enters adolescence he encounters another period of obligatory psychological emotional turmoil and adjustment, but at that point he is equipped with more fully developed ego armament. The adolescent passage functions as a strainer through which all the influences of the foundation years pass.[31] If the strainer is a fine one, it holds back certain rough ingredients; what passes through, therefore, is more refined.

Until they go through adolescence, youngsters are considered to have only character traits, i.e., they are thought to be either phobic, brave, shy, aggressive, or some combination of these, but they do not have a totally crystallized character. During adolescence, the youth has the chance to reexamine internally and overhaul the contents of his earlier (pre-oedipal and oedipal) experiences. The surface picture of this process is evident in the turmoil that accompanies adolescence. Once they go through adolescence, however, individuals develop a rather unalterable *total* personality which absorbs the various existing character traits. This final personality is not the sum total of the character traits of childhood, but includes the character traits that have been modified, newly created, or surrendered during the adolescent passage.[32] If the child's experience has been rather normal up to this time, he will gain more mature ego functions, and at the end of the overhaul he may either surrender or modify maladaptive character traits that had been brought into play during childhood conflicts. With the new ego functions now at his disposal, he is better equipped to deal with conflicts that had been impossible to resolve earlier. Moreover, as the individual loosens up and changes his psychic investments in the images of his parents and others who had influenced him during childhood, he is better able to invest in a wider range of what the world can offer him.

A person's ability to pass through adolescence triumphantly depends upon the psychic structures that have accompanied him to this phase in his life. There is a reciprocal effect here: successful adolescence may modify certain malignant effects of the earlier years, but success may also depend on the nature of the original earlier experiences. Traumatic environmental factors during adolescence may preclude the transformation of certain maladaptive character traits, allowing them to be absorbed unchanged into the total personality. In fact, youngsters who face trauma in adolescence may strengthen their earlier character traits as a defense and absorb the exaggerated versions into their total personality. The individual's newly crystallized personality will be a factor in propelling him toward this or that direction in his late teen years and in adulthood.

Unconscious Fantasies

An individual's personality also "absorbs" the impact of unconscious fantasies. One of the major differences between psychoanalysis and other psychotherapies is the emphasis on the reconstruction of the patient's unconscious fantasies. This is why a psychoanalytic biography must strive to illuminate the subject's unconscious fantasies even though supporting data may not be readily available.

Throughout childhood, unconscious fantasies affect the mother-child, father-child, and sibling-child relationships. In the child's formative years, the child cannot be considered a passive partner because he will modify reality according to private wishes and unconscious fantasies. It should be noted here that we are not speaking of conscious fantasies or daydreams, such as made-up stories of success in business or in our love lives. Instead, we are referring to a child's hidden fantasies that center around wishes and mental defenses against these wishes. Our adult conscious fantasies may or may not reflect our childhood unconscious fantasies.

In order to understand the concept of unconscious fantasy, imagine a child who perceives an event and "interprets" it according to whatever mental capacity he has at the time, who mixes it with his wishes and defenses against them, and who comes to a conclusion that, from an adult point of view, seems illogical. To illustrate, let us describe some typical unconscious fantasies. For example, a child may perceive of love-making between parents as a fight between them; if this unconscious fantasy is not effectively repressed later in life, it may induce in the individual some hesitation in making love. A child with a pregnant mother may unconsciously fantasize that he enters his mother's womb and "kills" his sibling so he will forever remain his mother's only darling; the symbolic expression of this wish may trigger fear of retaliation from the siblings, and may even result in a phobia about being in enclosed spaces.[33] At the oedipal age, as we indicated earlier, a male child has an unconscious fantasy that his father will castrate or mutilate him because of competition for the mother's love; any real or fantasized aggressive behavior on the part of a father-substitute may trigger these fears in the adult.

One common fantasy, which exists in some political leaders, is that of "rescuing" a caregiver too depressed or emotionally constricted to meet a child's needs adequately. To rescue a parent means to respond to the parent's wish, unconsciously, in order to gratify the wish and make the parent happy. As with other unconscious fantasies, rescue fantasies that are not effectively repressed can lead to either adaptive or maladaptive behavior patterns.[34]

Clinical work in psychoanalysis discloses much about the nature of unconscious fantasies, thus helping to reveal the hidden agents that influence a person's life. When something is brought out into the open its sinister power diminishes or disappears, and this enables the individual to find more adaptive ways of handling it. After all, it is easier to deal with a known enemy than with a hidden one.

Focus on Richard Nixon

In researching material for this psychobiography, we followed the premise that, just as in a clinical situation or with a creative endeavor, the psychobiographical subject has "products" and creations that are available for examination. In Richard Nixon's case, we looked at his political thinking, decisions, and actions as his "products" and creations and we selected certain ones for closer examination.

As with our clinical patients, clearly our goal here is to seek explanations. Why would a man with as much intelligence as Nixon had, and with the ability to govern the most powerful nation on earth, behave at times "irrationally" and in a self-destructive manner? Why did he collect "historical firsts?" Why did he behave like a tough man yet have anxiety about firing a person who worked for him? Why did he appear very moralistic and "clean" while he bypassed personal integrity and frequently used "dirty" words while talking with his staff and others? Why did he order the bombing of Cambodia when many of his aides advised him not to do so? Why did he become "frantic" during the 1972 presidential campaign against Senator George McGovern, at a time when there seemed little doubt that he would win the election? Why did Nixon hold onto the Watergate tapes instead of destroying them? These questions point to areas of Nixon's behavior that have remained a mystery.

In addressing certain aspects of Nixon's life we may at times seem to attach importance to trivial information, and sometimes our information may even appear to be a bit implausible. For example, the reader will note that we place great emphasis on young Richard being a "cry baby." We have information from various sources that Richard cried a great deal when he was an infant and a year-old child. However, we do not know the actual quality and quantity of his crying or the reason for it. Was he hungry? Was he furious about something? Did he have colic? Was he beaten? Was he afraid of adults? What were his mother's reactions above and beyond what we have been told indirectly?

Our lack of firsthand information is not necessarily an impediment to our psychoanalytic research. When we have an adult patient on the couch, he does not and cannot give us a direct account of what happened to him, let us say, in the first year of his life. Instead, he may only report what he has heard from others. During the analytic process, however, he may "recall" the specifics of whatever occurred in his early life through his involvement in his transference neurosis, by discussing the content of his dreams, and so on. After all, "psychic truth" greatly influences the mind, in spite of reality testing. It is important to realize that the reconstruction that occurs during analysis is *not* a replica of actual truth. Instead, it refers to the mental image of the actual truth, and it shows how the experiences of events settle in the mind.

Similarly, we should not concern ourselves too much with learning all the actual truths about Nixon, such as the reasons for his excessive crying as a child. We are more interested in determining what being a "cry baby" may have meant to him, and how it settled in the structure of his developing mind. Obviously our reconstruction of the meaning of his excessive childhood crying can be explained only within the framework of our observations concerning his repeated behavior patterns. Our ideas about Nixon will parallel findings based on our experiences with actual patients on our couches who had histories and adult behavior manifestations that were similar to Nixon's, but because each individual "interprets" life events differently, the similarities are not decisive. Our clinical experiences guide us to make predictions that we test by collecting data about repetitive behavior to see if the usual responses obtain. We are, therefore, dependent upon the availability of sufficient information about our subject. For instance, our patients' private sexual histories are remarkably helpful in illustrating the nature of their inner worlds.

Although data about Nixon's sexual nature were not available to us, we have been able to learn something about his relationships with women.

In spite of the difficulties associated with creating a psychobiography of someone who has not been treated by us personally, we have gathered sufficient material to make us confident in our assessment of Richard Nixon. In order, then, to present our findings about this complex man in the most thorough manner possible, we have organized some of our material chronologically (Part 1), some according to its relationship to Nixon's personality (part 2), and some according to what we call the "three different faces" of Richard Nixon (Part 3). At the end we wonder who was the 'real" Nixon and consider how he was able to resurrect himself after leaving the presidency in disgrace (Part 4).

PART ONE

The Life of Richard Nixon

2

Nixon's Parents

Our enigmatic 37th President was born in a small California town in 1913, forty-eight years after Robert E. Lee surrendered to Ulysses S. Grant at Appomattox Court House. Many aspects of Richard Nixon's conceptualization of the world can be best understood if placed within the context of the period of American history between Lee's surrender and Nixon's birth.

For four years brother had fought brother in a war that caused an agonizing loss of life, self-esteem, and fortune. When the fighting ended, a period of national mourning was necessary in order for a healing process to begin. Mourning is a human response to loss or threat of loss, and any loss inflicts an emotional wound of some kind, even for a large group like a nation. Under the umbrella of a large group, people share certain responses to a loss or change. This involuntary procedure, with its predictable phases, is similar to the physical process of the development of scar tissue. Just as an individual mourns after a personal loss, so should a large group like a nation be expected to share mourning after a historical trauma.[1]

The massive residual effects of the Civil War remain in evidence to this day in the United States, as exemplified by the North/South dichotomy and by various social, economic, and political transformations that have occurred since then.[2] In 1863, Abraham Lincoln urged the preservation of the Union in his Gettysburg Address; in his second inaugural address, in 1865, he exhorted the American people to "bind up the nation's wounds" to initiate and complete the process of mourning. By the time Richard Nixon was born, mourning over the war was so nearly complete that the nation was ready to mobilize; there was a new kind of energy that can become available only when the emotional investment over what has been lost is loosened.

The forging of the new nationalism that served to unite the house so recently divided against itself proved to be instrumental in this process of healing. The restoration of nationalistic pride contributed to America's expanding industrialism, with industries old and new spreading into virgin territory and pumping an urgent vibrancy into the nascent national economy. This expansionary process was facilitated by the measured development of a national transportation system and infrastructure. With the need for greater mobility having been met, an industrial marketing system was devised to satisfy increased consumer demands.[3] This new nationalism generated sufficient vitality to enable America to look beyond its geographical boundaries, as they were then defined.

Late-nineteenth-century and early-twentieth-century Americans viewed their continental arena from the secure vantage point of a solid domestic foundation that was based on expansionistic capitalism.[4] The driving forces of movement and change that dominated the American scene were fueled by such concepts as Manifest Destiny and Social Darwinism. British philosopher Herbert Spencer (1820–1903) merged his social ideas with those of British naturalist Charles Darwin (1809–1882), applying the developmental theories of Darwin's *Origin of Species* to the social sphere. Spencer propounded the suggestion that societies, like species, are influenced by the law of natural selection, and that only the most fit survive and progress. This doctrine, popular during the nineteenth century, was consistent with the notion of the new entrepreneurial American identity: those who were poorly motivated, people who refused to "get up and go" in order to meet the growing nation's demands, were not contributing to its progress. Political, economic, and social revisions, along with expansion and growth, permeated American society during this formative period.

Naturally, changes came about, but when they did they often proved too abrupt. As psychoanalyst Erik Erikson notes, America "subjects its inhabitants to more extreme contrasts and abrupt changes during the lifetime of a generation than is normally the case with other great nations."[5] America's transformations created two separate, antithetical "truths." According to Erikson, the American identity is based on a continuous oscillation between sets of polar opposites:

... the functioning American, as heir of a history of extreme contrasts and abrupt changes, bases his final ego identity on some tentative combination of dynamic polarities such as migratory and
sedentary, individualistic and standardized, competitive and coop-
erative, pious and free-thinking, responsible and cynical, etc.[6]

Richard Nixon's parents embodied this dichotomy of "truths" as
described by Erikson. Theirs was the generation most affected by
America's abrupt changes, casting them in the unsettling position of having to endure and contend with its growing pains.

Frank Nixon

The Nixon family background is deeply rooted in America, with ties to
European ancestry. In its various forms the name Nixon is Celtic for "he
wins" or "he faileth not." Richard Nixon's paternal ancestors were Scots
who had moved to Ireland during the seventeenth century. Later, in the
early eighteenth century, they joined the wave of Scottish-Irish immigra-
tion to America. James Nixon, who settled in Delaware in the 1730s, was
the first of the family to arrive. His two sons, George and James Jr., fought
in the War of Independence, the former crossing the Delaware with
George Washington to fight in the Battle of Trenton. When the war
ended, the two brothers went west and settled in Ohio. George Nixon III
served in the Civil War in Company B, 73rd Ohio. He died at Gettysburg,
leaving eight children, including a son named Samuel. On April 10,
1873, Samuel, then twenty-six years old, married Sarah Ann Wadsworth,
a schoolteacher. In time they had two daughters and three sons, including Francis Anthony (born December 3, 1878), who became known as
Frank. Frank was Richard Nixon's father.

From various sources we have been able to piece together an account
of Richard Nixon's father that portrays him as a distraught, frustrated,
and generally unhappy man.[7] An examination of anecdotes and impres-
sions provided by his family and friends, indicates that deep within Frank
Nixon there seems to have been an angry and basically mean-spirited
individual whom others took pains to avoid and feared encountering
face-to-face. Apparently, he made people uncomfortable in his presence,
for he evoked intense emotions and did little to appear amiable. His life,
in fact, consisted of hardships, bad luck, and losses, leading him to know
great frustration, discouragement, and humiliation. It seems he felt compelled to share his unhappiness with others.

We could gain some insight into Frank Nixon's adult behavior if we
could delve into his developmental years. However, since there are fewer

details available to us about his childhood than there are about his son Richard's, our perception of Frank's personality makeup is restricted and should in no sense be considered a complete picture.

We do know that young Frank had a difficult childhood and adolescence. When his mother contracted tuberculosis soon after his birth, his father took the family to the Carolinas in what would prove to be a futile search for a more healthful climate. Eventually they returned to Ohio, where Frank's mother died in her father's house, in January 1886. Frank, who was eight years old at the time, was emotionally scarred by her death. He was placed in the household of an uncle while his father worked at a variety of jobs.[8]

Unfortunately for Frank, real-world traumas sometimes coincide with critical developmental stages which make the individual more vulnerable to the effects of traumas. In Frank's case, his mother died while he was in the midst of what psychoanalysts call *latency*—the calm period between the ages of five or six and puberty. In normal development during this period the child is not impulse ridden. It is no accident that society is set up during this stage to provide an individual with education in both formal studies and social behavior, in an effort to help children find their place in the world while they still benefit from a close connection to their families. It shakes a young boy's psychological foundation to lose his mother when he is in the midst of latency, making it likely that he will encounter difficulties while learning and adapting to the requirements of his society and culture, especially if he cannot obtain an adequate replacement for the mother.

It is entirely possible that Frank Nixon might have become another kind of man if he had a comforting mother figure throughout his latency and adolescence, for the early teenage years can offer a chance to redo much of the developmental work hitherto unsuccessfully negotiated.[9] Frank was denied this opportunity, even though his father remarried when he was eleven. His stepmother seems, at least in his mind, to have been a prototypical "wicked stepmother": she was very harsh with the boy and beat him regularly. Under these circumstances, Frank was not able to tame his aggressive impulses and was prone to offensive outbursts all the while searching for a calm environment, which he never found.

We do not have further details concerning other factors that may have influenced Frank's personality development, so all we can offer is the above partial explanation. What is known is that Frank Nixon remained frustrated, angry, and discontented throughout his adulthood.

Lacking emotional support and money, Frank dropped out of school in the fourth grade. He would never return to the one-room schoolhouse where, as a poor newcomer, he had come to know humiliation and pain.

At the age of fourteen he left home. Becoming a drifter, he supported himself by doing a variety of odd jobs: he "drove an ox team . . . worked as a carpenter, managed a potato farm, sheared sheep and installed hand crank telephones."[10] According to his son Richard, Frank's life in Ohio left him "frustrated and discouraged."[11]

In Ohio, seventeen-year-old Frank had a brush with history. The town where he lived was a campaign stop for William McKinley, who was running for President in 1896. Frank owned a horse and some fancy accouterments, so he put on his best outfit and joined in at the tail end of a welcoming procession. When the parade marshal spotted him, Frank was brought to the head of the cavalcade and introduced to McKinley, who asked him how he planned to vote. Overlooking the fact that he was not yet of voting age, Frank staunchly replied, "Republican, of course!" Since his family had been Democrats, it is hard to say whether his conversion came about from the glory of the moment or from his growing unhappiness with the policies of Grover Cleveland and the Democrats, as some researchers would have us believe. In any case, Frank voted for McKinley's reelection in 1900 and afterward remained a lifelong Republican.

Frank went to Colorado in 1904, but was disheartened by the lack of opportunities there and returned to Ohio within eighteen months. He then took a job as a motorman on the trolley system operated by the Columbus Railway and Light Company. He enjoyed the image of himself in uniform, but other working conditions bothered him, such as having to drive the street car from an open vestibule and having his feet freeze in the cold weather. Rebellious, he organized the motormen. The group successfully supported a young lawyer who was running for the State Senate, and he reciprocated by lobbying for legislation that forced the company to enclose the vestibules.[12]

Characteristically for him, Frank did not capitalize on his victory. Following his tendency to search for something new as though his inner happiness was always waiting around the next corner, he pulled up stakes and headed for southern California. He was twenty-eight years old then. Armed only with his restless longings and a letter of recommendation from his Columbus employer, he quickly found work as a motorman with the Pacific Electric Railway Company. He drove the interurban between Whittier and Los Angeles until the day his car hit an automobile, whereupon he was dismissed summarily.

Falling back on his early farming experience, Frank became a ranch hand in the community of Whittier, which was predominantly Quaker. The solemn, hard-working lifestyle there did not allow for liquor stores, bars, or dance halls. In search of some social life, Frank began going to

Quaker meetings and participating in activities. There he met Hannah Milhous, the daughter of Franklin Milhous, a prominent member of the Quaker community. Frank was invited to the Milhous home after a Valentine's Day social in February 1908, and he became captivated with Hannah, whom he saw nightly throughout the remainder of the winter and during the spring. Although this did not please the Milhous family, they did nothing to keep the young couple apart.

Frank settled into his work as a ranch hand and into life in Whittier in general. His circumstances seemed to be improving. He had been able to form a romantic attachment, and in his future father-in-law, Franklin Milhous, he seemed to have found a father figure to stand behind him and bring a woman into his life. By coming full circle and facing up to the problems of his early years he might have been able to use Milhous's sponsorship to help him bring his childhood to some sort of resolution, but the evidence shows that he did not. Interviews with those who knew the situation indicate that the Milhous family never really accepted Frank as one of their own.[13] Many people, including his son Richard, have said that Frank continued to be aggressive and hot-tempered after his marriage to Hannah. Although he was industrious and energetic, he continued to be disgruntled and to inspire fear in others.

Hannah Milhous Nixon

Hannah's lineage was German—the family name originally was Melhausen—[14] but at some point her forefathers resettled in England, where they went into service with Cromwell's army and were rewarded with an estate in Ireland. There they embraced Quakerism and became followers of William Penn, and anglicized the family name to Milhous. In 1729 Thomas Milhous emigrated to America, settling at first in Chester County, Pennsylvania. The family moved to Ohio in the early part of the nineteenth century, and lived there in a Quaker community. In 1854 six-year-old Franklin Milhous, Richard Nixon's maternal grandfather, moved with his family to Jennings County, Indiana, where they became abolitionists. After the death of his first wife in 1879, Franklin Milhous, at the age of twenty-eight, married a schoolteacher named Almira Burdg. Together they raised two sons and seven daughters, including Hannah, who was born in 1885.

In 1887 the Quakers established a new colony in California named Whittier, after the Quaker poet John Greenleaf Whittier. Attracted by the weather and prospects of good, cheap land, the Milhous family resettled there. Franklin was a religious man who used the Quaker pronouns "thee" and "thou." He shared John Greenleaf Whittier's concern for

"Truth." The family was taught to stress individual conscience and responsibility, to the extent that Richard recalled his mother praying silently each night behind a closed door or even in a closet. In time Franklin Milhous became very successful, and he established a trust fund for the education of his grandchildren at Whittier College.

Nixon family members and Nixon biographers generally agree that Hannah, Richard Nixon's mother, was Frank's polar opposite in many respects. Julie Nixon Eisenhower wrote of her grandmother's inner reserve and extreme sense of privacy.[15] Where Frank would yell and "carry on," Hannah carefully guarded herself against anger and was more likely to write down her thoughts and feelings, keeping them confidential.

Hannah's general demeanor contrasted markedly with that of her husband. Richard wrote in his memoirs that "the principle that opposites attract aptly describes my father and my mother . . . two more temperamentally different people could hardly be imagined."[16] Apparently, Richard had been aware of their differences since the time he was in the eighth grade, when he wrote, "My father . . . is a very talkative man . . . [and] is a ready debater on any subject. My mother . . . does not like to travel . . . [and] is not very talkative."[17] In contrast to her husband's vociferous and caustic temperament and loud, aggressive manner, Hannah was soft spoken, and this is what attracted people to her.[18]

Hannah's demeanor is not surprising in view of the Quaker faith in which she was reared. Its philosophy, based on the Gospel of John, prescribes "the doctrine that there is in all men a light which is the source of religion and ethics."[19] For orthodox Quakers everything revolves around this inner light, which they believe all people share. Since their faith places an emphasis on inward emotions and self-control, Quakers are generally quiet in behavior, restrained and unemotional, with a deep regard for privacy. Hannah suited the description of "a pious Quaker and a strong, hard worker,"[20] and as such she was almost a facsimile of her mother.

Almira Milhous, Hannah's mother, established the emotional tone in her own family and, subsequently, by the force of her personality and attachment to Hannah, in the Nixon household as well. Heir to this Milhous work ethic, Richard Nixon once explained, "My grandmother set the standards for the whole family. Honesty, hard work, do your best at all times-humanitarian ideals."[21] Evidence of Hannah's steadfast adherence to humanitarian ideals can be found in the intense and firm resolve she exhibited in everyday life, a natural consequence of having been reared in an orthodox Quaker environment.

Physically, Hannah could be described as having plain features, and was not really considered attractive. After graduating from Whittier High

School, she attended Whittier College for two years and then became a schoolteacher. She married Frank Nixon on June 20, 1908, following a courtship of just four months. Whatever romantic reasons there were for the union, it is likely that an additional factor may have been Frank's unconscious quest for a home and a parental figure who would approve of him. Thus, this somewhat unlikely marriage began with much unconscious "unfinished business" and was destined to be subject to many tribulations.

The Nixon Marriage Before Richard's Birth

Although Frank Nixon renounced his Methodist faith and became a Quaker when he married, he never embraced Quaker principles quite as fervently as did his wife, nor did he ever attain her level of control over the expression of emotion. His conversion may have been a condition of his marriage into a family that was less than enthusiastic about the match. The feeling remained that since Frank was merely a common laborer with just a fourth-grade education, Hannah had married beneath her. Hannah, though plain, came from a good family and had been to college. Frank's brash and argumentative nature, in addition to his having been born a Methodist, exacerbated the general disapproval.[22]

Nonetheless, Franklin Milhous offered his son-in-law the job of foreman in his citrus operation, and when Hannah became pregnant he took the couple in with him, to live in his home. Although the town of Whittier circa 1968 has been described by one of Nixon's biographers, Garry Wills as a suffocating place "heavy with moral perspiring,"[23] California in the early twentieth century was a delightful area whose unravaged natural beauty and future promise drew many people to it. Ostensibly, the young Nixons stayed in the Milhous household for economic advantages. For Frank, the arrangement may have also temporarily fulfilled his longings for an accepting home and made him feel encouraged about his prospects. He remained a Methodist and a Democrat in spirit while in Whittier, in spite of having become a nominal Quaker and a Republican.

Hannah bore her first son, Harold, a year after her marriage. For the young family these seem to have been " . . . times of struggle, sorrows and deprivation, but they had pleasant experiences too; they had the security and contentment that characterized so many of the well-knit, small-town families of a past generation."[24]

Before long, however, Frank came to look upon this security as constricting. In addition to being an incurable drifter, as we have seen, he routinely sought external solutions to help him solve his internal problems and to fulfill his largely unconscious needs. Wishing to separate himself from the Milhous family either because he felt some emotional rejection on their part or because he found the environment too confining—because of his own internal psychodynamics—in 1910 he decided to take his family north of Bakersfield to work on another Milhous ranch; and in 1912 he moved them to Yorba Linda. Hannah was then pregnant with Richard.

We can only surmise Hannah's reactions upon leaving her parents and the supportive and familiar Quaker environment of their community. She may have sensed Frank's restlessness early in their marriage. Beneath his gruffness was an insecure man who searched repeatedly and unsuccessfully for stability. Although Hannah has been described as a "saint,"[25] one wonders if she did not feel quietly rebellious about the turmoil her husband brought into their life together, or if, at the same time, she might not have welcomed the change from her hitherto rather dull and uneventful existence.

In Yorba Linda, a village situated thirty miles southeast of Los Angeles, Frank expected to strike it rich. It was a tiny desert town then, and its inhabitants were the kind of people Nixon would later call "The Silent Majority." They were farmers, shopkeepers, churchgoers—hard-working people who respected authority and believed in the American dream.

There Frank Nixon bought a small lemon grove with his father-in-law's money and supported his family by doing odd jobs while building a two-story frame house. Weighing eleven pounds, Richard Nixon was born in Yorba Linda on January 9, 1913 and as a child was subjected to the turmoil his family experienced, for Mother Nature proved to be as treacherous for Frank as had his stepmother during his adolescence, and the lemon grove project eventually foundered. The clay subsoil on the land did not drain well, adversely affecting production, and Hannah Nixon would later state that she ended up working for the Sunkist lemon packing house in Yorba Linda, taking her children, Richard (then six) and Donald (then four and one-half) with her where they performed menial, somewhat humiliating, tasks such as sweeping while she labored.[26] Thus, the move to Yorba Linda was disastrous economically and emotionally. Frank was reduced to doing odd jobs again and Hannah, separated from her extended family, must have been prey to considerable anxiety, depression, and emotional hunger.

3

Childhood and Adolescence

Richard Nixon's birthplace was a modest white clapboard house built by his father. Born in 1913, he was named after a king—Richard the Lion-Hearted.[1] He was the second of five sons in the family, all of whom were named after kings—Harold (1909–32), Donald (1914–), Arthur (1918–25), and Edward (1930–). This naming system may have reflected a wistful parental hope that the sons might defend and save the family, whose fortunes were at a low ebb most of the time.

As the mother of two very young children Hannah literally had her hands full after Richard's birth. Her recovery from childbirth had been long and difficult, thereby reducing the attention she could give the newborn Richard. Then, six months after Richard's birth, Hannah also agreed to care for the infant son, Russell Harrison, Jr., of her ill sister Elizabeth.[2] For a time, she even nursed her nephew along with Richard.[3]

When Richard was nine months old, he was separated from his mother when she had to be hospitalized for a mastoid operation. In 1914, during Richard's second year of life, Hannah bore Donald, who placed even more demands on her.[4] While she did her best during his first year or so of life, the future President of the United States seems to have lacked what psychoanalyst Donald Winnicott called "good-enough mothering."[5] To elaborate, when the experience with the mother or her substitute is not enough to soothe the child's unpleasant feelings and anxiety, so that the child cannot establish a sense of inner security, technically we say that the mothering is not "good-enough." This may account for Richard's habit in infancy and early childhood of crying a great deal.[6]

It seems that he retained his crying habits for some years. Paul Ryan, a childhood playmate of Nixon's, has a clear memory of little Richard's loud crying.[7] Richard Nixon himself once remarked, "I was the biggest crybaby in Yorba Linda. My dad could hear me even with the tractor running."[8] Even if we consider Hannah to have been comfortable with her maternal role and even if we assign little Richard's crying to a physical cause such as a colic, the child-mother experience still would not be considered adequate and nurturing. The infant depends on a strong relationship with the mother; anything that disturbs this relationship makes the mother "bad." All indications are, in fact, that Hannah was not emotionally comfortable and, indeed, was depressed during Richard's infancy.

When what is provided falls short of need, one must depend on oneself if one is to survive. This prolonged crying of infant Richard's may have marked the beginning of his documented tendency toward enhanced self-reliance, which became more obvious the older he grew.

During his mother's convalescence Richard stayed with his grandparents. Richard became a great favorite of his grandmother. Rather than being annoyed by his constant crying, or perhaps in order to deny her annoyance, she predicted that with such an authoritative voice he would become a preacher or a teacher.[9] The family's notion of his being destined for great things seems to have appeared early in his childhood. Both his grandmother and mother considered him to be a "special" child rather than a "distressed" one. Unlike his siblings, Richard was granted an extra degree of specialness.

In 1916, Richard was seriously injured in an accident: while riding into town in a wagon he was thrown to the ground because he refused to sit down and, as a result, he sustained a scalp wound severe enough to require suturing.[10] Furthermore, when Richard was four, he had an almost fatal attack of pneumonia. These episodes acquainted him early on in life with the experience of having his bodily integrity attacked.

In turn, little Richard began to display a tendency toward self-reliance. He enhanced his independence by beginning to exploit his mental abilities, partly because he had the intellectual strength and partly because he sought his elders' approval. There is ample evidence to show that at this early point in his life he was serious and quiet, almost aloofly precocious. His mother remembered his being "mature far beyond his years."[11]

Hoyt Corbit, a childhood friend, recalled that as a child Nixon was "one of those fortunate people who seemed to be able to grasp the thing that he's studying quicker than most of us. He obviously showed a natural ability."[12] Virginia Shaw Critchfield, a childhood friend three years Richard's senior, described how he had impressed her with his talent and remarkable memory. As a kindergartner visiting his brother Harold's classroom, he once recited a long poem. Critchfield recalls being amazed and "very, very envious." She related how she and Harold Nixon entered a recitation contest sponsored by local friends a year later, as did Richard, who, in spite of being so much younger, won.[13]

Nixon was in the midst of his oedipal period when, in 1918, his brother Arthur was born. A sibling's birth is not necessarily a traumatic event for an older child; in fact it may be a pleasurable experience unless the home environment is filled with anxiety or the older child has suffered previous separations from his mother that have left his inner security vulnerable. The birth of a new sibling is traumatic for the older child whose inner security is threatened. Whenever the birth of a sibling is experienced as traumatic—and Nixon appears to have been unhappy about this new arrival—a child will find a way to cope with the tension, using whatever psychic mechanisms are available to him.[14] In Richard's case, Frank Nixon's behavior toward his children complicated this process: he frightened them with his belligerent ways and never hesitated to punish them, sometimes savagely, as illustrated by the following anecdote.

One day, Richard and Harold decided to play in the Anaheim canal, which flowed past the Nixon property. When Frank found them there, he hauled them out, only to fling them right back into the water, yelling, "Do you like water? Have some more of it!"[15] An aunt, who witnessed the event, recalled screaming, "You'll kill them, Frank! You'll kill them!"[16] Although Richard was no more than six or seven years old at the time, such punishment for disobedience was not unusual. It should also be acknowledged that by now the father of this growing family was ailing, suffering from partial deafness, arthritis, and gastric ulcers,[17] which no doubt added to his irritability.

Accelerated Maturation and Latency

It was obvious to the people around him that young Richard possessed greater than average intelligence. His precocious intellectual activity may have begun unconsciously, as a way of dealing with the traumas and conflicts he had experienced during his early years. The more this behavior gained approval and support from those around him, especially on his maternal side, the greater were his unconscious and conscious efforts to absorb himself in intellectualization to an excessive degree. Nixon's father, too, approved of and encouraged his son's intellectual specialness. Nixon wrote that during his developmental years "My biggest thrill . . . was to see the light in his [father's] eyes when I brought home a good report card."[18]

Nixon's intellectual proclivities were encouraged by his parents, who clearly considered him to be a gifted child with great potential. His display of excess in this area is analogous to a situation where a boy who is a skillful bicycle rider takes unnecessary risks in order to demonstrate his prowess. He may engage in dangerous stunts because unconsciously he is reacting to the encouragement he receives from his father, who is proud of the son's abilities and who perhaps secretly pushes the boy to show his masculinity in this manner. In times of stress children will use, in an exaggerated way, whatever available mechanisms they have mastered. Thus, a bright child may make similar use of his intellectual capabilities. The foundation of Richard's personality was laid down: overtly, he depended in an exaggerated manner on self-reliance, intellectualism, and self-adulation; covertly, he would remain a child of deprivation and physical abuse.

When Hannah found herself pregnant again in 1918, she hired a young girl, named Elizabeth Guptill Rez, to help her with the children and household chores.[19] The girl read poetry to Richard at various times. Unlike most of his peers he was already able to read when he entered grammar school. One of his teachers even reported that he read between thirty and forty books besides those required for class work, all while he was in the first grade.[20] The books he read were said to have been "beyond his years."[21] In elementary school Nixon was such a good student that he skipped the second grade. He was quiet, reserved, and gifted at reading poetry. Athletically, he was clumsy but determined.

Reading was Richard's main interest: apparently he was content to stay indoors reading while the other children "played out." His brother Donald recalled, "Dick was always reserved. He was the studious one of the bunch, always doing more reading while the rest of us were out having more fun."[22] Hannah Nixon noted that even at the age of six or seven Richard was fascinated by concerns that usually interest much older children.[23] He enrolled in Sunday School at the age of five and read newspapers at six. *The National Geographic* was his favorite magazine.[24] He learned to play the piano before he was seven, and then took up the violin. Although he liked football and baseball, he was too small and too slow to play very well, so he took refuge in fastidiousness and detachment. The discipline and self-control he gained from his Quaker background led him to say his prayers daily and to attend Quaker meetings on Sundays.

As Frank Nixon's family expanded in size, the prospects for his lemon grove continued to dwindle. Eventually, in 1922—when Richard was nine years old—Frank sold the grove and moved his family back to nearby Whittier, where he built another house and went to work in the oil fields. Two years later he bought a gas station along the highway, to which he subsequently added a general store. The establishment became a kind of "neighborhood club,"[25] where men gathered to discuss politics and other matters. These discussions may have planted in Richard the first seeds of an interest in politics, although, as we shall see, there were unconscious motivations at work as well.

Throughout his latency period Richard continued to read a great deal. He had no intimate friends and confided only in his mother and his brothers Harold and Donald. He was not popular in school and took little notice of girls.[26] Intellectual concerns continued to hold his interest. When he was given a large volume of American history on his tenth birthday, he practically memorized it.[27]

Because of his family's financial circumstances, Richard started doing odd jobs at an early age—he was a part-time bean picker at the age of ten—and helped out in the family store. When he was eleven years old, Nixon applied for his first serious job by answering an advertisement in the *Los Angeles Times*, but did not secure the position.[28]

When the Teapot Dome scandal erupted in 1924, it was of particular concern to Californians; coverage in the newspapers was intense. Frank Nixon, disturbed by the corrupt politicians and their expensive lawyers, no doubt spoke heatedly of the scandal. Richard seems to have followed the newspaper accounts, and they may have prompted him to declare that when he grew up he would be "an old-fashioned kind of lawyer who can't be bought."[29] This may have been his first mention of wanting to be a lawyer. Earlier dreams he had of becoming a railroad engineer and of visiting far-off places most likely had been influenced by his father's accounts of his own travels.

Adolescence

During adolescence Richard experienced a number of tragic losses that kept alive the memory of earlier misfortunes—both physical and emotional—that he had experienced in childhood. He spent the first half of his twelfth year living with his aunt, Jane Beeson, in the town of Lindsay, which was more than a hundred miles from his home. Clinging to the notion that he was gifted, Richard's mother agreed to the separation.

Indeed, Beeson, a piano teacher, helped him develop his musical talents. His aunt noted that "it was outstanding to have accomplished what he did in the length of time that I had him."[30] As in the case of his earlier crying bouts, once more the emphasis was on the positive; the negative aspect of the separation between the mother and the son most likely was denied. Although Richard did not go on to pursue a career in music, his attention to his lessons may have helped him cope with the pressure of the separation and the perception of his mother pushing him to excel.

During Richard's adolescence his father served as a butcher in the Nixon family store. Apparently he was in the habit of engaging in arguments with customers and creating scenes. According to one account, Frank was "often brutal and frightening, especially in a rage when he was wielding butcher's knives and cleavers."[31]

In the summer of 1925, soon after Richard returned from Lindsay, his younger brother Arthur was stricken with tuberculosis. Richard was sent off again, along with Donald, to stay with an aunt. Although some found Arthur "hard to take," apparently Richard was fond of him. He took it hard when Arthur died, on August 11; Richard fell into "a deep and impenetrable silence," according to his mother.[32] She recalled sensing that Arthur's death first stirred in Nixon the determination to try to ease his parents' grief by making them proud of him. (We suspect, however, that his unconscious fantasies of rescuing her from depression had formed earlier). His mother thought Richard may have felt guilty because he had outlived Arthur, and later, Harold as well.[33]

Richard was becoming well acquainted with loss as he entered his teenage years. The various upsets in his life did not slow him down, however; his intellect continued to mature rapidly, and he continued exceeding expectations and proving himself over and over again. Driven to excel, he did so even in the most minor of endeavors. Because he needed to help support his family, he worked at a variety of jobs: in a packing house, as a janitor at a swimming pool, and as a barker in a carnival. He ran the Wheel of Fortune booth for three successive summers, reportedly making more money than anyone working at any other concession stand.[34] He made straight A's in school and scored fifty-nine on an intelligence test, the norm for which was thirty-five.

Tuberculosis struck the oldest son, Harold, who was the family favorite, in 1927. Richard was fourteen at the time, and at an age when youngsters normally are involved with peer-group relationships, an expanding environment, and the assimilation of new ideas and values presented by new associates. Refusing to send Harold to the county tuberculosis sanitarium, Frank Nixon sold some of the land behind the family store[35] in order to send his son to a private sanitarium in Arizona, and then to another one in California. Harold returned home in 1928, but when his health faltered again, his mother insisted on taking him to Prescott, Arizona. There she rented a cabin and took in other patients in order to make ends meet. Richard stayed behind in Whittier where, once more separated from his mother, he experienced "the roughest period of his boyhood"[36] and contracted an intractable sinus infection. The all-male Nixon household was far from peaceful—quarrels predominated between Frank and his sons and between the boys themselves. Hannah sent for Richard to join her in Arizona in the summertime.[37] Frank visited the family there occasionally and, at the age of forty-five, Hannah became pregnant again. Her pregnancy forced her to return with Harold to Whittier. Edward Nixon was born in 1930.

Earlier, in the autumn of 1926, Richard had entered Fullerton High School, where, although a poor player, he became involved with several athletic teams. Two years later a change in the school system enabled him to attend Whittier High School, where he enrolled in debating, distinguishing himself by winning an oratorical contest on the Constitution in his junior year. He did not, however, win his bid to be president of the student body. This proved to be the only election he would lose for thirty years. Throughout his high school career he was described as dedicated, serious, and intense. History and Civics were his favorite academic subjects, and he continued to participate in athletics by joining the football team. It is remarkable that he could do so well and remain unshaken, on the surface, in view of family emergencies that must have made him anxious and that inflicted deep psychological hurt, fear, and conflict upon him.

After finishing high school, Richard took advantage of the trust fund established by his grandfather for the education of his grandchildren and went on to Whittier College. He also continued to work in his family's store, as bookkeeper and manager of the vegetable department. This assistance was crucial, for the family experienced deep financial stress at the time due to expenses associated with Harold's care. In his 1978 memoirs, Nixon cited monetary difficulties as the reason for his choice of Whittier over Yale University, to which, along with Harvard, he had been invited to apply for scholarships.[38] Nixon's dreams of attending a prestigious eastern university crumbled because of circumstances at home: Harold was ill, 1930 was a depression year, and there was a new baby, Edward. However, Nixon said later that he never regretted going to Whittier College-that he liked being a big man on a small campus.

Harold died suddenly, in 1932, when Richard was not quite twenty years old. He had been studying in the college library when he was summoned home to find a hearse parked in front of his house, ready to take

Harold's body away. Later that evening, Richard gave his mother the gift Harold had purchased the day before for her birthday. In true Quaker fashion, Harold's death was seen as God's will. The Quaker philosophy about death added to Richard's inability to express his feelings, because the control that was demanded of him meant that he could not grieve openly.

As his teenage years ended he was, on the surface, a loner—bright and aloof. He was also reserved, fastidious, serious, and intense, using his mind systematically to good effect. He had worked hard for everything he had, and this was reflected in the sober, industrious demeanor he acquired.

4

Adulthood

College Years

Full of energy, Richard Nixon hit the ground running when he began his studies at Whittier College. During his first month at the Quaker institution he helped found the college's second men's society—the Orthogonian Club. The club, designed as an alternative to the exclusive Franklin Society, whose members were socially elite undergraduates, adopted its name from the Greek word for corner or angle to indicate "square shooters." Nixon wrote in his memoirs that Orthogonian members were dedicated to the Four B's—Beans, Brawn, Brain, and Bowels.[1] Whereas the members of the Franklin Society wore tuxedos, the Orthogonians dressed in shirt sleeves and did not even wear ties. Nixon later denied the existence of class distinctions between the two clubs, but throughout his life he drew parallels between his modest beginnings and the wealthy, privileged background of many of his political opponents.

Nixon devised the society's constitution, composed its theme song-*Ecrasons l'infâme*, translated as "Stamp Out Evil"—and collaborated on and directed its first play, "The Trysting Place." Although he was a mere freshman at the time, he successfully competed against juniors and seniors to become the society's first president. Encouraged by the sweetness of victory, his youthful ambition propelled him into a contest for freshman class president in 1930, in which he won over ninety percent of the votes. Later, he became a member of the college's Joint Council of Control. Nixon quickly gained a reputation among his fellow students— as well as within the college's bureaucracy—for being a mover and a shaker. Although his peers clearly thought of him as someone upon whom they could depend to get things done, he was also gaining a reputation for being ruthless and cocksure. The "deprived and fearful" aspect of his personality was in the shadows.

Nixon remained involved in student activities throughout his college years. As a sophomore he was elected to the Society of Knights, which was an organization of campus leaders. He ran for Vice President and won by a margin of more than three to one. As a junior he was made chairman of the annual Whittier College bonfire.

Apparently, Nixon was driven to find "a number of issues that made him a leader without making him, in the customary sense, popular."[2] He seemed friendly enough, but he was a loner and was without close friends, although the football coach, "Chief" Newman, did offer him counsel and guidance. Nixon considered Newman, who was an American Indian, to have had the greatest influence on him after his father.

As a senior, Nixon aspired to the most prestigious office available, that of student body president. He ran on a platform that supported student dances on campus, although Nixon himself was not an avid dancer. This was a popular issue a leader like Nixon could champion. By doing so, Nixon challenged the Quaker school's policy against on-campus dancing. He used the argument that the college's tradition had to change with the times, that it was better to allow campus dances that were supervised by college staff than to have the students slink off to the "dens of iniquity" in Los Angeles.[3] His opponent's platform, based on support for a student center, was far less compelling. Nixon easily won the contest. As a true Orthogonian he had stamped out an evil—the lure of the big city—but at the same time, he had flouted a Quaker tradition.

Student leader, activist, and athlete, Richard Nixon also was a serious scholar. He graduated second in his class in 1934 and won a full tuition scholarship of $250 to Duke University's new School of Law. Twenty-five such grants were made to an entering class of forty-four, although only twelve of the scholarship recipients returned for their second year. Nixon's fellow students referred to the program as "the meat grinder," in recognition of the fierce competition it engendered. Knowing that it would be financially impossible for him to stay in law school without a scholarship, Nixon pushed himself to the limit throughout his three years at Duke. He rented a room for five dollars a month during his first two years there, and in his last year he lived in a one-room clapboard shack about two miles from the campus, sharing it with three other students. He supported himself by doing afternoon work in the law school library, where he also studied in the evenings. Eventually his lifestyle earned him the nickname "Gloomy Gus" because he lived so frugally and studied so hard.

Nixon's hectic schedule threatened to wear him out both physically and emotionally. He tells how one evening, while he was in the library, he found himself suffering from fears and doubts about his ability to compete with the large number of Phi Beta Kappas in his class. He poured out his anxiety to a classmate who reassured him, saying "You don't have to worry. You have what it takes to learn the law—an iron butt."[4] In his second year at law school Nixon ran for the presidency of the Student Bar Association, which was a highly prestigious position, and won. He graduated third in his class—behind two of his housemates—in 1937, and was admitted to the Order of the Coif, the national law school honor society that was limited to the top ten percent of the graduating class.[5]

The Graduate

On close examination, Richard Nixon's high school and college years reveal a peculiar paradox in his behavior that proved to be characteristic of him in his political life as well: more than once he acted as though the success that came his way was too good to be true and he either punished himself for it or compromised the success in some way. Nixon's "self-punishing side"[6] was evident by his behavior while he was a member of the football team at Whittier. He was too slight to count for much in the roughness of line play so he served as "cannon-fodder"—a human tackling dummy.[7] Nixon earned praise for this early display of team spirit and enthusiasm. It is interesting to note that he seldom missed practice, although he was usually not brought into a game until it was either well won or definitely lost. His chief harvest from all this work seems to have been bodily punishment.

In his last year of law school, Nixon applied for a job with the Federal Bureau of Investigation. He never followed up on the status of his application, however, because he was not confident that he would be accepted. Not until years later, when he was President, did he mention to the long-term director of the FBI, J. Edgar Hoover, that he had once applied. Only then did he learn that the FBI had been on the point of making him an offer when a sudden budget cut made hiring impossible.[8] Nixon also passed up an opportunity to gain employment with a prestigious New York law firm upon his graduation. He had interviewed with

Donovan, Leisure, Newton, and Lombard, but when asked to return to New York for another interview, he decided he "was no longer keen on the idea of starting out in that cold and expensive city."[9]

With few solid prospects in view, Nixon sought the advice of some of his law school mentors. Dean H. Claude Horack, of Duke's Law School, encouraged him to consider returning to Whittier in order to go into practice there, as a stepping-stone to a political career. We believe that at that point in his life Nixon was most comfortable with this direction. He decided to follow the Dean's advice, but missed the deadline for applying to take the California Bar Exam, an uncharacteristic oversight. One might at first attribute his "failure" to take the necessary steps to sign up for the Bar examination to his having thought he was going to work in New York and thus he did not need to prepare for the California Bar. But we speculate that Nixon's success in graduating among the best in his class led him to find it necessary, at least unconsciously, to suffer some discomfort, and that this accounted for his "forgetting" to make appropriate application to the Bar on time.

In the end, Dean Horack intervened on his behalf. Through a Stanford colleague, he managed to help Nixon attain eligibility for the examination.[10] Nixon then had to cram into two months' study what normally would have taken five. Dean Horack wrote to him that his was the honor of being the first Duke Law School graduate to take the California Bar examination, whereupon Nixon divulged to a friend at Duke his fear that "the first graduate to take it has a darn good chance of failing."[11]

As a Young Lawyer

Following his successful completion of the California Bar examination, Nixon set about finding employment. With the help of his mother, he was interviewed by Whittier's busiest law firm, Wingert and Bewley. The Bewley and Milhous families had had a business relationship back in Indiana, and Thomas Bewley was happy to follow up on Hannah Nixon's suggestion that he talk to her son. Nixon was hired and taken on as an associate: his first assignment was to "straighten out" the office law library.[12] Instead of simply putting the books in order, he took this to mean that he was supposed to remove the many volumes from the shelves, dust them, varnish the shelves, and then arrange all the books appropriately.

At the outset, it looked as though it would be a long time before Nixon proved himself worthy of a partnership in the law firm. He mismanaged his very first serious case—a suit for repayment of a substantial loan—and Bewley had to rescue him from a malpractice suit by securing an out-of-court settlement.[13] Nixon's subsequent assignments were mainly divorce cases, estate settlements, and accident suits. Work on divorce litigation embarrassed the prudish young lawyer. He wrote in his memoirs: "At first I was surprised by some of the intimate matters people argued about, and equally surprised by the fact that they could calmly sit down and tell a stranger, even a lawyer, about them."[14] The intimate revelations of a beautiful young woman seeking a divorce caused him "to turn fifteen colors of the rainbow."[15]

Nixon's dedication, intelligence, and hard work made a good impression despite his initial failings, and after a year he was taken into the firm as a partner. In his memoirs, Nixon has acknowledged the importance he attached to this promotion: "Now for the first time I was no longer Frank and Hannah Nixon's son—I was Mr. Nixon, the new partner in Wingert and Bewley."[16] He approached his work with considerable single-mindedness. His first secretary once commented that she could be at her desk in the morning for twenty minutes before Nixon, already hard at work, would take time to greet her.[17]

Nixon adopted a similar pattern of hard work in his private life by immersing himself in community affairs. He joined the Kiwanis Club and the "20–30" Club (a group of business and professional men under the age of thirty), soon becoming president of its Whittier chapter. At the age of twenty-five he was elected president of the Whittier Alumni Association, and a year later he became the youngest member of the college's Board of Trustees. An enthusiastic proposal was made to nominate him, at the age of twenty-nine, for the presidency of the college. It was generally believed that had it not been for the war, he would indeed have become Whittier's youngest president.[18]

Ever driven, Nixon was also elected president of the Duke University Alumni Association of California, and of the Orange County Association of Cities. In spite of his increasing success, the "collection" of presidencies that he was building, and many associations with prominent people, he continued to take his own counsel and to make his own decisions. It was not his style to share his thoughts, reactions, and feelings with associates, so he made few close friends. In this way, Nixon expressed exaggerated self-reliance in his personality. He was like his mother, who also kept her thoughts and feelings to herself.

Romance and Marriage

While our knowledge of Nixon's relationship with women is limited, we can sketch some details of his romantic life. We know that as a Whittier student he was regarded as "too intelligent to be much fun" by the women there.[19] Yet he did have a steady girlfriend for a number of years, beginning in his senior year of high school.

Nixon dated Ola Florence Welch off and on up until the time he was in law school at Duke. She has been described as bright, pretty, vivacious, and well liked. Their relationship was a stormy one, characterized by quarrels and frequent partings.[20] According to his contemporaries, Nixon was to blame for many of the difficulties because of his "combative rather than conciliatory" nature and his "nasty temper."[21] Although Nixon had asked Ola to marry him, they never settled on a date and, in fact, both felt free to date others. Their separations were usually prompted by Nixon, whose "urge to punish and to be vindictive was evident throughout their relationship."[22] Ola later said there was something missing in the alliance: "Sometimes I think I never really knew him, and I was as close to him as anyone. I still feel some of that—that he was a mystery."[23]

When Nixon was named student body president at Whittier in his senior year, Ola recalled feeling a sense of inferiority.[24] Their far from serene relationship continued to disintegrate after Nixon left for law school. He sent Ola long letters in which he wrote of his homesickness as well as his expectations of marriage. But Ola had formed a new relationship with Gail Jobe, and when Nixon returned to Whittier for the summer, she told him. He was hurt and angry, and they quarreled. The day after he received the news, however, he went back to Ola's house, acting as though nothing had happened. Throughout the summer he repeatedly asked Ola to marry him. She responded in vague answers, and when Nixon returned to Duke in September, he continued to send her letters. Eventually, Ola decided to marry Jobe. She wrote to Nixon before Christmas of 1935, telling him of her decision. It took him a long time to accept the reality of the situation: he continued to send her letters, but they went unanswered. His final letter was a pathetic one. Later Nixon was so embarrassed by Ola's rejection that he downplayed their relationship. He never spoke to anyone at Duke "about the girl to whom he wrote love letters for more than a year and a half at law school and her decision to marry another man."[25]

When Nixon resettled in Whittier he mostly kept to himself, busily pursuing his career. Since he had acted in college, the local Little Theater held some appeal for him. He volunteered to work on lighting and set design before deciding to audition in 1937 for the part of District Attorney Flint in the Ayn Rand play, *The Night of January 16th*; a fellow professional had suggested that an appearance on stage in the role of a lawyer might bring him business.[26] When, in January of 1938, the Little Theater prepared for a production of *The Dark Tower*, a mystery by George S. Kaufman and Alexander Woollcott, Nixon read for the part of Barry Jones. At the same time Pat Ryan, a schoolteacher new to Whittier, also auditioned for a part, and both were chosen for the play.

Although Nixon states in his memoirs that theirs was a case of love at first sight and that he proposed marriage to Pat the night they met,[27] their falling mutually in love does not seem to be the actual story. He may have taken to her immediately, but she refused to date him even after meeting him twice. When she refused him again with a laugh, Nixon remarked to her as he drove her and a friend home from rehearsal, "Don't laugh! Some day I'm going to marry you!"[28] That outburst was so unlike Nixon's usual calculating decisionmaking that, in light of his prior experience with Ola Welch, one might wonder whether he had planned even before meeting Pat how he would propose to any girl!

Apparently, Nixon's attentions and marriage proposal took Pat very much by surprise, as she indicated in one interview: "I thought he was nuts or something. I guess I just looked at him. I couldn't imagine anyone saying anything like that so suddenly. Now that I know Dick much better, I can't imagine that he would ever propose like that. Because he's very much the opposite; he's more reserved."[29]

Thelma Catherine Ryan was nicknamed Pat by her father, because she was born on March 16, 1912, the eve of St. Patrick's Day. She moved with her family from Nevada to Artesia, California, when she was a baby, so that her father could take up farming rather than continuing in his previous and more dangerous occupation of mining silver.

The Ryans were a typical farm family, close-knit and hard-working. Pat's mother died when she was thirteen years old, and her father passed away five years later. Just out of high school, she suddenly found herself completely on her own. She worked a variety of jobs, among them an X-ray technician in New York, before returning to California. Enrolling at the University of Southern California (USC), she continued to support herself by taking on whatever employment she could find—as a switchboard operator and as a sales clerk—and red-haired Pat even played bit parts in several movies. She graduated in 1937 with a degree in merchandising and a teaching certificate. Although she would have preferred work in the merchandising field, when she was asked to teach a course in business education at Whittier Union High School, she accepted. Her monthly salary then was more than three times as much as Nixon's.

It is possible that at this time in his life, Nixon experienced an internal urgency to find a mate—an urgency that cracked open the defensive shell he had created for himself by his tendency to be cautious, aloof, calculating, and controlling in his interpersonal relationships. It is also possible that Richard found in Pat an echo of "sameness" in his heart, for she too was self-reliant, accustomed as she was to hard work and adversity. Determined, Nixon launched a relentless campaign to win her heart in his "cloying, undaunted, often unrequited pursuit of Patricia Ryan over the next two years."[30]

Seemingly content with the quality of her life at the time, Pat did not appear to appreciate Nixon's attention. He persisted in requesting dates (that she refused) and in making frequent, unannounced appearances at her home. She arranged a blind date for him with her roommate, to gently communicate her lack of interest in him, but he did not take the hint. In desperation, she took to locking her door from the inside and not responding to his knocking, although it was probably obvious to him that she was at home. His response was to write notes such as the following, which he would leave under her door:

> Miss Pat:
> I took [a] walk tonight and it was swell because you were there all the time . . . the wind blowing thru the tops of the palms making that strangely restless rustling, a train whistle sounded just as I got to the bridge. The Dipper . . . was pouring down on you all the good things I've wished looking up at it in the past. . . . Yes, I know I'm crazy, and that this is old stuff and that I don't take hints, but you see, Miss Pat, I like you![31]

Eventually, Pat decided to confront the issue of Nixon's unannounced visits by pointedly "throwing" him out of her lodgings. Nixon adopted an unabashedly high-handed stance in return, in another of his notes to her:

> But I can honestly say that Patricia is one fine girl, that I like her immensely, and that though she isn't going to give me a chance to propose to her for fear of hurting me! and though she insulted my ego just a bit by not being quite frank at times, I still remember her as combining the best traits of the Irish and the square-heads.
> Yours,
> *Dick*[32]

Blema Steinberg, who studied these letters, suggests that while Nixon talks of being "honest," he is, in fact, being dishonest in his reaction to Pat's rejection of him. He chides her indirectly, refusing to admit to himself that he doesn't see her entirely as "one fine girl," because she has assaulted his self-esteem, and "insulted my ego just a bit."[33]

At the same time that she was trying to discourage Nixon's advances, Pat was touched by the mournfulness of Nixon's note. However, she continued to see former boyfriends from USC on weekends, using her sister's apartment in Los Angeles as a base. Nixon was not happy about her seeing other men, but he also did not want her to take public transportation to Los Angeles. Consequently, when he offered to drive her to the city himself on Friday nights and pick her up on Sunday evenings, she accepted. If she was out on a date, he would wait for her, passing time at a movie until she was ready to return to Whittier.[34] Pat did make one stipulation, however. She insisted that there be "no declarations of love or proposals of marriage."[35]

Nixon pursued Pat for two years. We assume that he had felt "humiliated" by Ola's rejection of him. Now, he was determined not to be "humiliated" by Pat. As we stated earlier, he had told Pat not to laugh at him, that he was firm in his determination in making her his wife. He showered her with flattery, telling her that she was destined for greatness. Eventually, she agreed to marry Nixon. Her decision was not free of reservations, however, as substantiated by her daughter Julie: "Even as she consented, she was not sure she wanted to marry. She was twenty-eight years old and had been independent for a long time."[36] Nixon was rewarded for his tenacity in the end, and he and Pat were married on June 21, 1940. Almost six years later their daughter Tricia was born, followed by Julie in 1948.

Nixon's relationship with his mother, which will be explored later in greater depth, was a crucial factor influencing his attitude toward women. In any event, once Richard and Pat were husband and wife, Nixon underwent a transformation of sorts. His "behavior shifted from a humble self-deprecatory stance in which he seemed prepared to accept mere crumbs from his beloved's table while he was courting her, to that of chief architect of her humiliation once he had married her."[37] Nixon seemed to demonstrate an unconscious need for revenge. He targeted his wife, "as a way of alleviating the sense of humiliation he had previously suffered at her hands."[38]

According to observations supplied by friends and acquaintances of the Nixons, their marriage was notably lacking in warmth. Tom Dixon, Nixon's radio coordinator during 1948 and 1950, said he never saw

Nixon even touch Pat's hand.[39] Evelyn Dorn, a secretary in the Wingert and Bewley law firm and a Nixon family friend, said she too never saw Nixon "reach out to touch his wife save once, when they were standing together in the back of a car in an election rally, and he put out his hand to steady her."[40]

Tom Dixon's ex-wife, Georgia Sherwood, reported that Pat "had only two interests, her daughters and her husband, and that she talked incessantly about what a great man her husband was." She also observed that Nixon's treatment of Pat was generally churlish: "He would always hold the door for me," she said, "but would walk through in front of Pat as if she wasn't there at all."[41]

Tom Dixon related in an interview how once the two women were sitting on uncomfortable chairs outside a radio office waiting for him and Nixon. Pat went into the office at one point, but "Nixon flared at her like a prima donna," ordering her out "with as little ceremony as he would have a dog," saying, "you know I never want to be interrupted when I'm working!" Dixon said he saw a new side of Nixon that gave him fresh insight into the man. "If he had been doing a brand new speech, I could have understood it, but this speech he knew by heart." Pat attempted to cover up her embarrassment by telling the Dixons, "You know Richard doesn't like to have me in there. I don't know why but I make him nervous. He's such a great man."[42]

Nixon's coldness toward his wife contrasts with the Quaker custom of kissing on the cheek. When Nixon accepted the vice-presidential nomination in 1952, he turned his face away from his wife even as she tried twice to kiss him.[43] Then, on Pat's sixty-first birthday, Nixon surprised and delighted his wife by playing "Happy Birthday" for her on an upright piano that was wheeled onto the stage of the Grand Old Opry in Nashville, Tennessee. Nixon was there for an opening and used the occasion to honor his wife, but he was in front of an audience—when he finished playing, he perfunctorily brushed her aside as she came toward him with outstretched arms, and resumed his ceremonial duties.

Nixon was clearly not a warm husband, nor did he display affection toward women in general. He seemed to view women as "an extra appendage, a different species," according to James Bassett, a campaign aide in 1952, 1956, and 1960. Bassett felt that Nixon had "a total scorn for female mentality."[44] His ambivalence toward women extended to disdain for their participation in traditional male activities, such as Eleanor Roosevelt's wartime visit to the troops in New Caledonia. Nixon was particularly appreciative of the nonpolitical first ladies—Bess Truman, Mamie Eisenhower, and Grace Coolidge—and he would conjecture a passive image of the behavior of Harry Truman's wife in times of trouble, saying "I'm sure Bess stood there like a rock."[45]

Pat was expected to accompany her husband on his campaigns, but only as an accessory. Her function was to do little more than be pleasant and greet the crowds. Nixon wrote in his memoirs, "Pat is one of those rare individuals whose ego does not depend on public attention."[46] After 1970, Pat did travel on her own and, as far as reporters were concerned, she seemed to come alive on these occasions. Nixon often praised her campaigning skills. Shortly before his resignation he called her "the best ambassador the United States has,"[47] but this did not stop him from slighting her on public platforms and privately in front of friends.

Blema Steinberg writes:

> Nixon's fear of strong women and his desire to keep them in their place is suggested in his intense dislike of pant-wearing opinion-ated women. He made this obvious to the women in the press corps when he was President. His daughter Julie, it is said, was the only student at Smith to wear skirts during her entire four years in college.[48]

Nixon advised political wives to content themselves with a supportive but subordinate role. "Never embarrass your husband" and "Always look at your husband when he is talking" were two of his self-proclaimed adages.[49] The implication seems clear: "uncontrolled and uncontained, women are a potential source of shame and humiliation for men. Their job is to reflect their husband's glory, not to take away from it."[50]

In the Military

After the invasion of Pearl Harbor, Nixon became convinced that his Quaker pacifism had to be set aside in a war with such a "barbarous foe."[51] He volunteered for military duty in January 1942 and for an over-seas assignment in the Navy. While awaiting his orders, he and his new wife moved to Washington, D.C., where he had accepted a post in the Office of Price Administration.

In August 1942 he was assigned to a naval air transport unit in the Pacific, as a lieutenant junior grade, and eventually was promoted to lieutenant commander and sent to the Solomon Islands. He seems to have been a tireless worker: while stationed in the South Pacific he was known to strip off his shirt and join the enlisted men in heavy physical labor. He became known as a good "horse-trader" too. It was said he could start out with a single sheet of plywood and soon have his unit housed and well-equipped. He also achieved some popularity as a scavenger: he somehow managed to obtain food and liquor supplies for his grateful men, who called him "Nix." He learned to play poker quite well in the South Pacific, and found it highly profitable, always playing in a quiet, careful way with his cards close to his chest. This violation of the Quaker rule against gambling netted him a tidy sum that, when combined with Pat's salary and his own, made for a nest egg of ten thousand dollars—not a negligible amount at that time. It proved to be an auspicious nest egg too, because these poker winnings helped Nixon finance his first political campaign.

As a Young Politician

When the war in the Pacific started to wind down Nixon returned to the United States, first to California and then to the East Coast. Pat followed him everywhere he was assigned. After the surrender of Japan, while Nixon and Pat—now several months' pregnant—pondered their future, Herman Perry, a leading Whittier Republican and a fellow trustee of Franklin Milhous at Whittier College, wrote to ask if Nixon would be interested in running for Congress from the Twelfth District.

Jerry Voorhis, a New Deal Democrat, had been entrenched as congressman from this district for five terms, and the Republicans despaired of ever unseating him. He was a Yale graduate who came from a wealthy family. He supported labor and opposed the big financial and oil companies, while championing social welfare programs.

A group of Republican bankers and businessmen from Whittier went so far as to advertise in the local newspaper for a candidate who was willing to undertake the seemingly hopeless task of running against Voorhis. Nixon made it known to Herman Perry that he was willing to run. He then learned that he would have to win the support of an ad hoc committee-the Committee of 100—that had been established to find a candidate. Nixon went to California to appear before this committee, which eventually approved his candidacy. The Whittier Republicans considered him an attractive choice for several reasons: he came from good Quaker stock, he was aggressive, and he was a World War II veteran. The committee felt Nixon was highly marketable as a candidate, and Pat agreed to spend half their savings on his campaign.

Nixon took to campaigning like the proverbial duck to water, but he soon found out that he was up against very stiff competition. Voorhis was a veteran politician who knew how to work his constituency. For example, he sent a pamphlet on child care to all new parents in his district. When Tricia Nixon was born he sent the Nixons a pamphlet too, adding a note saying that he looked forward to meeting Richard in public. Nixon saw this as an opportunity to challenge Voorhis to a series of debates. True to form, Nixon outshone Voorhis in the match. In this, his first political campaign, he also adopted an approach that he would use over and over again for three decades—that of appealing to voters as a hard-working family man, a believer in individual enterprise, and a supporter of the "little" man.

During the campaign Nixon showed himself to be a fierce adversary who possessed a determined ruthlessness. When distorting the Congressman's voting record, Nixon chose to emphasize Voorhis's close connections with organized labor, particularly the militant CIO. Nixon also conducted an intensive telephone campaign through which he spread this message about Voorhis to the voting public. Later, Nixon told a Voorhis aide that he had distorted Voorhis's record, but that "I had to win. That's the thing you don't understand. The important thing is to win."[52] Many Nixon supporters were surprised by the character of the campaign that Nixon waged, but even Voorhis had to admit that Nixon was a good, clever debater, although he delivered a lot of "below-the-belt punches." Nixon, whose success was part of a national Republican surge that election year, went on to win the election by an overwhelming margin—he won sixty percent of the vote. This totally unexpected victory brought him into the national spotlight briefly through coverage in *Time* and other publications.

5

Nixon as a National Figure

When Representative-elect Richard Nixon arrived in Washington, D.C., in December 1946, he had taken his first auspicious step into the national political arena and had achieved his boyhood goal of entering politics. His routinely successful attempts to assume a leadership role in any group with which he associated proved true for the Congress of the United States as well. Upon entering that august body, Nixon made it a priority to organize a club with other freshmen congressmen that would meet every Wednesday. It was a good time to be a Republican as the party controlled both houses of Congress for the first time in twenty years.

At their weekly meetings Nixon and his peers planned activities for the week, requested research reports, and designed strategies to influence legislation and to penetrate the sacrosanct precincts of power in the House. Nixon's efforts, backed by his energy, paid off. "Within eight weeks Nixon, with the strength of his club behind him, had marched . . . his way into the inner sanctums of the most powerful leaders in the Republican-controlled House."[1]

Representative Nixon was assigned to various significant committees. He supported the Marshall Plan and other foreign aid programs, and he helped write the Taft-Hartley Act. He also became a junior member of a controversial headline-making body, the House Un-American Activities Committee (HUAC).

The Alger Hiss/Whittaker Chambers Controversy

In 1948 Nixon was re-elected to the House of Representatives. Following the stamp out evil theme of the Orthogonian Society of his college days, he took on the Alger Hiss/Whittaker Chambers controversy, which he would later identify as the first of six political crises in his life.[2]

Alger Hiss was a former State Department official accused of spying for the Soviets and giving them secret information during the 1930s. The controversy started when Whittaker Chambers, as a witness at a House Un-American Activities Committee meeting investigating subversives in the government, charged that Hiss was a Communist. Chambers, an editor for *Time* magazine, acknowledged that he had once been a member of the Communist party and that he had been a spy. There was no concrete evidence against Hiss, however. It was largely a matter of Hiss's word against his accuser's. Nixon's successful assault on Hiss began on August 3, 1948. With it, Nixon gained national exposure. Nixon was undeterred by Hiss's impeccable credentials: graduate of Johns Hopkins University and Harvard Law School, clerk for Supreme Court Justice Oliver Wendell Holmes, past president of the Carnegie Endowment for International Peace, aide to Franklin Delano Roosevelt at Yalta, and one of the organizers of the United Nations. While many of his fellow members on HUAC preferred to drop the charges, Nixon persisted in his attack. After discovering that Hiss had been under suspicion for some time, Nixon focused on the fact that Hiss had never stated explicitly that he did not know Chambers, only that he "did not know a man by the name of Whittaker Chambers."[3] Nixon was convinced that this was a deliberate attempt on Hiss's part to avoid a perjury charge.

For the next few months Nixon dedicated himself to uncovering supporting evidence. As the controversy surrounding the charges grew, partisan issues were introduced. President Harry Truman claimed the proceedings were politically motivated, and he ordered government agencies not to cooperate in the investigation. Realizing he had committed himself to securing a conviction against Hiss and fearing he might be hurt politically if Hiss was exonerated, or not found guilty of every charge, Nixon countercharged that it was a Democratic cover-up.

Nixon visited Chambers at the latter's Maryland farm and questioned him. He wanted information that only someone close to Hiss would know. Later, when Nixon took a long-delayed vacation to ponder his next move, a search was conducted at Chambers's farm that yielded microfilms of secret documents that were found hidden inside hollowed-out pumpkins—"evidence" that both Chambers and Hiss had acted as espionage agents; the microfilms became known as the "Pumpkin Papers."

With the Pumpkin Papers providing the "evidence" and publicity that Nixon needed to secure Hiss's conviction of perjury (neither man could be indicted for espionage because the statute of limitations had expired), Nixon flew back to Washington by helicopter for a press conference.

Although some people eventually came to regard Nixon as a hero, there were those who would compare him unfavorably to Senator Joseph McCarthy for the questionable tactics he had employed. The style of the man who later became known as "Tricky Dick" had helped him accomplish his goal: it landed him squarely in the political arena. Hiss was indicted for perjury on December 15, 1948, and convicted in 1950. Many people, including former president Herbert Hoover, credited the conviction of Hiss solely to the patience and persistence of Richard Nixon.[4]

The Race for the Senate

In 1950, Nixon ran for the U.S. Senate from the state of California, in a race that would prove to be one of the most vicious political contests in the state's history. National opinion toward the thirty-seven-year-old Nixon had been polarized by the Hiss case: conservatives enthusiastically supported him as a hero who had succeeded in exposing a seditious government official; liberals opposed him as a dangerous man who had destroyed an honorable American, thereby setting the stage for future witch-hunts against Communists.

Nixon's opponent in the Senate race was Representative Helen Gahagan Douglas, a former actress. She was a three-term Congresswoman who, like Jerry Voorhis, was wealthy, well-educated, and an outspoken New Deal Democrat. She was considered an extreme liberal by the conservatives in her own party, a weakness that Nixon astutely seized upon as a theme in his campaign. Douglas publicly condemned as irrational the idea of the Communist peril, and openly opposed the House Un-American Committee. Members of both political parties called her a bleeding-heart liberal, a do-gooder. During a time when the Soviets had already exploded an atomic bomb, the Rosenbergs had been accused of spying for the Soviets, and Mainland China had been overrun by Communists, a candidate like Douglas was a perfect target for what Nixon called his "rocking, socking style of campaigning."[5] Even young Democratic Congressman John F. Kennedy contributed one thousand dollars to Nixon's campaign.

Given the anti-Communist sentiments of the time, basically all Nixon had to do was charge that his opponent did not take the threat of

Communism seriously enough. But he went further and put out a flyer on pink paper criticizing her voting record. He charged that she was "pink" down to her underwear, leading Douglas to coin the phrase, "Tricky Dick."

Nixon won the election easily, by almost seven hundred thousand votes. He had gained the largest plurality of any candidate in the history of Senate elections and became a U.S. Senator in January 1951. Once more he was involved in a first-time event. He later said he won on the basis of the issues, but in a 1979 interview Douglas drew a parallel between the campaign Nixon ran against her and the one he ran against Voorhis: as she saw it, the real issues of the campaign were masked by the creation of bogus issues and by Nixon's manipulation of people's fears. If he had talked about the real issues he might have lost votes. Nixon later said, "People react to fear, not love. They don't teach that in Sunday School, but it's true."[6]

The Vice Presidency

After a year and a half in the Senate, Nixon lobbied hard for the vice-presidential slot on the Republican ticket in 1952, with General Dwight D. Eisenhower as the presidential nominee. Nixon was an attractive choice. He was well-liked not only by the conservatives and the isolationists who supported Ohio Senator Robert Taft and his anti-Communist ideas but also by the more liberal internationalist faction of the party Eisenhower represented. Eisenhower's supporters also liked Nixon because of his support for the Marshall Plan and his commitment to rebuilding postwar Europe. In addition Nixon represented the growing power of the West Coast. However, he basically had no set ideology or principles. "He was a Nixon Republican," said early Nixon biographer Ralph de Toledano in a 1990 television interview.[7] Nixon succeeded in securing the nomination and set about helping Eisenhower win the election by taking responsibility for one important but delicate task: it was Nixon's job to attack Adlai Stevenson, the Democratic presidential nominee. Using now-familiar tactics, he did so by claiming the Democrats were soft on Communism and crime.

It was in the midst of this election campaign that Nixon faced his second major political battle—the Fund Crisis. Accusations that he maintained a "secret" fund containing more than $18,000 through which millionaires surreptitiously supplemented his congressional salary seriously threatened his chances of continuing in the election. Many of Nixon's supporters advised him to fight the charge of wrongdoing, but some of the upper-echelon Republican leaders recommended that he resign from the ticket in order to preserve Eisenhower's chances, regardless of his own guilt or innocence.

Confronting overwhelmingly negative press and public opinion, Nixon's plight seemed even more dire because of the only tenuous support that Eisenhower gave him. After keeping Nixon waiting for three days for a decision as to whether he would be dropped from the ticket, Eisenhower finally came up with the suggestion that Nixon make a nationwide speech from California to test the public reaction. Nixon decided to follow this advice and address the charges head-on. Using the young medium of television as it had never been used before, he delivered an emotional speech, broadcast nationally on radio and television, that became known as the "Checkers Speech." In it he defended the legality of the fund on the basis that it was used solely to pay for the political expenses he incurred while supporting Republican programs and candidates. He gave a full accounting of his financial history, adding that the accusation was "unprecedented in the history of American politics." He insisted that the fund did not benefit him personally, saying: "Pat doesn't have a mink coat. But she does have a respectable Republican cloth coat." The "Checkers Speech" was so named because in it Nixon announced that he intended to allow his daughters to keep Checkers, a cocker spaniel that had been given to them as a gift during his term of office.

Throughout this crisis Nixon received no public support from Eisenhower, who had decided to wait to make a statement until after the opinion polls were tabulated. The speech widened the gap between Nixon's supporters and critics. Some viewers found him humble and sincere; others found him sanctimonious and openly manipulative. In the end, the outpouring of praise that Nixon received after his speech secured his place on the Republican ticket. The next time he saw his running-mate, at the Wheeling, West Virginia, airport, Eisenhower greeted him with the words, "You're my boy!"[8]

They won the 1952 election, making theirs the first Republican administration in two decades. At the age of thirty-nine, Richard Nixon became the second youngest Vice President of the United States (John C. Breckinridge was thirty-six when he served one term under James Buchanan, 1857–61).

It was Nixon's job to be the point-man in the Eisenhower Administration, to address the political issues. After the 1952 campaign and the fund episode, Nixon became the target of harsh criticism from the media. When Eisenhower had his first heart attack in 1955 Nixon decided it was best to avoid attracting attention to himself: he quietly went about running the government while Eisenhower recuperated.

Then, when the President recovered and announced that he felt well enough to seek re-election, rumors began that Nixon would be dropped from the ticket in 1956. Eventually, however, he regained Eisenhower's support. The press began to write of a new Nixon—he was less aggressive in 1956—but he remained the Democrats' favorite target. Adlai Stevenson, again the Democratic presidential candidate, spoke contemptuously of him. Yet Eisenhower and Nixon proved a strong combination, and they won by a landslide. Nixon showed himself to be a survivor: he overcame Eisenhower's indifference, the hostility of the press, and bitter partisan attacks. He entered his second vice-presidential term as the Republican heir-apparent.

In 1960 Nixon succeeded in being named the Republican candidate for the presidency of the United States. The events of the past four years had made him one of the most highly visible Vice Presidents in history. During a tour of South America he faced down angry leftist mobs who spat on him and his wife and attacked their motorcade, shouting "Muerte a Nixon" (death to Nixon). He returned home to a hero's welcome. In Russia he also faced down Nikita Khrushchev in an impromptu television debate. His display of toughness helped him gain support in his bid for his party's nomination.

Defeats and a Remarkable Comeback

Fourteen years after winning his first election to Congress, Nixon faced the young Senator from Massachusetts, John F. Kennedy. Their four televised debates hold historic significance, marking the first time candidates campaigned in this way. Their debates changed the way the American public chose elected officials, as the images on a television screen came to make a difference in the casting of votes.

The feeling at first was that it would be a mismatch, with Nixon having the upper hand. Since Nixon had been hospitalized with a knee injury, however, his preparation for the first debate was not up to his usual high standard.[9] In addition, as events would prove, Nixon did not do well on television—he refused to wear make-up and alongside Kennedy's healthy tan he had a transparent pallor; he appeared haggard and drawn. He also lost the television audience in his unconvincing attempts to relate to the average viewer by emphasizing his humble background and ability to identify with the poor and the unemployed. The first debate cost him dearly and Kennedy picked up many new admirers. The election proved to be a close one, with Nixon losing by only 100,000 votes. He refused to demand a recount though: despite his bitterness he did not want to be tagged a sore loser.

Defeated, Nixon returned to California, where he decided to run for governor in 1962. He had been away from his home state too long, however, and lost the election to Pat Brown. He felt humiliated; he became angry and resentful; his political career seemed to be over. His anger at the press came out when he lost. Believing they had treated him unfairly, he announced his departure from the public eye with the words, "You won't have Nixon to kick around anymore."

In 1968 he made a remarkable recovery. He won his long-sought-after bid for the presidency. In the six intervening years between his humiliating defeat in California and his nation-wide victory, Nixon worked as a Wall Street lawyer. His wife was happy being out of politics, but he missed the limelight. He appeared on the Jack Paar television show six months after losing the governor's race and enthusiastically displayed his musical talents, playing a tune on the piano that he had written himself. Then came the assassination of President Kennedy in 1963. Nixon claims he chose not to be a candidate in 1964, perhaps because he expected Kennedy's Vice President and successor, Lyndon Baines Johnson, to win by a landslide. Instead, Nixon worked hard for the Republican Party. He collected favors while paying his dues. He may not have liked it, but he realized that was the way to win. As a private citizen he traveled to four continents, thereby keeping himself in the news and staying abreast of foreign policy. Through it all he kept a wary eye on the presidency.

When Nixon announced his candidacy in February 1968, he seemed to be in the right place at the right time once again. The events of the preceding four years had helped him a great deal: The Vietnam War had escalated and anti-war sentiment was mounting against Johnson; there had been two more heart-wrenching assassinations of national figures—Robert F. Kennedy and Martin Luther King; and riots and demonstrations were taking place throughout the country. Nixon presented an image of safety and stability. He won his party's nomination and pledged to bring order out of turmoil.

The press wrote that Nixon was better prepared in 1968 than he had been in 1960. They joked about still another *new* Nixon, but the fact is that the widespread anti-Johnson sentiment also helped him. The Democrats were clearly hurt by the Vietnam War and yet their candidate for President, Hubert Humphrey, had declared his support of the administration's stand against withdrawal. During the campaign Nixon avoided commenting on the issue. He saw an opportunity for the possibility of open warfare among the Democrats and unity among the Republicans. He invoked the memory of Abraham Lincoln, saying that he too wanted to bring the American people together, and he reemphasized the issue of law and order. He blamed the liberal Democrats for the upheaval in the country and rallied the Republican majority behind him. Nixon appealed to the middle American voters because he focused on the issues that concerned them. He aimed his campaign at the "forgotten" American—a white, middle-class, hawkish, patriotic group that felt ignored during the 1960s.

When President Johnson suddenly stopped the bombing of North Vietnam, the presidential race became neck-and-neck between Humphrey and Nixon. But it was too late. The damage to Humphrey's campaign had already been done. In the end, Richard Nixon won. His victory proved to be one of the most astonishing political comebacks in history.

The Thirty-Seventh President of the United States

Richard M. Nixon was elected President of the United States on November 5, 1968. He garnered 31,770,237 votes, or 43.4 percent of the ballots cast, to Hubert Humphrey's 31,270,533 votes, or 42.7 percent of the ballots cast. Alabama Governor George Wallace received 13.5 percent of the vote, numbering 9,906,141, which clearly spoiled the chances for a Democratic win. In the new Congress, the Republicans would be a minority government, with only 42 senators out of 100, and 192 representatives to the Democrats' 243. These numbers meant that Nixon would have to tread carefully regarding the war in Vietnam, policies dealing with the economy and inflation, racial integration, and foreign affairs with the Soviet Union, China, and the Middle East.

Having attained the goal of the Presidency which had previously eluded him, Nixon set about forming his team of closest advisers and confidants. The litmus test for membership on the governing team was one's status as a Nixon loyalist. The main players were Spiro Agnew as Vice President, H. Robert Haldeman as White House Chief of Staff, John Ehrlichman with responsibility for domestic issues, Daniel Patrick Moynihan for urban affairs, John Mitchell as Attorney General, Melvin Laird as Secretary of Defense, John Connally joining later as Secretary of the Treasury; Henry Kissinger as National Security chief with eventual special responsibility for foreign affairs (overshadowing William Rogers, the Secretary of State until Kissinger's appointment to that office in September 1973), and Alexander Haig as assistant to Kissinger. A number of other appointees to the White House staff had served Nixon before and would continue to serve him loyally. Some of their names would later become enmeshed in the Watergate episode—Charles Colson, John Dean (moving over from the Justice Department to be Nixon's Counsel in July, 1970), Egil "Bud" Krogh, Patrick Buchanan (a part of the Nixon team since 1966 in charge of political intelligence, allowing him to make good use of his decided partisanship), Jeb Magruder, and Alexander Butterfield, assistant to Haldeman and the one who would later reveal the existence of the presidential tapes during the Watergate affair.

Some of these individuals would belong to Nixon's "inner circle" and some would not. For example, Spiro Agnew never belonged to it. Kissinger used his own "dirty tricks" to block access to the President in order to enhance his own position in the inner circle. Nixon, priding himself on his knowledge of and ability in foreign affairs would talk to Kissinger about global affairs as a "big system," but Secretary of State Rogers, was kept out of such discussions. The Kissinger and Rogers dichotomy was taken care of by Haldeman.[10] Nixon was fascinated by John Connally who was a macho person. Dean and Colson, who would perform any task delegated to them, were lower in status than others, but still within the inner circle (the circle contained a hierarchy). Sometimes members of the inner circle lost their status in it. Ehrlichman was cut out twice, and in late 1972 Nixon had a falling-out with Kissinger.[11] Nixon was capable of dividing and uniting his advisers, but had difficulty in firing them. He had both inept and very talented subordinates, and Nixon perceived and related to them differently. Some were there to be ordered around, and the talented ones were there to bolster his sense of superiority and intelligence as extensions of himself; the latter played roles similar to that played by "Chief" Newman of his younger years, who protected him.

The longevity of the terms of many of these and other members of Nixon's team of advisers is perhaps directly attributable to Nixon's inability to fire anybody, and his well-known desire to avoid confrontations at any costs. It was Haldeman's job to handle any dismissals. A case in point was J. Edgar Hoover, long-time head of the FBI. Hoover stopped accommodating the President's requests for wiretaps on people in government whom Nixon either wanted to monitor or whom he suspected of leaking information to the press. Knowing that Hoover had files on everyone and that he also knew a great deal about Nixon's "dirty tricks," the President preferred trying to get Hoover to resign rather than dismiss him. The problem resolved itself upon Hoover's death in office on May 2, 1972.

In domestic affairs, Nixon's legislative attainments were not outstanding, but as Joan Hoff has shown, he did more than he has been given credit for.[12] One of the main reasons for this was that he neither cared about nor enjoyed the rough and tumble of domestic issues. Ehrlichman served as the main policymaker for internal affairs. The major issue confronting Nixon in the domestic arena dealt with the economy and the inflation driven by that economy which was geared up to fight the Vietnam War. As the war waxed and waned, unemployment crept up, especially at Boeing Aircraft. Nixon had to stabilize the economy.

The standard Republican bromides of cutting social programs and reducing the size of the government did not work, and the deficit related to the war rose to $25 billion—well past the $15 billion mark predicted by Lyndon Johnson. Although he hated government regulation of the economy, Nixon was responsible for more regulations than any other President since Franklin Roosevelt. He was even advised and pressured into using price control and wage freezes, upsetting labor leaders. For example, in an attempt to strengthen the dollar by closing the gold window, he did away with pegging the price of gold at $35 an ounce and let the dollar float, which served only to devalue it. He also imposed a ten percent tax on imports. All of this was largely the work of John Connally, Secretary of the Treasury. Other additional regulations involved environmental issues. Although Nixon personally detested these attempts at cleaning up the environment, William Ruckelshaus at the Environmental Protection Agency (EPA) kept trying to improve the quality of air and to protect the environment, requiring these regulations.

Desegregation was another issue that plagued Nixon. In the South desegregationists sought to use the courts to further the interests of greater integration. The major question was how to achieve quality education for everyone, and the answer was forced busing. Southern members of the Congress pressured the President to force the courts to relent on this issue. Nixon's stance, which he promulgated to all his staff, was to observe the law but not to do one extra thing. He felt that the blacks would never give him any credit if he enforced the law. In addition, his Secretary of Health, Education, and Welfare, Robert Finch, was interested in running for the Senate from California and wanted to amass a good record on desegregation. It was a no-win situation for Nixon. At best, he wanted the problem to just go away. At the least, he hoped for voluntary compliance with the law of the land, which was highly unlikely in the South.

Another area in which Nixon attempted to make an impact was welfare. Here he had the assistance of his adviser on urban affairs, Daniel Patrick Moynihan, who had enlisted Nixon's support for a comprehensive program of welfare reform. Moynihan, an intellectual from Harvard, enlisted the President's support despite the opposition he encountered from Federal Reserve Chairman Arthur Burns, a conservative, who tried to temper the liberalism of Moynihan.

The plan that finally emerged was the Family Assistance Plan (FAP), which had the capacity to transform the welfare system radically. It was nothing short of a plan to guarantee income for all Americans. Initially, the response was favorable, but as so often happened, Nixon lost interest in the program as the Left and the Right complained of its being too much or too little. It got through the House, but foundered in the Senate where the Finance Committee voted it down 14–1. Despite Nixon's conservativeness, he respected the liberal Moynihan's intellect, and had been won over by him during this time, at least for a while.

Nixon was perhaps at his worst on the domestic front when he had to fill two vacancies on the Supreme Court. He set his mind on appointing what he called "strict constructionists," and if they were Southern strict constructionists, so much the better. This fit in with his desire to get the courts to stop pushing bussing as the best way to achieve school integration. He first appointed Warren E. Burger to replace the retiring Chief Justice, Earl Warren. Burger was a party activist and a "law and order man." He easily won confirmation. The next opportunity Nixon had to nominate a judge, however, was a disaster. It started badly and ended badly.

When another vacancy occurred, Attorney General John Mitchell suggested a South Carolinian Appeals Court Judge, Clement F. Haynsworth. For reasons to be discussed in chapter 9, his nomination was turned back by the Senate 55–45. Still committed to his Southern strategy, Nixon then nominated another Southerner, G. Harold Carswell, judge of the Fifth Circuit Court of Appeals in northern Florida. His nomination too was derailed. This was another first for Nixon—the first time a President had had two Supreme Court nominations rejected in a row!

Having demonstrated his solidarity with the conservatism of the South, Nixon then appointed someone whom the Senate would confirm. Burger recommended fellow Minnesotan Harry A. Blackmun, who was quickly confirmed 94–0. Blackmun would proceed to have an enormous influence on the court, especially through his position in support of abortion in the landmark case Roe v. Wade. Nixon had two more opportunities to fill seats on the bench and he did so with Lewis Powell, Jr. and William Rehnquist. This was done despite Pat Nixon's obvious support for the appointment of a woman.

What interest Nixon lacked in domestic affairs, he more than made up for in the sphere of foreign policy. He inherited the war in Vietnam from LBJ and was determined to bring it to a successful conclusion. Peace with honor was his driving ambition. He wanted to end the carnage, bring the men and women home, heal the nation's wounds, and reorient a's foreign policy so that the policies of the United States were ...ore in tune with its capabilities. He managed to bring about détente with the Soviet Union and forge an arms control policy that made the world a safer place. He also repaired the rift in Sino-American relations, becoming the first American President to be received in both Beijing and Moscow. All this was done by a man who had made his early reputation as a doctrinaire anti-Communist.

Nixon's strategy in foreign policy matters represented a shift from reliance on the doctrine of military superiority to the recognition of the need simply for "military sufficiency." While never fully defined, this strategy boiled down to giving the United States, in any situation, a range of options from doing nothing to engaging in nuclear war. The U.S. would also let her allies play a greater role in world affairs so that it would no longer have to be the world's policeman. In essence, that was the new "Nixon Doctrine." It would allow the United States to reorder its priorities by cutting the defense budget and eliminating the draft. Elimination of the draft would also have the added advantage of getting the nation's youth off of the President's back as he worked to achieve peace in Vietnam.

The first step toward that goal of ending the war in Vietnam, which had divided the nation and undermined its self-confidence, was to negotiate with the North Vietnamese. Here Nixon relied greatly on Kissinger as they engaged in secret talks with the North Vietnamese while official talks were being carried out simultaneously.

Bombing raids on North Vietnam were to be halted. Large numbers of American troops would also be withdrawn as part of the policy of the Vietnamization of the war—that is, the building up and training of the South Vietnamese forces so that they could assume a greater part of the burden of the war. It is impossible to underestimate the difficulty of achieving an end to the war without appearing to abandon South Vietnam to the communist forces, and making sure that Nixon did not become the first American President to lose a war.

While the war continued Nixon achieved a strategic arms agreement with the Soviets and opened the door to China. Part of his strategy was to enlist the Soviets and the communist Chinese in bringing pressure on the North Vietnamese to end the war. His attempts to end the war ultimately spread the war to Laos and Cambodia as he ordered bombings of those regions in an attempt to halt the flow of armaments to the North Vietnamese troops. Those bombings also damaged Nixon's credibility on the homefront.

All this led to what would prove to be Nixon's downfall: Disclosure of his secret negotiations was leaked to the press. Nixon became "paranoid" and sought to ferret out the persons responsible through the use of illegal wiretaps and other means. Then excerpts from the Pentagon Papers, a top-secret study of the origins of the Vietnam War and its conduct, were given to the *New York Times* by Daniel Ellsberg, who had worked for former Secretary of Defense Robert McNamara, who had served in the Kennedy and Johnson administrations. When these excerpts were published by the newspaper on June 13, 1971, Nixon's rage was unbounded. A group that became known as "The Plumbers" was organized in the White House to contain the leaks. From here it was only a small step to the Watergate break-in and the downfall of the Nixon presidency.

Even as applause for his successes rang in Nixon's ears and he was surrounded with the adulation and attention that he seemed to need, the stage was being set for his downfall. Nixon had managed to avoid disaster many times in his life, but within a brief six years, he would prove that ultimately he could not evade the inner hand that guided him.

PART TWO

The Mind and Personality of Richard Nixon

6

A Bird's Eye View

We will now focus on the many events that we believe were traumatic for Richard Nixon and that we think induced conflicts in him during his formative years, i.e., infancy through adolescence. Our clinical knowledge of human development allows us to make good "guesses" as to how these events affected him at the time and how he dealt with them as an adult. We will describe observable behavior patterns and events in Nixon's adult life to provide evidence supporting those guesses. In this way, we can be sure we are on the right track. The meanings of the behavior patterns and events can then be explained through our "construction" of Richard's childhood mental experiences which became the building blocks of his personality.

Traumas and Conflicts

"Hunger" and Crying in Early Childhood

Psychological influences on the infant Richard evolved from the state of his mother's mind while she was pregnant with him. At that time, as explained earlier, Hannah's husband had been frustrated in his efforts to find an external solution for his own internal needs and wishes, and this, we feel, affected Hannah as well. It was at this critical period that the pregnant Hannah was uprooted; she had to struggle internally with the move to Yorba Linda around the time of Richard's birth. Since character traits are defensively exaggerated during times of stress, it is likely that Hannah, already someone who kept her emotions under control, felt the strong grip of her Quaker conscience even more so while living in Yorba Linda. We surmise that Hannah was depressed at this time.

The timing of the Nixon family's move and its effect on Hannah were important to the infant Richard's development. It might seem that, due to her own emotional state, Hannah could not be a "good-enough" mother in some ways. During these first months of life a child must psychologically feed off of the interaction with the mother to acquire and nourish the first components of the organized mind, which develops within the framework of the infant's biologically given potentials.[1] We believe that Hannah's depression, together with her deeply implanted reserve and self-control, prevented her from responding to her child's cues and from building mutually rewarding interactions between herself and her child.

Another complicating factor during infant Richard's first year of life was the invasive appearance of his infant cousin when Richard was six months old. He suddenly had to compete for the physical and psychological nourishment at Hannah's breast. Sensing unconsciously a decrease in the amount of attention and milk he was receiving, it was likely that Richard did go "hungry" at times, at least psychologically. Then, at the age of eighteen months, Nixon had even more competition for his mother's attention when his brother Donald was born. The reality of having to be concerned about physical and psychological food and hunger during early childhood created an unconscious foundation of deprivation of food/love in later childhood and adulthood. He thus would have to deal with this sense of being deprived in order not to have unpleasant feelings.

Later on, John Ehrlichman, Nixon's chief domestic policy adviser, tells of bringing poverty legislation to the President for review and listening to him recall how his mother had grown tomatoes in her garden so that her family could at least have soup to eat. Ehrlichman concluded that Nixon must have once known what it was like to go hungry.[2]

Elizabeth Wirth Marvick, who compared Nixon's and Churchill's early childhood (Nixon admired Churchill), reminds us that the President was self-denying with respect to food and that he was notorious for choosing meager lunches.[3] His adult eating habits probably reflected his early childhood experience. Nixon in his memoirs described as a noteworthy occurrence having been served country sausage for breakfast (instead of his usual wheat germ) while a houseguest of John

Connally.[4] Churchill knew of his own "oral rage" and its connection with his search for power. He was known for his indulgence in food and drink. In contrast, Nixon denied his "oral" anger and denied himself any indulgence in good food.

In order to understand Nixon's infantile anger, we must make sense of the fact that the infant Richard cried so much. Donald Winnicott, addressing infant development in his book *Mother and Child*, titled one of the chapters "Why Do Babies Cry?" He concluded that crying "gives the baby the feeling that he is exercising his lungs (satisfaction) or else it is a signal of distress (pain), or else it is an expression of anger (rage), or else it is a song of sadness (grief)."[5] An infant's crying may be caused at times by physiological difficulties, such as colic, at which time the mother's efforts to comfort the child may be fruitless. But crying also signifies a baby's reaction to not finding a "fit" between his needs and the satisfaction he is able to derive from his mother or caregiver. Regardless of the reasons behind the infant's frustration, i.e. physiological or psychological, the unpleasant experiences are internalized. Eventually, the infant's crying may change function, and he may come to cry for purely psychological reasons.

Unable to quiet him, Nixon's mother and grandmother tried to deny that his crying was a sign of need. Instead, they placed value on it by declaring that he had a strong, laudable voice that bespoke leadership. Despite their belief that Richard's continuous crying during his first year of life was a positive sign, it would appear that his crying was, in fact, a clue to disturbances in the crucial mother-child experiences.

Throughout Nixon's life this act of crying—which means "Help me! I am hurting!"—was *transferred* to behavior that stems from using the mouth, the lips, the tongue, and the upper digestive and respiratory systems. This area of the body, especially the mouth (psychoanalysts call it the oral zone), is associated not only with crying but also with eating, receiving physical and psychological nourishment, and later using language. Nixon's oral zone thus became excessively utilized for functions that defended him against his early traumas and conflicts. Eventually, his crying would change function as he began to command attention through speech. For example, he became interested in public speaking and in drama, excelling in both.

Most children, especially young ones, cry at times to get attention. Richard seems to have cried often, however, not only to express possible physiological distress—pain, rage, and later, grief—but also because crying is an oral means by which he could focus attention upon himself. As he matured, he came to sublimate this process: he turned instead to related devices that involved the use of speech, which served to help him influence and control others. For example, one may consider the Checkers Speech as a derivative of his early crying, in that they were both means of attracting attention and of putting the spotlight on himself.

One can "bite" with words, making others cry; or "soothe" with words, making others happy. Nixon's use of his tongue, mouth, and lungs for both purposes is well known. Nixon's brother Donald noted that "Dick used his tongue more than his fists."[6] Richard's grammar school years yield many such recollections and examples of derivatives of his (oral) aggressiveness, which were mostly sublimated at that time. In addition to winning a church recitation contest over much older participants— including his brother Harold—Richard, when still a young boy, often spoke at parent-teacher association meetings. Elizabeth Glover, a Nixon family friend, recalled that "whenever [Richard] performed at a PTA meeting . . . everybody turned out."[7] Yoneko Dobashi Iwatsura, a grammar school classmate, also remembered that during the class "show and tell" periods, Nixon "would always have more to say than all the rest, and it was always interesting."[8] As a fifth grader Nixon participated in his first debate. His position was "Resolve that it is better to own your own home than to rent."[9] Nixon researched the subject extensively prior to the debate.[10] Most likely he did so in order both to ensure that his knowledge of the material would impress his classmates, and to direct attention to himself.

During his high school years Nixon's oratorical abilities were sharpened, as is evidenced by the many friends who commented on his debating and forensic abilities. James Grieves, a classmate and teammate, recalls that Nixon was "outstanding in forensics . . . and won many *firsts* in this field. He was an excellent public speaker."[11] Sheldon Beeson, Richard's cousin, observed, "If you ever got in an argument with Dick, you would lose. . . . You just can't argue around Dick because he would always win."[12] During his junior year he won the prestigious National High School Oratorical Contest with a speech entitled, "Our Privileges Under the Constitution." His main opponent and the favorite in the contest, Herton Wray, declared, "Nixon was a tremendous orator then. He had a tremendous empathy to communicate with his audience. He had a way of reaching out and getting hold of them."[13] In assessing his former debating teammate's oratorical abilities, Wayne Long commented, "He was so darn good."[14] Another classmate recalled a speech Nixon delivered to his junior English class: "He gave it before the class and Miss Jennie B. [McGregor, chairman of the English Department] as though we were Congress. It was great."[15] Yet another classmate recalled that when Nixon won the championship for the Whittier Union High School debating team, "He became pretty much of a hero in all of our

eyes for that put Whittier Union on the map for the first time. We
n't help but recognize his outstanding ability as a public speaker, even
then."[16]

To summarize, we can see in young Richard attempts to change the
"memory" of his crying and the unpleasantness (i.e., anger, envy) he
experienced through oral means, in this case through public speaking,
as a way to gain attention and control. Nixon had an image of having
been blessed with a "silver tongue" since early childhood. He considered
debating a crucial tool, even though it did not always ensure success for
him—sometimes factors other than oratory ability affected the outcome.
The result of the television debates of the 1960 presidential campaign
illustrate that his physical presence sometimes detracted from his performance, for, although those who listened to the debates on the radio
felt that Nixon had surpassed Kennedy, those who viewed them on television perceived that Kennedy clearly had overshadowed his opponent.

Trauma at the Age of Nine Months

The reader will recall that when Richard was nine months old he was
exposed to a physical separation from his mother because of her mastoid
operation, at which time he moved to his grandmother's house temporarily. This external event coincided with a certain psychobiological
developmental event that happens to every small child. At this time of
life a toddler experiences what one researcher on child development,
Henri Parens, calls a "biological upsurge" of the child's natural aggression.[17] Parens notes that infants feel uncomfortable when this upsurge of
aggression is directed toward their mothers, upon whom they depend
and whom they now perceive more distinctly. As the child's aggressive
actions result in the mother saying "Hush!" or "Don't bang on the table
with your toy!" or "Don't hit me!" infants begin to learn to inhibit their
aggression within their relationships with their mothers. Although the
baby wants to continue to gratify his aggressive expressions, he restrains
himself because he wants to be loved by his mother. However, the baby
cannot "think out" this conflict in the same way an adult can. The experience of going through this struggle is more a psychobiological process
than an intellectual exercise. Internalized curbing signals the very beginning of the formation of the *superego*, the theoretical entity that embod-
ies the strictures of parental discipline and societal standards. In lay-
man's terms this is known as the conscience, with its emphasis on control. Its form in early life is obviously far more primitive than what will
develop later. In its early stages it simply stresses obedience as a way to
avoid distress, but as the child grows and develops mentally, the curbing

process gradually refines itself. At the same time, the prohibiting aspects of the parental images become more integrated with the idealized aspects of the parents.

Since the nine-month-old child wants to be loved by his mother, he begins to learn to make use of *displacement,* the unconscious substitution of one object (or person) for another, and of *projection,* the unconscious feeling that someone or something out there is the source of an unacceptable impulse or thought. Instead of being angry with the mother, the child may direct his anger, through displacement and projection, toward another person or thing—e.g., a doll. The other person or thing then becomes "the enemy," while the child continues to remain dependent on the mother.

In Nixon's situation, his biological upsurge of aggression came at a time when his mother was not present, so he faced a dilemma. There was no mother to check or soothe his aggressive upsurge. From his mother he could have "learned"—through identifying with her prohibiting functions—to find a comfortable balance between his impulses and the prohibition of them. His grandmother, who took care of little Richard during his mother's absence, could not stop his crying; she actually "joined" him by praising the way he cried. Without his mother and without needed empathy from his grandmother who served as a mother substitute for a while, he was left to his own devices—thus the beginning of his superego (conscience) formation was traumatized, while his use of displacement and projection and "enemy"-making increased.

We consider it possible that a few of the character traits in the adult Richard Nixon's personality might be traced back to his trauma at the age of nine months. We must emphasize here that we are referring to *the root* of these character traits. Certainly the effects of other traumas and associated conflicts that occurred later in life subsequently *condensed* with the effects of the trauma he experienced at the age of nine months. Richard Nixon, under some circumstances, utilized excessive displacement and projection. While his mother remained a "saint" in his conscious mind, he was for a while preoccupied with "enemies" out there. During his presidency he made a list of them and felt that they might harm him in one way or another.

His utilization of his conscience (superego) under certain circumstances was not benign. Either he would punish himself or, conversely, with a sense of entitlement, he would be ruthless toward others in pursuing his goals. Stubbornly, he would want to attach himself to women and deny their rejection of him, just as he wanted to deny separation from his mother, from Ola, and from Pat while he courted her. Once he got their attention, however, he would treat them as though he wanted revenge, or, as is the case with his mother, he would attempt to deny the feelings caused by the separation and consider them "saints."

We therefore believe that "losing" his mother at the age of nine months—combined with later separations from her, which required him to take care of himself emotionally— stimulated the premature maturation of his mind. We can say that young Richard utilized the "normal" upsurge of his infantile aggression in asserting his will prematurely. Such a child begins to develop an "I am above these difficulties" personality and attempts to avoid the hurt, rejected, and devalued aspects of his personality. The foundation of Nixon's "I am first" and "I am above hurts" (narcissistic) personality most likely appeared in the first year of his life. Individuals who develop this type of psychic organization depend on their own assets, denying their dependency needs. However, the dependency remains in the shadows. To shore up their denial of being dependent and emotionally hungry, such persons are driven to become nonpareils, gaining an exaggerated sense of self-love and self-reliance. Sometimes this can be a positive influence in a person's life: for instance, a study of politicians in Washington, D.C., by Lloyd Etheredge revealed that the narcissistic personality organization is common among such individuals.[18] In the case of Richard Nixon, a compulsive seeker of acclaim and leadership bent on recognition, it is clear that a narcissistic personality organization contributed to his observable behavior in both positive and negative ways, as we will show.

A Special Being

Clinical studies have shown that the way a parent regards his or her child affects the child's own developing sense of self. For some famous statesmen, parental high regard became self-fulfilling prophecies, even though the parents in question probably did not consciously think of their children as being future leaders of men and nations. The rescue fantasy of the Turkish leader Mustafa Kemal Atatürk for example, dovetailed with his mother's perception of him as a rescuer and as a replacement for siblings born earlier but who had died in childhood.[19] It is said that when David Ben-Gurion was born frail and with an uncommonly large head, his family defensively concluded that he was destined for great things.[20]

Although the mothering Richard received as an infant was deficient in some important ways, his mother and grandmother clearly regarded him as a special being. For example, they associated his loud crying with a future talent for oratory. His early childhood traumas made Richard incorporate into his developing personality the idea that he was above hurts—while remaining covertly dependent. In Yorba Linda, the Nixons' four sons slept in the same room. However, when the family moved to Whittier, Harold, Donald, and Arthur bunked together while Richard was given his own small room because his mother thought he needed privacy for studying.

In summary, Richard definitely was perceived as "special," fitting psychoanalytic findings that parental perceptions of specialness propel talented youngsters toward great achievements and, at the least, play a role in their developing a grandiose personality.[21] As an adult, Richard wished to be perceived as "special" by the public as well. While he was aloof in his relationships with individuals, he had great appeal to the public; he succeeded in making a great number of people see him as "special," e.g., a hero after he won combats against South American mobs, against Hiss, and against Khrushchev. He also succeeded in making the public see him as needy and vulnerable, awakening in some of them a protective instinct. His interaction with the public paralleled his interaction with his mother. As Tom Wicker has demonstrated, by exposing his ambition and his vulnerability Nixon made himself "one of us," just another American pursuing the American Dream.[22]

The Second and Third Years of Life

The formation of Richard's narcissistic personality began during the first year of his life, and his experiences during the next couple of years further deepened narcissistic characteristics in his personality. Psychoanalysts use the term "the anal phase" to refer to a period between 12 to 18 months and three years of age, during which children physically gain control of the anal sphincter and other muscles. This biological advance is also reflected in their mental development, and they become able to move away from or toward their mothers at will. Utilizing a large repertoire of parallel mental mechanisms, children at this age discover that they can control what they keep in and what they expel, when to be close to someone and when to be distant from that person. At times, "bad" thoughts or words have to be expelled impulsively; otherwise the individual would feel unworthy. Other times, that which is in the body— i.e., feces—is perceived as a "jewel," and the child may not want to give it up. This may be the mental beginning of miserliness.

Between the ages of two and three, a child expands the repertoire of his mental functions so that they now include what psychoanalysts call *intellectualization, rationalization, isolation, and undoing.* To use one's mind in an intelligent way and to think rationally are obviously necessary developments for all of us. However, those who welcome anal-level control may utilize such necessary functions excessively to cover up their emotions and hurts. It should be recalled that Nixon's mother and others encouraged Richard to use his brain. He excelled in this, which is admirable. He had the ability to separate feelings from deeds, to calculate cooly. He used his intellectualization and rationalization as his mental armament to solve problems, to adapt to new situations, and to defend himself against realistic enemies. But he also used them to defend against fantasized enemies. In addition he practiced undoing, in that "good" and "bad" acts had to follow each other; and, instead of simply utilizing these functions, Nixon exaggerated them, as we will demonstrate. The mental mechanisms associated with his second year of life development became so habitual that they became part of his everyday personality makeup.

Richard may have felt more comfortable when he reached the anal phase and developed mental capacities which, psychologically speaking, helped him to control his anxieties from the first year of life. The individual who holds onto his "anality" may later become a *collector* of that which he considers to be "good" and necessary for his self-esteem. In other words, he tightens his "mental sphincter" to support his sense of self. When he perceives items he has collected as "bad," he impulsively tries to get rid of them, at least symbolically.

Indeed, Richard Nixon was a collector. He collected many "first time events," presidencies, taped interviews, and so on. He needed these for his self-esteem and his sense of control. His baffling insistence on keeping the famous White House tapes that later incriminated him can be understood from a psychological point of view. In this event he intertwined "oral" and "anal" issues. Under the influence of anality he had an urge to stockpile the tapes (which, to him, were anal gems that could not be given away), while at the oral level they, like a mother's milk, supported the inflation of his sense of self. Since his inner reality triumphed over the prudent dictates of outer reality, he could not let the tapes go, despite the danger of keeping them.

Nixon obsessionally controlled his feelings, keeping them within. With this behavior he not only expressed the effects of the controlling behavior of his second or third year of life, but also indicated an identification with an obsessional mother. However, things kept within sometimes turn sour, just as the unabsorbed portion of "good" food has to be expelled. On the White House tapes Nixon's obsessional discharge of "dirty" words represents the elimination of "bad" contents held in too long.

Richard as an Oedipal Child

Richard Nixon was unable to resolve his Oedipus complex adaptively partly because his father seems to have had his own unresolved oedipal problems. In normal development, the male child between the ages of three and one-half and five and one-half competes with his father for his mother's love. Being scared of the father, he gives up this competition and instead identifies with his father, thus becoming a little man himself. In Richard's case, identification with the image of the father did not help him much, because in spite of his father's menacing outside ("the aggressor"), he was a weak man inside.

A strong oedipal father can absorb his son's oedipal struggles, allowing them to be directed toward himself without having to retaliate or become threatening or frightening. It seems that Nixon's father was not able to help Richard through his oedipal difficulties. Furthermore, Richard was not prepared to have a "normal" oedipal phase because of the influence of traumas and conflicts of his earlier life. He therefore entered his oedipal struggle with the beginnings of a narcissistic personality which had absorbed controlling and obsessional (anal) maneuvers to protect his budding grandiosity and to deny and project onto others his "hungry" and devalued parts. Persons with such mental developments split the images of themselves into a "good/idealized" unit technically called a *grandiose self* and a devalued *hungry self*. During daily life he tried to hold on to his grandiose side while attempting to hide his devalued side. The narcissist "splits" others as well, placing them in one of two categories: either idealized beings whose task it is to love and adore the grandiosity of the narcissistic individual and/or reflect the individual's self-sufficiency like a mirror; or devalued entities who can be reduced to nothingness. The latter, even though devalued, still inspire fear, for they are psychic reservoirs for the individual's hungry self, which the individual tries to deny. This combination of devaluing and fearing leads to the kind of "enemy-making" prejudice and suspiciousness that we think infant Richard found difficult to manage at nine months of age, and this way of being gained ascendancy in his developing personality as he grew older.

Thus, while Nixon retained his "good" mother image to serve his grandiosity he split off a separate image of the mother that was not "good enough." At times, Pat Nixon served Richard in the same way. As a "narcissistic object" for him, like a mirror image,[23] he placed her on his "wanted" list—he had idealized her and he "had to" have her. We stated earlier that Nixon's initial attraction for Pat was partially her similarity to him: she, too, seemed self-sufficient and intelligent. After their marriage, her function changed, however. Instead of reflecting his grandiosity, she now served to enhance it. He accomplished this by devaluing her, humiliating her. Then, in comparison to a devalued person (or other), he was the greatest; Pat would reinforce this by saying in public "My husband is a great man."

Approaching his oedipal phase of life, Richard also split his father representation into the "bad one" (i.e., the communists), and the idealized, "good" father he longed for but did not have. In later life he imposed the "good" image onto others, then used them to shore up his self love. This seems evident in his association with men such as "Chief" Newman and Dean Horack, both of whom he made into protectors of himself.

Nixon attracted the attention of "Chief" Newman because of his self-sacrificing behavior while on Whittier's football team; their relationship supplied Nixon with a much-needed "good" father figure who rewarded his suffering by boosting his self-esteem. Dean Horack played a similar role later by protecting Nixon from the repercussions of his failure to sign up for the California Bar examination at the proper time.

It seems likely that Nixon used Whittaker Chambers in a similar way, leaving aside the issue of whether Chambers merited such idealization. Chambers was a necessary party in the attack on Alger Hiss who, as a communist sympathizer and a "spy," represented a devalued but dangerous image in Nixon's view. The relationship with Chambers in the real world was important for his political future, but, we believe, it also responded to Nixon's internal need for an idealized father. This alliance persisted even though Nixon became angry with Chambers at one point—as noted earlier, when he learned that Chambers had suppressed certain evidence. In other words Nixon expected Chambers to have protected him from bad consequences as one would expect a father to do.

Ralph de Toledano called the Nixon/Chambers relationship "poignant," noting that, "At times of stress, even when he was Vice President, Nixon would drive to Westminster (in Maryland) for a visit, informing only friends such as myself and the most reliable members of his staff."[24] de Toledano believed that Nixon was seeking "intellectual replenishment and emotional stability"[25] from Chambers, who was well educated. "Never one to open his heart or his mind unstintingly, (Nixon) came as close to this with Chambers as he had with any man."[26] Chambers allegedly was a man who also displayed feminine characteristics. In view of this, it is likely that he combined elements of a much-needed total parent for Nixon.

During his political life Nixon often sought the company of his friend and confidant Charles G. (Bebe) Rebozo, who sat with him by the hour in times of crisis. Rebozo seldom talked, always deferred to Nixon, and could keep a secret.[27] It is possible that in Nixon's mind Rebozo, like Chambers, combined idealized elements of the "good" mother and the "good" father.

Nixon's search for an idealized father is dramatized by his lifelong wish to identify with Abraham Lincoln, a dream that began in childhood. When, as a twelve-year-old, Nixon was sent more than a hundred miles away from home to study music with his aunt, he received a picture of the sixteenth president from his grandmother and hung it over his bed.[28] He apparently admired Lincoln from that point on. The six-month separation from his mother during his adolescence, when a youngster internally revisits his oedipal phase, seemed to increase his desire and his anxiety to be close to her. In order to be able to deal with them he continued to seek a strong father image, which he found in the image of Lincoln.

However, the American people never quite managed to support the notion that Nixon was another Lincoln.[29] Fluctuations in Nixon's behavior were a big obstacle. When his "hungry" self appeared he acted paranoid and the public perceived him as weak. When he gave his "Checkers Speech" he was no longer the combative hero stamping out evil, but a hurt child who wanted the public to protect him in a motherly way. And when he confronted an opponent, even one whom the public wished him to fight, he sometimes resorted to such questionable maneuvers to protect his grandiose self that his followers saw him as a controversial figure, not an idealized one like Lincoln.

Crystallization of the Personality

Nixon's traumatic years of latency and especially adolescence appear to have prevented him from successfully working through his conflicted attachment to the images of the parents of his childhood. During his adolescent passage he was unsuccessful in his attempt to modify and tame the images of the others and the world around him. The death of his brother Arthur (and later Harold) supported his sense that danger existed in the environment, causing him to retain, as a defensive adaptation, a dominant narcissistic-obsessional-suspicious orientation to life, which interfered with his ability to modify his maladaptation to trauma as a child. He continued to experience the world as a hazardous place, as symbolized by his view of a "bad" oedipal father, a potential castrator who lived in the body of his biological father. (As noted, Frank worked as a butcher and actually used knives and other cutting tools.) Additionally, his guilt over unacceptable feelings or thoughts was deepened by a kind of *survivor guilt*: his sibling, Arthur, had died while he had been spared!

The character traits that centered around his exaggerated narcissism and (anal) control of his childhood crystallized in his total personality during his adolescence. We provide evidence for this in the next section.

Anxieties

Anxiety Concerning the Loss of the Mother or Her Love

Richard developed certain character traits (aloofness, for example) and the beginning of his narcissistic personality along with obsessional elements to deal with his anxiety concerning the "loss" of Hannah or her love. The events during his passage through adolescence made him retain his anxiety about such occurrences rather than diminishing them. His mother's psychological absences, compounded by frequent physical separations, meant that young Richard was often left without her or her love.

Thus, for the child Richard, the fear of losing his mother had some foundation; he did actually "lose" her through separation more than once. He was forced to share her and her love with an infant cousin and with his brother Donald. He had "lost" her at the age of nine months during Hannah's hospitalization, at the age of twelve, when he went to stay with his aunt in order to take advantage of piano lessons, and during adolescence when his mother departed for Arizona. Physical separations were compounded by emotional ones created by his mother's depression when he was born and her grief (hidden though it may have been) when Richard's siblings died. These separations may have caused him to feel rejected. We believe that the memory of early absences stayed alive in him, and the maintenance of his grandiose self supplied him with the illusion that he was above such hurts. However, the threat of losing his mother and her love and his reaction to this threat sometimes emerged in spite of his efforts to deny them. According to Abrahamsen, "Behind all his actions as a child, and later as an adult, was a person who had been cheated out of love. He wanted it back at all costs."[30]

Children who have actually experienced loss of the mother, either physically or emotionally, will find it difficult to separate from their mothers emotionally (intrapsychically), a necessary step for achieving individuation. The process of achieving individuation is known as *separation-individuation*.[31] Richard Nixon's life experiences made it so hard for him to negotiate his way through this process that he developed certain behavioral patterns. For example, as an adult, he had to maintain a link to the image of the mother of his childhood, in order to sustain the illusion that she would not be totally out of reach, and that she would feed and protect him should his self-sufficiency fail. Evidence of Nixon's need for emotional refueling, or his need to maintain links to his mother, is provided by Nixon's attachment to a letter Hannah wrote to him after his inauguration as vice president in 1953. Nixon is known to have carried this letter with him in his wallet long afterwards:

To Richard
You have gone far and we are proud of you always—I know that you will keep your relationship with your maker as it should be for after all that, as you must know, is the most important thing in this life. With love, Mother[32]

By carrying this note around with him in his wallet, Nixon made it a kind of a "linking object." The concept of a linking object has been described by Vamık Volkan and refers to objects some mourners use to deny their loss.[33] For these individuals an object such as a photograph or handkerchief becomes magical and it symbolically represents an emotional connection to the dead person. Apparently, Nixon felt a need to keep his mother's letter near him. Even though his mother died before Nixon was elected President, he was still linked to her through the note in his wallet which reinforced his unconscious illusion that she would always be available to him for emotional refueling. Being dependent on someone (however it may be hidden) means that that someone can "make" the individual or "break" him. Therefore, the dependent individual remains ambivalent regarding the person on whom he depends.

To compensate for his early and repeated physical losses, for losses of love/food, and for the emotional loss of his mother during his separation-individuation struggle, Richard Nixon was driven to attain control over his feelings, with power over others as a ready substitute. This drive for power can become self-enveloping, especially if, as was the case with Nixon, other unconscious forces contribute to it as well. He had a profound need for protective armor as embodied by titles and awards.

Although Nixon could handle tense confrontations in the political sphere, such as negotiating with Khrushchev or Zhirinovsky, in day-to-day living he avoided conflicts as much as possible. The idea of dissension in his everyday surroundings made him uncomfortable, as though it was some kind of force that would impel him to set aside his wish to be loved. He was a paper President rather than a people President, and he avoided the heated arguments that occasionally broke out among members of his administration. He preferred having arguments presented to him in writing.

John Ehrlichman, in 1982, discussed Nixon's inability to fire staff members;[34] later, in 1986, Ehrlichman elaborated on three particular cases. The first involved Walter Hickel, Secretary of the Interior. According to Ehrlichman, Nixon

> ... wanted to persuade Hickel that there was a better job for him as Governor of Alaska. He started out on this tack, and it became evident that he [Hickel] was not interested in doing that. Then Nixon did not know what to do . . . It was like killing a chicken with a spoon. It was a mess, just terrible.[35]

Pat Hitt's case was Ehrlichman's second example. At one time she had been Nixon's neighbor, and she had acquired her job through him. When a shift in the Cabinet occurred, Casper Weinberger, the new Secretary of Health, Education, and Welfare, tried to dismiss her from her position in his department. She maintained that since she had been hired by the President, she would have to be fired by the President. Ehrlichman quipped that "anybody who knew Nixon knew that that was a big insurance policy." He then told the following story:

> I set up an appointment for her to see the President, and then I programmed him with a memo telling him that Cap [Weinberger] hadn't been able to make this stick. Nixon called me because he was very upset that this had been scheduled. "Why me? Why can't you guys handle these things? . . ." It was dreadful! It was a two hour meeting. It just went on and on and on and he went all around the barn in every direction. I finally had to say to her that the President has asked for this meeting to confirm what Secretary Weinberger had already told her: that "your services are no longer required." And Nixon said, "Yeah, that's right Pat." And that was all he could bring himself to do. Otherwise we would be sitting there yet going over hill and dale.[36]

To reiterate our belief, Nixon's difficulty in firing people did not stem from any genuine concern he had for their welfare. He was narcissistic and he was a loner, and being so meant that he was preoccupied with protecting his grandiose self: he couldn't fire people because this would mean a loss of their love and adoration.

Ehrlichman's final example concerns his own firing on April 30, 1973. This, he said, was one of the few times he had ever seen the "real man to the bone." Nixon told Ehrlichman that he had prayed that he would not wake up that morning. It was too emotionally wrenching for him to fire his two closest advisers. Further insight above and beyond the real world reasons for the firings of Ehrlichman and H. R. Haldeman is provided by a Nixon interview with David Frost. Nixon said:

> And so it was late, but I did it. I cut off one arm and then cut off the other arm. . . . And I suppose you could sum it all up the way one of your British Prime Ministers summed it up, Gladstone, when he said that the first requirement for a Prime Minister is to be a good butcher. Well, I think the great story as far as a summary of Watergate is concerned, I did some of the big things rather well, I screwed up terribly in what was a little thing and became a big thing. But I will have to admit I was not a good butcher.[37]

In the cases of H. R. Haldeman and John Ehrlichman, who really were loyal to him, Nixon unconsciously felt they were there to support his superiority. Haldeman had been a former advertising executive; he had been at Nixon's side since 1956 and Nixon made him Chief of Staff. Ehrlichman was a lawyer; he handled the domestic policy. Together they controlled access to the President and were called his "Berlin Wall." When he thought they were politically "dangerous" to him, however, he dismissed them. Since he considered them to be extensions of himself at some level, to "butcher" them or any other staff member meant "butchering" himself.

Anxiety Concerning Mutilation

As described earlier, castration anxiety develops from the young boy's fear that his father will remove his sex organ if his (sexual) yearnings for his mother continue; it arises during the boy's struggle with oedipal issues. Frank Nixon's "prickliness"[38] and his physical attacks on his son did little to allay Richard's castration fears. Nixon saw his father as a castrator, separating this "bad" image of his father from the "idealized" one for whom he continued to search (by becoming a father figure himself—the leader of a nation—and by identifying with Lincoln).

During Richard's adolescence, a time of a normal reactivation of oedipal strivings for review, Frank Nixon was a butcher in actuality. To have a father who is a butcher or a surgeon does not necessarily cause the son to fear the older man, unless the child already has developmental reasons to fear castration. Most likely, his father's wielding of knives in the market seemed threatening to young Richard.[39] Later, when he became a politician, one can hear in his speeches the echoes of unconscious castration fears, along with an attempt to identify with the aggressor.

For instance, on election eve 1969, Nixon conducted a radio telethon in which he answered listeners' questions over the air. Columnist William Safire wrote, "Late that night, too late for it to really matter, he slipped and said 'now let's get down to the *nut-cutting.*' " He meant to say "brass tacks" . . . but instead used the vernacular based on castration that was often used in the political backrooms.[40] In a speech about the war in Vietnam, in 1970, Nixon spoke of "the pitiful, helpless giant" rendered impotent ("impotent" equals "castrated" in psychoanalytic terms). In the midst of Watergate he said, "The Congress *should not cut off the legs* of the President."[41] To Edward Cox, his son-in-law, on the day of his resignation on August 9, 1974, Nixon remarked, "Well, at least this *cuts it off,* Ed."[42] To David Frost he confided: "By the time I resigned I was crippled. I was crippled even before that . . . I brought myself down. *I gave them the sword. And they stuck it in.* And they twisted it with relish. And, I guess, if I'd been in their position, I'd have done the same thing."[43]

On becoming President, Nixon had the Press Room moved from the West Wing of the White House, where its occupants were privy to the intimate details of his administration, to a more isolated office.[44] Demonstrating the belief that the press was trying to mutilate him (which means to castrate him, psychologically speaking), Nixon told David Frost that his supporters "had to resist the pounding they took night after night from television commentators who were *tearing me to pieces, limb from limb.*"[45]

Self-punishment

We have found that some individuals who undergo analysis actually seem to become more distressed as the analysis continues even though well-timed and accurate interpretations during their treatment might be expected to help them maximize their gains. The cause is a clinical phenomenon known as *negative therapeutic reaction.* Sigmund Freud originally attributed such a reaction to the patient's unconscious guilt and consequent need for punishment.[46]

Stanley Olinick described how a person displaying a negative therapeutic reaction may be fixated on early phases of life. If his relationship with his mother was stressful, he may have resented her helplessness and responded to it by forming an alliance with her against dependency and fear of abandonment. If such a person's father was not psychologically available to interfere positively with the mother-child alliance, no positive resolution of the Oedipus complex can occur. Olinick found that the type of patient prone to negative therapeutic reaction often has superior intelligence, creativity, or talent. Moreover, he is likely to have experienced severe illness or the death of a sibling or a friend, and to have gastrointestinal disturbances that reflect conflicts from the first years of life.[47] (Richard Nixon's psychosomatic symptoms will be described in the next chapter.) Olinick concluded that the presence of negative therapeutic reaction indicates an unconscious need for punishment beneath which lies an injured narcissism.

Nixon's behavior resembles that of analysands who exhibit negative therapeutic reaction. At times when he needed love and support, he would "buy" them with acts that he later resented. Thus, he performed acts such as driving his wife-to-be to meetings with other men and waiting to drive her home after her dates. He would collect "love" through "being good," which would hurt and humiliate him; and then after he collected the "love" he would try to get revenge. But his retaliation might cause him to lose the "love" and then he would feel helpless again.

Nixon manifested self-punishing behavior when he accepted the position of live tackling dummy on his college football team. Most of the team members were also members of the Orthogonian Society that he had co-founded and of which he was president. We can only surmise that unconsciously he felt it necessary to pay his dues—to endure physical punishment in order to balance his superior position. Nixon's success on the California Bar examination despite his lack of time to prepare for it must have reinforced his sense of superiority; it also demonstrated how he forced himself, in a masochistic way, to punish himself to prove his superiority.

His self-punishing side had layers of significance: his need to "buy" love, his fear of surpassing his "bad" father, and his inability to enjoy success without being suspicious of the motivations of others. His reactions to the Watergate situation, which came when he was "riding high," once more exhibited his "negative therapeutic reaction." We think Nixon would have met his "Watergate" even if he had simply continued practicing law without entering public office: one can imagine his winning a major case after much persistence, only to have his triumph sullied by the revelation that he had withheld important evidence or that he had some undisclosed past association with a member of the jury.

Clumsiness

From Woodward and Bernstein we learned that Nixon was not well coordinated physically.[48] Yet this must have been apparent selectively since he had enough manual dexterity to play the piano. On the other hand he required assistance for even the simplest of tasks. For instance, his White House aide, Steve Bull, often had to help him open cardboard boxes containing souvenirs such as cufflinks, tie clasps, pens, and golf balls. Nixon had been handing out such souvenirs for years, but he was clumsy with his hands and constantly needed help opening the boxes. He could not hammer a nail or turn a screw properly. Woodward and Bernstein describe how the President once called on Bull to help him open a bottle containing allergy pills. The bottle had a child-proof cap on it, with instructions to "press down while turning." Bull saw teeth marks on the cap where Nixon had apparently tried to gnaw it open.

Dr. Salman Akhtar, a Philadelphia psychoanalyst who brought the fact of Nixon's selective clumsiness to our attention, has studied such patterns in some of his adult patients.[49] Clumsiness is multidetermined. It may stem from constitutional factors or, as Dr. Akhtar has observed in his patients, it may also derive from unconscious fantasies regarding both the struggle with separation from the mother's image and oedipal issues. The adult who seems efficient in many areas may manifest clumsiness in other areas so as to be able to summon a caregiver to the rescue. The clumsiness, like a flag, represents dependency and a plea for assistance. Nixon was not clumsy in playing the piano since it pleased his mother and got her attention through achievement. His selective clumsiness— especially in relation to using his hands—may also correspond to anxieties related to masturbation or to murderous fantasies directed toward the oedipal father. If one is clumsy, neither the masturbation nor the murderous wish regarding the father can be carried out!

A Complicated Man

It should be evident that in the case of Richard Nixon we are dealing with a most complicated man, filled with contradictions. For example, Nixon could mercilessly order the bombing of Cambodia, but he could not fire people face-to-face. He could take liberties and stretch the law to suit himself, while exhibiting a moralistic attitude. He could use curse words habitually in his office, while appearing with the utmost decorum in public. He could seek high ideals at the same time that he could initiate self-punishment.

We have shown that Nixon had difficulty integrating the image of an idealized father with that of the "bad" butcher father (the castrator). He simply could not identify with an idealized father image, see himself as "number one," and be done with it—he had to deal with an image of his father too ferocious to assimilate. Whenever he tried to defeat the "bad" father image within him he would also defeat himself, so he punished himself for it by spoiling his successes. "Playing Lincoln" seemed to validate his self-esteem, but the ever-present frightening image of the "butcher" father within him prevented him from successfully crystalliz-ing an identification with the "good" father.

Beneath the oedipal issues concerning his father's images, Nixon's maintenance and regulation of his self-esteem were handled according to psychological processes typical of a narcissistic personality. Since his habitual defenses and his adaptations could not be relied upon to keep his inner turmoil and splits in check, he had to strive continually to prove his specialness, by becoming the head man—from class president to President of the United States of America. By making himself special, he attempted to dissociate himself from any negative, unwanted aspects of himself or of his internalized images of important others in his life. We believe that President Nixon's narcissistic personality and fluctuating self-esteem explain many of his decisions and actions regarding his domestic and foreign policies. We do not mean to imply any lack of capa-bility in the political arena; on the contrary, he was quite talented at con-sidering political moves. What we are saying is that certain patterns moti-vated by internal demands were associated with his conscious delibera-tions and manipulations. At times, however, these internal motivations became highly influential, such that he would lose his perspective on what was trivial and what was politically significant. At worst, his internal demands would lead him to irrational and/or self-defeating decisions and actions. To understand how this occurred, we devote all of the fol-lowing chapter to a detailed study of his narcissistic personality.

7

Nixon's Personality:
Exaggerated Self-Love and Dependency

Psychoanalysts speak of narcissism as self-love. The word comes from the Greek myth in which Narcissus, a young man, saw his reflection in the water and fell in love with it. If humans are to function positively in their daily lives, they require a healthy narcissism. A healthy narcissism depends on the individual's ability to master the psychological dangers he encounters in the course of his development. It balances dependency on the self with dependency on others.[1] In this particular context narcissism can be considered a prerequisite for self-esteem and it reflects a normal sense of entitlement.[2] Psychoanalyst Leo Rangell notes in his insightful study, *The Mind of Watergate*, that: "Narcissism is an important mechanism of self-preservation, as normal within the human psyche as sex, aggression, or anxiety. It is not only desirable, but necessary for survival. But as with other traits, it is subject to frustration, expansion, and lack of containment."[3]

A leader who has a healthy kind of narcissism feels comfortable with leadership and can sustain it. However, there are distinctly different forms of narcissism encompassing a broad spectrum: at one end is a normal feeling of entitlement and healthy self-esteem, at the other end is exaggerated investment of love (libido) in the self, with "malignant narcissism" at the extreme end.[4] In the latter type, the person utilizes aggression in order to gain self-esteem, as in the case of a serial murderer such as Ted Bundy,[5] who kills to feel alive psychologically and to feel superior to others. Another example would be a leader such as Adolf Hitler, who crushes other groups in order to advance his own, to support his pathological need for self-esteem. Iraqi leader Saddam Hussein attracted our attention by his utilization of destructive behavior toward other individuals and groups in order to maintain his sense of superiority.[6] Often we see leaders who have exaggerated self-love but who are not malignant narcissists. Technically we say that such individuals have a narcissistic personality.

Narcissistic Personality

Personality refers to the customary patterns of an individual's day-to-day behavior under ordinary circumstances. This pattern is relatively stable and unquestioned by the individual. It allows the individual to maintain a style of reciprocal relationships between himself and others (or things) in the environment. Sometimes an individual's personality becomes habitually maladaptive and he will have problems in dealing with the external world. The narcissistic personality is considered a maladaptive personality.

Persons who possess a narcissistic personality are preoccupied with self-importance and fantasies of endless success and lofty rank. Although they demand admiration, even adoration, they are aloof, cold, and without empathy. They exploit others and feel entitled to anything they want. They have a split (a contradiction) in their personality. Overtly they exhibit grandiosity. Technically we say they have a *grandiose self*.[7] Covertly they have a *hungry self* which depends overmuch on others. The dominant grandiose self has to be maintained at any cost while the hungry self has to be devalued and denied. If the grandiose part is not maintained, the individuals feel humiliated, may suffer from psychosomatic symptoms, and experience envy, rage, and paranoid fears. They then may attack those whom they consider agents of their downfall and those whom they envy, in order to recapture their grandiose self.

The typical person with a narcissistic personality has a limited repertoire of feelings. He can easily feel envy, rage, and entitlement, but it is usually impossible for him to feel grief, remorse, and empathy. He has an illusion of being "number one" and above hurt. In pursuing positions of supremacy the individual may step on others without sorrow or concern for their feelings, may lie, and even blur reality. While very ambitious, such a person constantly seeks and demands reassurance, approval, and praise, and is at a loss when he does not get them.

The person with a narcissistic personality organization who is intelligent, talented, and creative may be able to change his environment in accordance with his internal demands.[8] He may become a leader who seeks to alter external factors in such a way as to bring into harmony his inner wish for power and the outer world, which recognizes his superiority. One might say that if successful in this endeavor he "gains" from his personality organization,[9] but success is not always forthcoming.[10]

The beginning of a narcissistic personality organization can be traced to repeated frustrations encountered during the first year of life. These frustrations increase the infant's rage as well as envy; at the same time the mother sees something special in the child early in life, which encourages the child's sense of importance. For example, a mother grieving over the loss of an important person in her life may not be able to respond adequately to her baby's emotional needs. She may be too preoccupied with her own grief to minister to the baby. However, at the same time, the mother may unconsciously perceive of the child as being special, as being a replacement for her loss. For example, she may hope that her child will bring back the family's lost fortunes. The child reacts unconsciously to his mother's perception of him as a special being and develops a corresponding sense of self. As he grows older he assimilates anything "good" and idealized into his specialness and develops a grandiose self, while he splits off and devalues anything he considers "bad" and not supporting his grandiosity.[11]

With Richard Nixon we see exaggerated narcissism, but *not* malignant narcissism. Nixon organized his personality at such a level that he had an exaggerated need to be "number one" in his own eyes as well as in the eyes of others, to maintain his self-esteem and to avoid the anxiety of acknowledging his "hungry self." His need to be "number one" found an echo in reality since he was in fact successful most of the time. It is this congruence with reality that ultimately differentiates successful people with narcissistic personality organization from those who, having such an organization, try to maintain their grandiose selves in the absence of realistic validation.

We will now observe the manifestations of a narcissistic personality in Nixon, providing examples of how he repeatedly attempted to prove to himself and others his right to be "number one" and how he denied his dependency, rage, and envy. At times when the reality of his environment or his own internal turmoil threatened his grandiosity he would feel humiliated, enraged, envious, physically ill, paranoid, and willing to strike back at "unloving" others or dangerous things in order to reaffirm his grandiosity.

Maintaining Grandiosity and Denying Dependency

Collecting Titles

Pat Nixon once said that her husband had always been "president of some group like the 20–30 Club, and this, that, and the other thing."[12] Richard Nixon collected leadership roles obsessively. Running for the presidency of nearly every social, professional, or political organization he ever joined guaranteed Nixon considerable attention, which aided him in the cause of pumping up his self-esteem. To win the title of president, general manager, or leader wrapped him in protective armor, accumulating evidence of his worth. Out of the thirteen such elections in which he ran, Nixon lost only three—a high school office, the Presidency to John F. Kennedy, and the California governorship to Pat Brown.

At those times when Nixon did not have a title to brandish before the world, he resolved to reenter the political arena to acquire one and to erase the devalued image he felt he possessed. His political "resurrections," a most intriguing aspect of his career, derived from an inner psychological urgency; it was psychologically "obligatory" for Nixon to try to be "number one" again because his personality demanded it. Without "resurrecting" himself he would feel humiliated, envious of others, enraged, and empty.[13] After his 1962 gubernatorial defeat in California he conducted his famous "last press conference," saying to the journalists present (many of whom had attacked him over the years), "You won't have Nixon to kick around anymore." Yet, only six years later he was a candidate for President again. Why did he change his mind? Etheredge suggests that a narcissistically oriented individual develops an "idealizing transference" to the institution or office which is desired: the higher the office, the more desirable it becomes.[14] Nixon was driven to attain high office for the intrinsic pleasure he derived from titles that stirred his grandiosity. Without a title to support his grandiose self his defensive armor would atrophy and expose his hungry self, making the grandiose self susceptible to penetration and attack. Even when he had the title and the power of the presidency, he still had to protect his sense of superiority and deny his hungry self. For example, when reality clearly indicated that he would beat Senator George McGovern his inner world still propelled him to take extraordinary and irrational steps to assure an overwhelming victory. An overwhelming victory would feed his grandiosity.

Applause

It is apparent that despite the titles he won, these were not the only means Nixon used to satisfy his need for acceptance and adulation. His earlier attempts at amateur dramatics indicate that some manner of stage performance seemed to have attracted him. Perhaps the stage provided vital cohesiveness for his grandiose self: adoration from his audience/ constituency helped him to maintain dissociations from his devalued aspects. Thus, "in Whittier College Nixon sought applause as though it were a substitute for love, and the student vote fed this special hunger."[15]

There are other instances of his preoccupation with applause. Elliot Richardson, who wrote Nixon's vice-presidential renomination speech in 1956, recalled that after Nixon read it he said: "The problem with the last paragraph was that [it] lacked cheer lines. He pointed out that this was a speech to be given in a large auditorium to several thousand delegates. . . . It was at least indicative of the extent to which he thought about the processes of communication."[16]

Roger Ailes, who was Nixon's media consultant during the 1968 campaign and communications consultant in the Nixon White House, remembered that Nixon was adept at delivering stump speeches and that he had a natural talent for spotting cheer lines.[17] It is of course true that a well-made speech with appropriate cheer lines is simply good politics, but Nixon's preoccupation with creating an effect was evidence of the value he placed on applause.

Most revealing of Nixon's unconscious preoccupation with applause and cheers, however, is a diary entry in which he recounted a dream he had one night: "I had a rather curious dream of speaking at some sort of rally and going on a bit too long and Rockefeller standing up in the middle and taking over the microphone on an applause line. Of course, this is always something that worries a person when he is making speeches."[18]

It is difficult to understand the hidden meaning of a dream (*latent content*, as it is called in psychoanalysis) of a person who is not on a psychoanalytic couch and who cannot add free associations to it. It is possible to look at the *manifest content* of this dream, however, and to examine the surface themes. In the case of Nixon's dream, we can see that the dreamer worries that a rival will take something from him; the dreamer fears experiencing a loss. What the dreamer fears to lose can be understood within the framework of the dreamer's anxiety at different levels of the developmental ladder. Here we focus on the issue of receiving love and attention (oral-level issues) and we may speculate that Nelson Rockefeller, aside from being Nixon's main Republican rival in the political arena, symbolically represented rivals from his childhood—the unwelcome infant cousin, or brother Donald—who were rivals for Hannah Nixon's attention and care. The microphone and the applause line might represent the mother's milk. By crying (as an infant) and speaking (as an adult), Nixon could summon the representation of the "good" mother, now the national audience, and make them notice him. He was envious and anxious if someone else received adulation instead.

An illustration of his need to collect adulation occurred when Henry Kissinger would occasionally garner much of the applause the President felt he personally deserved. When Kissinger was awarded the Nobel Peace Prize, Nixon became "jealous."[19] What we see here is that Nixon perceived adulation from the public as a kind of feeding, like the availability of a glass of milk. If someone else drank part of it, there would be less for Nixon, making him feel empty to some degree. We believe that the opposite was true for Nixon, too. If he kept the glass of milk for himself, he perceived his competitors as envious of him. Nixon's reactions to thoughts such as these made him appear paranoid to others. Kissinger received so much adulation from crowds at airports that eventually Nixon ordered Kissinger's handshaking routine to stop; it stole away the attention and applause that Nixon desperately wanted for himself.[20]

Nixon often felt that he "was not getting commensurate credit for his accomplishments."[21] Whenever he lost an election he had a "totally empty feeling."[22] Without adoration and applause (representing mother's milk and love) Nixon went hungry emotionally and this meant that he had to acknowledge his hungry self. This was unacceptable to him.

"Historical Firsts"

Nixon's obsession with "historical firsts" and other successes was a form of collection. By collecting firsts he ensured the reflection and maintenance of his grandiose self. In his book *Witness to Power*, Ehrlichman discussed Nixon's frequent claims to achievement of "historic firsts," even applying it to events of no great significance. "There was a running gag on any Nixon campaign; everything that happened was "a historic first." Every campaign speech claimed at least one, however mundane. The Hawaiian trip to four islands was Nixon's first stop as a nominee, Hawaii's first Presidential campaign, and Oahu's and Maui's and Kauai's too."[23]

Nixon's preoccupation with the "historic first" continued even after he left the presidency. In a *Meet the Press* interview on April 10, 1988, Nixon congratulated President Reagan for having achieved a "historic first" in influencing the withdrawal of Soviet troops from Afghanistan, claiming that this was the first time the Soviets had given up an occupied land. When the Nixon library opened in Yorba Linda, California during the summer of 1990, Nixon seized the opportunity to declare another "historic first." As he gave his speech outdoors, three other Presidents (Bush, Reagan, Ford) sat in the audience with their wives, and Pat Nixon. When Nixon stepped up to the podium one of the first sentences he uttered made reference to the fact that for the first time four former first ladies were appearing together. This was a trivial point to make on the occasion of the immortalization of his presidency, but he *had* to say it— he had to announce a historic first. Their presence at the ceremony meant that he was "loved" or "acknowledged" by four first ladies.

Lying

Fawn Brodie's psychologically informed biography, *Richard Nixon: The Shaping of His Character* especially emphasizes the theme that Nixon lied in matters both important and trivial. She stated that "Nixon lied to gain love, to store up his grandiose fantasies, to bolster his ever-wavering sense of identity. He lied in attacks, hoping to win. . . . And always he lied, and this most aggressively, to deny that he lied. . . . Finally, he enjoyed lying."[24] She gives examples of Nixon's lying in matters large and small: He lied about his college major, about his wife's first name and birth date, about his own secret slush fund in the 1952 Presidential campaign, and in the Watergate cover-up. She added that "almost every one of Nixon's victories and political achievements save the elections to the vice-presidency had been won as a result of lying, attack or the unexpected and fortuitous death of others."[25] Brodie's work attributes Nixon's lying from boyhood to maturity to the characters of Nixon's parents. His mother denied what was uncomfortable and she stretched the truth. The father was brutal and the son learned to lie in order to avoid punishment. Brodie does not distinguish between lying as an ethical transgression and lying as truth-bending utilized by politicians for political ends. It should be recalled that, for example, Kennedy denied having Addison's disease and Lyndon Johnson repeatedly understated the U.S. commitment in Vietnam. Nixon's reliance on truth distortion was absorbed in his narcissistic personality structure, becoming an armament in maintaining his grandiose self and in his skillful dealings with the political process.

Nixon exhibited, when not under stress, great "ego strength" in effectively capitalizing on the time and circumstances. He knew when to lie and ruthlessly exploit the electorate. Peter Loewenberg, a professor of history as well as a psychoanalyst, states that we may listen to Nixon's Checkers Speech today "and find the emotional tone unctuous and revolting, but at that time he knew what would sell and he produced it."[26]

The Infamous White House Tapes

The ultimately self-destructive installation and use of a taping system in the White House may have reflected Nixon's need to collect proof of adoration and power—as supplies for his narcissism. We have already referred to his need to collect tapes as evidence of his (oral) greediness and (anal) retentiveness. Now we shall examine this same phenomenon from a different angle, as an expression of his narcissistic personality.

For Nixon, the permanent capture of information and exchanges on tape would ensure that his grandiosity would never go hungry. Volkan has described a patient who always kept a hundred cans of food in his apartment and had an anxiety attack whenever the supply fell to ninety-nine.[27] Like the hundred cans of food, a surplus of titles or tapes gave Nixon a certain degree of security in maintaining his grandiosity. This, along with the oral and anal motivations mentioned earlier, may explain why he did not destroy the tapes even after their existence was disclosed, and why he protested and fought so fiercely once they were subpoenaed. Aside from his public constitutional arguments concerning the importance of the separation of the branches of government, there was a concurrent, underlying unconscious need not to allow the tapes, which secretly represented verification of his grand presidential position, to be released. To destroy or to relinquish the tapes would have been tantamount to inviting an anxiety attack or psychosomatic reaction. (Readers may recall that Nixon was afflicted with pneumonia during his court battles to retain control over the tapes.)

Interestingly, even after leaving office Nixon continued legal action to prevent further disclosure of the tapes and papers. Nixon filed several suits seeking a restraining order concerning the release of the material. By 1986 all the legal battles over regulations ended, but in 1987 a review still pended regarding objections Nixon raised to having special files made public that contained sensitive White House material. Approximately 15,000 documents containing about 150,000 pages were involved. After Nixon's death it was learned that his will calls for continued efforts to gain custody of the tapes. According to the will, Nixon gave control of his tapes, personal diaries, and transcripts to his two daughters and instructed them to continue court action seeking to regain custody of thousands of hours of tapes. The Nixon library does own certain tapes, but only in abbreviated format.

Nixon's acquisitive urges combined with another factor to produce a compulsive collection of what might be called narcissistic supplies. The other factor was his identification with his mother, who had an extreme sense of privacy and "collected" her own thoughts and feelings inside herself; she did not share them with others. Nixon's collecting trait was generalized and included gathering intelligence about the activities of other people, whether they were political opponents or collateral family members. An individual who secretly has a hungry aspect wants to know about others' (siblings') food/love supplies. Haldeman recalled that Nixon "was expecting to have and insisting that we get intelligence on what the opposition was doing."[28] This, of course, might have been a politically astute strategy, but knowing what we do about the man we believe that his need for information about others stems also from his internal demands. His "need" to know was a part of him, and, as we will show, it also manifested itself in a need to know about his brother Donald, one of his childhood rivals. He posted his supporters at every speaking engagement of his Democratic rival, George McGovern, to record McGovern's remarks during the 1972 presidential campaign. Nixon "wanted to know what was going on, and what kinds of turnouts they were getting, and how they were handling them."[29]

Senator McGovern was pressing the issue of hunger in America. Nixon was skeptical that many Americans were in need of food. At one point, while he was being interviewed he asked, "How wide is the hunger problem in fact?"[30] as though to challenge the stress McGovern was placing on this issue. Once he was persuaded that hunger was a substantial problem, Nixon came up with his own plan. We think that the topic of hunger induced uncomfortable feelings in Nixon. By denying or minimizing the problem he could deny and minimize his childhood experiences with both physical and psychological hunger and he could deny his hungry self as well.

What is interesting is that at the same time he demanded that Haldeman gather information about the McGovern campaign, he asked Ehrlichman to check up on his brother Donald. Apparently, Donald and Donald's wife Clara were busy collecting Richard's old furniture and baby clothes and toys, and Nixon specifically wanted to know their motivation. Ehrlichman indicated this collecting "was a source of constant irritation for him because he did not like Don's wife. He didn't like the idea that she had that stuff."[31] Nixon declared that it should be made available to a foundation, and claimed that Clara planned to sell it.

Dropping "M"

When success permits a narcissistic leader to change the environment, the effect of the new environment in turn influences the leader's perception of his inner world. The leader may feel that he is transformed. Sometimes this transformation is only a wished-for illusion; at other times it may become crystallized. During the presidential transition period Nixon dropped "M," his middle initial. Perhaps he unconsciously felt that the achievement of his final goal would allow him to drop a symbolic connection to his mother by no longer acknowledging her maiden name. As President he meant to be a man who had no dependency needs![32] When Nixon dropped his middle initial he did it in a grandiose fashion, announcing it to his entire staff. From that time on he signed his name simply "Richard Nixon."[33]

The "Glass Bubble" Syndrome

People with a narcissistic personality sometimes fantasize consciously and often unconsciously that they are living by themselves in glory, protected from the rest of the world and the common herd by a shield made of something impervious, like a glass bubble. From this vantage point, they can look out at the world with disdain and without fear of challenge. Volkan wrote that patients of this sort have been known to contemplate their place of isolation for some time before allowing themselves to succumb to sleep at night. He described how one of his patients fantasized about being Robinson Crusoe living on an island *without* his Man Friday: The patient basically envisioned himself surviving quite well without anyone else's assistance, and he could not sleep until he had confirmed his self-sufficiency and denied his dependency in his fantasy.[34]

Nixon's style of relating to others and his habit of turning within himself—to make decisions, or to look for comfort—seems to fit this same pattern, and individuals such as Haldeman and Ehrlichman provided a "Berlin Wall" for him, as noted earlier. Theodore White in *The Making of the President—1968* wrote of seeing Nixon stroll down Fifth Avenue in New York City one day, "smiling as if amused by some inner conversation. His habit of great concentration lent itself to inner colloquy."[35]

What became known as "The Nixon Method" of presidency we believe reflects the Glass Bubble Syndrome. Harold Saunders, who was an Assistant Secretary of State during the Carter Administration, and who has served under five presidents on the National Security Council (1961–74) and in the State Department (1974–81), has made a comparison of presidential decisionmaking styles. His observations support the view that although Nixon listened to others, he was so much a loner that he seems to have arrived at decisions on the basis of talking to himself, in private.[36]

Nixon was always well prepared and had such a thorough grasp of his administration's policies that he invariably seemed to know in advance what would happen and was not a patient listener. According to Roger Ailes:

He had a very fast mind. He had an instinctive political nature so he knew why you were there when you first came in. He knew what you were going to talk about. He generally knew what your opinion was, already knew what his answer would be. Nixon used to say over and over, "ah hah, sure, fine, OK, good . . ." It was a way of hurrying you along. When I asked a friend who had just been in to see Nixon how he was today, the guy responded, "He must be fine because I got two goods, a well, and three fines."[37]

Ailes concluded that one who could not present his case to Nixon within thirty to sixty seconds would be lost.

Nixon's emphasis on time management and his ability to focus on the specific task at hand explain to some degree his discomfort when faced with the need to engage in small talk. Richard Helms, former director of the Central Intelligence Agency, has described Nixon as an intensely concentrated man, always concerned with serious world issues that he would rather discuss, even at inappropriate times, than indulge in conversation about everyday trivialities.[38] Elliot Richardson, who held several Cabinet posts in the Nixon administration, confirmed Helms's assessment, saying "He was all business . . . I do not think he took any recreational pursuit seriously."[39]

The fund crisis seemed to underscore for Nixon the value of self-sufficiency, and the urgency of always being on one's guard. In his memoirs Nixon concluded: "Eisenhower had not saved me in the fund crisis; *I was saved because I had been able to save myself.*"[40] An Eisenhower White House aide recalled, "You must start with the basic psychological fact—that Nixon is an introspective man. He just can't ask anybody for help. He could have had our help any time he wanted . . . but Nixon couldn't bring himself to ask for help of anybody."[41] When asked to whom Nixon turned during times of crisis Roger Ailes responded, "I think he went inside himself in crises almost every time."[42]

The Media

One may speculate that Nixon's dislike and distrust of the media stemmed in general from the possibility that his power and success might directly depend upon media coverage and/or might be challenged by the media. A person like Nixon who fails in controlling other influential persons or organizations may look upon them as potentially able to make or break him. They can provide adoration or love, or they can deny nourishment and produce "dry breasts." James David Barber of Duke University wrote that Nixon "believes his power to be dependent upon his public reputation,"[43] which for most politicians hinges directly on the media's portrayal. Elliot Richardson concurred, remarking how Nixon's "accomplishments were presented as directly dependent upon what the media said about him."[44] His emaciated appearance on television during the debates with John F. Kennedy, for example, is often given as the reason for his defeat in the 1960 presidential election; his 1962 gubernatorial defeat was blamed on slanted news reporting.

Entering the 1968 presidential campaign, Nixon was distressed by the notion that in order to be elected president one had to rely on television as a "gimmick." He approved a television campaign program to circumvent television journalists and to avoid depending upon them. Dubbed "The Man in the Arena" series by its director, Roger Ailes, it featured Nixon alone on a stage without a podium or notes. He was the only one or number one in this setting and this strategy fit well with his personality organization. He fielded questions from a panel of ordinary citizens in order to erase the "Would you buy a used car from this guy?" image. Ailes explained that "it was difficult to find anyone in the press who would give him a fair shake, so we blatantly made an attempt to put him on television and let him speak for himself."[45] This series appealed to Nixon not only because he could speak to the issues of the campaign, but also because he could transcend the media by communicating directly with the American people. Haldeman commented that:

> There was a strong feeling of trying to go over the heads of the press. What Nixon was saying in speeches . . . was being strained through the press. And he felt that we had the opportunity to go over their heads directly to the people. He wanted to figure out ways to be covered live in ways that could not be distorted or diluted by the press.[46]

Nixon's self-sufficient strivings materialized as a positive force insofar as this particular media strategy was concerned, for Nixon did win the election.

Reaction to the "Pentagon Papers"

Excessive preoccupation with self-sufficiency, combined with a need to have absolute control over one's environment, can create problems. In Nixon's case, an example of this was the establishment of the "plumbers" unit. Daniel Ellsberg had intentionally leaked some classified material— which later came to be known as the "Pentagon Papers"—to the press. Speech writer Ray Price recalled that Nixon was in a "ferocious mood"[47] over the Ellsberg leak. He was having what psychoanalysts call a "narcissistic rage." He was especially upset with the FBI for not having assigned a higher priority to the case. The "plumbers" were detailed to work under the direction of John Ehrlichman to thwart such leaks in the future. In his *Memoirs*, Nixon noted:

> J. Edgar Hoover was dragging his feet and treating the case on merely a medium-priority basis; he had assigned no special task force and no extra manpower to it . . . I did not care about any reasons or excuses. I wanted someone to light a fire under the FBI, and to keep the departments and the agencies in active pursuit of leakers.[48]

When it became clear that the FBI would not increase its "leak-seeking" forces, he impatiently decided to take charge of controlling the leaking for, as he said, "if the FBI was not going to pursue the case, then we would have to do it ourselves."[49] Assistant to the President Charles Colson recalled that Nixon said, "I want to know who is behind this, and I want the most complete investigation that can be conducted. . . . I don't want excuses. I want results. I want it done; whatever the cost."[50]

Leaking, with its anal symbolism, indicates loss of control, and Nixon was not going to tolerate the possibility of not being self-sufficient. Acting upon Nixon's demands, the "plumbers" broke into the office of Ellsberg's psychiatrist—Ehrlichman has acknowledged that this was done on the President's orders—to acquire information that would publicly discredit Ellsberg.[51] Nixon later claimed that this was a matter of the highest national security, but it is clear that the "plumbers" went beyond normal legal limits in order to compromise Ellsberg. This break-in, the impetus for which was Nixon's unconscious need for exaggerated self-sufficiency, controlling others, and denial of his "hungry self," marked the beginning of his downfall.

Other leaks besides Ellsberg's disturbed Nixon, who authorized, under the guise of guarding national security, the wiretapping of some administration staff members and popular columnists. In 1978 Haldeman wrote that "Nixon was one hundred per cent behind the wiretaps."[52] He also stated that Nixon and Kissinger kept spreading the electronic surveillance net farther and farther. The order to put a tap on journalist Joseph Kraft came directly from the President. When the FBI claimed that Kraft's phone was untappable, Nixon assigned Ehrlichman the task of generating alternative ways to circumvent the FBI. Nixon's persistence clearly shows how the President's personal intrapsychic processes dominated his decisions and activities; they overruled any ability he may have had to govern in a logical way and in a way that was not contaminated by pressures emanating from his inner world.

Psychosomatic Expressions

Having the support of his followers helps a narcissistic leader maintain his grandiose self more effectively.[53] Consequently, he may behave as though he were immune to physical illness and too powerful for germs. His followers may also believe it impossible for so powerful a leader to succumb to illness.[54] But under conditions that threaten the grandiose self, a person with a narcissistic personality is likely to manifest (in addition to psychological responses to be described in chapter 10) hypochondriacal preoccupations (concerns about being physical ill) and a tendency toward psychosomatic illnesses (actually having physical symptoms).[55] The psychoanalytic study of psychosomatic illnesses is very complex; we cannot say for sure how the psyche and the body interact. However, we have observed this interaction clinically again and again. Various theories about the relationship between the mind and the body have been formulated, and work in this area continues.[56]

At the beginning of life an infant lacks psychological content; its rage is discharged in a bodily way.[57] For example, we see how the body tightens up during moments of anger, as when we hear screaming or feel kicking. These are physiological mechanisms that discharge tension. While infants have the potential to develop many mental functions, they do not possess organized psychological content, nor do they have sophisticated psychological tools (i.e., verbal expression) with which they can declare their rage or other emotions. It is thought that psychosomatic illnesses operate similarly. Ideational and emotional expressions become partially retransformed into somatic and physiological expressions.[58] Contemporary research on psychosomatic conditions shows that psychosomatic illness results from disorders in processing specific aspects of experience during childhood development. The child's tension-regulating mechanisms are not adequately internalized (i.e., assimilated into the developing psychic system). Furthermore, the child is unable to use words to signal to his environment the state of distress in a regulated manner, but communicates primitively through the early mother-child relationship. Psychosomatic illness is due to the deregulation and miscommunication activities of the developing child.[59]

Nixon's life crises generally triggered respiratory disturbances. Franz Alexander, a pioneer in the psychoanalytic study of psychosomatic conditions, stressed the influence of emotion on respiratory functions, noting that it occurs in everyday life. We sometimes describe an anxiety attack as taking our breath away, and sighing is a common expression of despair. According to Alexander: "Crying is another complex expressive phenomenon in which the expiratory phase of respiration is involved.

And above all, respiration is an important component in speaking."[60] In the case of Richard Nixon we observed, as mentioned earlier, how he could summon his mother's—or fantasized mother's—attention first by crying and then by speaking. In certain situations we think he also summoned his mother through psychosomatic illnesses that were mostly upper-respiratory.[61]

Therefore, it is not surprising that at the age of fifteen—when there were so many tragedies and hardships in his family—Nixon began having a sinus infection that plagued him every year thereafter. It should be recalled that the Quaker tradition called for accepting death as God's will. His chronic sinus infection probably included elements of his family's and his own inability to express grief openly.

Nixon was under considerable stress when his sinus troubles began. His mother had just moved to Arizona, where she would remain for two years for the sake of Harold's health. Nixon continued to have annual bouts with sinus trouble as an adult; they began on the fifth of September and subsided on the first of October.[62] Since his father died on the fourth of September, and his mother on the thirtieth of September, it is likely that through this illness he was "crying out" for his parents as an anniversary reaction even after they were no longer alive. Similar cases where anniversary reactions occur with such clarity have been described in detailed psychoanalytic studies.[63]

Nixon was also susceptible to pneumonia during periods of severe crisis. In 1973, at the height of his stonewalling the Senate Watergate Committee's request that he release the White House tapes, Nixon awoke at 5:30 A.M. on July 12 with a stabbing pain in his chest.[64] White House physicians diagnosed his difficulty later that day as viral pneumonia. Although pneumonia is obviously caused not by emotions but by pathogenic agents such as viruses, our emphasis here is on how the effects of a life crisis may combine with physiological factors to trigger an illness.

During the Watergate investigation Nixon remained faithful to his pledge to travel to the Middle East and the Soviet Union. In June 1974 however, while he was en route to the Middle East, he developed phlebitis—an inflammation (blood clot)—in his left leg. He refused to alter either his Middle East schedule or his planned trip to the Soviet Union for Summit III. Four months later, the phlebitis reappeared, rendering the then officially resigned ex-President Nixon helpless and requiring his hospitalization. It is important to note that June 1974 marked the height of the critical Watergate revelations, and that October 1974 was an equally stressful period for the disgraced Nixon, who had forestalled the impeachment process by submitting his resignation. His grandiose self was threatened and he felt humiliated. Just a few days before his phlebitis returned President Gerald Ford had granted Nixon a "full, free and absolute pardon . . . for all offenses against the United States which he . . . has committed or may have committed." Psychiatrist Samuel Silverman told *Time* magazine that the pardon may have triggered a reactivation of the phlebitis: "I have no way of knowing whether Mr. Nixon has any unconscious guilt, but if he does, with the threat of legal punishment now removed, the only punishing force left is himself. That's why pardons can kill."[65]

Pneumonia struck again in November 1974, while Nixon was in the hospital recovering from his phlebitis surgery and shock. One may surmise that his bouts with pneumonia, the development of his sinus condition, and perhaps his phlebitis condition were contaminated with psychological elements. The anniversary reactions and threats to the maintenance of his grandiose self led Nixon to communicate his distress in a psychosomatic manner.

Immortality

The ego cannot conceive of its own annihilation.[66] Thus, it can be said that at some level we all believe in immortality. Furthermore, although we "know" that death is inevitable, we continue to go about our daily lives as though death does not concern us; emotionally we are able to deny the knowledge of our own inevitable demise. In other words we "know" that death is inevitable, but at the same time we "know" how to behave as if death will never come. This denial itself may play a role in our wish to remain "alive" after we die. The person with exaggerated self-love has a greater than average investment in the notion of immortality. Richard Nixon's preoccupation with it reinforced his sense of self-sufficiency, and his wish to be "number one." This, in turn, affected his actions and decisions.

Nixon had "beaten death" a number of times. Not only had he survived where two of his siblings had not, but he was told over and over again about how he had crawled under a team of horses at the age of two. An associate of his father's later declared, "I grabbed him just in time before the animals passed over him. They backed up and their hoofs tramped the spot where the little boy had been crawling only seconds before."[67] Nixon had also been told he had once fallen out of a buggy and cut his head, his scalp hanging down and bleeding profusely. The doctors who treated him said that he was taken to the emergency room just in time to save his life.[68] We can guess that once exaggerated narcissism became part of his personality organization, immortality became a defense against losing life, losing bodily integrity, and losing self-esteem. If he were above mortality, he could then deny his vulnerable, hungry self. On the other side of the coin, Nixon's sense of immortality clashed with his tendency toward developing psychosomatic illnesses. In any case, the recurring theme of "beating death" sharpened his unconscious illusions. A sense of immortality served as a defense against his anxiety about losing his own life and assuaged his guilt over surviving where his brothers did not.

Nixon's reaction to his phlebitis attack in 1974 exemplifies these illusions. He had been told that his phlebitis was extremely serious and that to continue with his travel plans to the Middle East and the Soviet Union would jeopardize his life. Even so, he steadfastly refused to slow down, and ordered his staff to keep his condition secret from the press.[69] General Brent Scowcroft, who later became President George Bush's National Security Advisor, accompanied Nixon on this trip. Scowcroft said he was told by the President's doctor that "he didn't know how he [Nixon] could stand the pain."[70] When phlebitis struck again in the wake of President Ford's pardon, Nixon refused to enter the hospital, telling his former aide, Ken Clawson:

> They say it's bad, but I've already told them to go to hell. I told them I wasn't setting foot outside the wall around my property, no matter what. They can cut off the damn leg, let it rot, or just wait for the clot to reach the end zone. I don't care. . . . You see, don't you? You've got to be tough. You can't break, my boy, even when there is nothing left. You don't admit, even to yourself, that it is gone.[71]

Nixon never did admit final defeat because he never believed that he was finally defeated, only temporarily set back. When he slipped off into shock after surgery for his phlebitis, he heard voices calling, "Richard, pull yourself back." At that moment, he later told an aide, he felt "as if he had a choice: whether he should give up or whether he should continue."[72] Perhaps in that moment of shock he unconsciously recalled the words his mother had spoken just before she died, "Richard, don't give up. Don't let anyone tell you you are through."[73]

Apart from surviving his own illnesses (pneumonia, undulant fever, phlebitis, etc.), Nixon also survived where others succumbed. He witnessed his brother Arthur's sudden death, apparently from tubercular meningitis, and he watched his brother Harold's agonizingly hopeless struggle with tuberculosis. Political rivals also fell. After John F. Kennedy was assassinated, Nixon would remarked, "I think it would not have happened to me."[74] Robert Kennedy, a long-time nemesis and Democratic adversary in the 1968 campaign, was also struck down by an assassin's bullet. George Wallace, yet another political rival, was paralyzed by an assassination attempt. Haldeman said "Nixon was fatalistic about assassination attempts. He often got in arguments with the Secret Service because he didn't take precautions that they recommended."[75] Death hovered over him like a vulture, but it struck only those around him. His own body seemed impervious, until his death from "natural causes" at an advanced age.

Final symbolic political death seemed impossible as well. Narrowly losing the 1960 presidential election to John F. Kennedy, Nixon departed Washington thinking "that this was not the end—that someday I would be back here."[76] In his farewell speech to the White House staff on August 9, 1974 he could not bring himself to say good-bye, only *au revoir*, with the addendum: "We'll be back." Nixon was unable to admit defeat, even to himself; he never truly believed that his public career was over. The following excerpt from a personal letter written August 2, 1972 to Terry Eagleton, the son of Missouri Senator Thomas Eagleton, who had just been removed from the Democratic ticket—partially because of revelations that he had once undergone electric shock therapy—perhaps echoes Nixon's unconscious belief that though down, he was never out:

> Politics is a very hard game. Winston Churchill once pointed out that "politics is even more difficult than war. Because in politics you die many times, in war you die only once."
>
> But in those words of Churchill we can all take some comfort. The political man can always come back to fight again. What matters is not that your father fought a terribly difficult battle and lost. What matters is that in fighting the battle he won the admiration of foes and friends alike because of the courage, poise, and just plain guts he showed against overwhelming odds.[77]

Nixon admired those leaders who could beat the odds and return to public life after losing a battle. He was one himself. If other leaders, such as those he singled out in his book entitled *Leaders*,[78] could rise from the depths of despair to return to public life and ensure their places in the history books, Nixon could also. Like the mythical phoenix that crashes to earth, burns, and then rises again from its own ashes, he would do the same.

PART THREE

Three Faces of Nixon's Personality in Policymaking and in Defeat

8

Reflections of Grandiosity

In *Six Crises*, Nixon wrote that a leader must possess "the emotional, mental, and physical strength to withstand the pressures and tensions created by necessary doubts and then at the critical moment, to make a choice and to act decisively."[1] The fact is that many condensed elements, ranging from reality factors to unconscious forces, go into making a political decision, taking a new diplomatic course, and providing leadership. Obviously, a leader must first be able to evaluate the issues at hand in a logical and intellectual manner. Level of intelligence, the ability to function whether in normal surroundings or in a crisis situation, relationship with advisers, and so on are all important factors in leadership caliber.

In our system of government, there are many checks and balances that blunt a leader's idiosyncratic and/or irrational responses to political or diplomatic events. However, we cannot altogether avoid the consequences of a leader's personality and unconscious motivations and defenses against them: they have a way of intruding in political situations even in a democratic system. For example, if in a crisis situation a leader unconsciously perceives a connection between real-world issues and his own internal dangers, his subjective/individualized response to the crisis may overshadow his objective/rational response. Leaders also develop likes and dislikes, transferences and countertransferences, toward other leaders and other countries. Sometimes leaders may project their internal dramas onto the historical arena, and attempt to find solutions for them there.

In this chapter we show how Richard Nixon's grandiose self was reflected in his activities in policymaking, both domestic and foreign. We call this Nixon's first political face, that of his grandiose self. As long as he maintained a sense of superiority, he desired and attempted to accomplish superior achievements. His grandiose self motivated him to be bold and active and to respond to the demands that came from within in his attempts to change his environment and to secure a lofty place for himself in history.

In the next chapter we will explore examples from Nixon's political policies that reflect his inner attempts to integrate his grandiose self with his devalued hungry self. This integrative urge belongs to Nixon's second face, that of his peacemaker self. The reader may recall our description of the split within the narcissistic personality where the grandiose self is cordoned off from the devalued self. Remember that this is an unnatural condition. In the course of normal development an individual is able to integrate his black and white aspects and make grey, because accepting reality means acknowledging both loving and hateful aspects of ourselves and others. The integration of opposite aspects heals a person developmentally. Since there is a psychobiological push in all of us to develop, to live up to our developmental potential, the ability to integrate is especially significant. Traumas in life that result in fixations at various rungs of the developmental ladder, and identifications with important others, affect functions that may be crucial in determining how much we can heal ourselves in times of stress or danger. The potential to integrate always exists, but whether one is capable of using it is another matter. Richard Nixon made use of this potential in the political arena at some times but not others. The times when he sought to forge or repair alliances, as a peacemaker, were the times when he showed his second political face.

In chapter 10 we will shed light on the situations where Nixon was at his worst. This happened whenever he could not maintain his grandiose self and his devalued hungry self threatened to come into his consciousness with a full force. Such a possibility made him anxious and humiliated. When the threat was displaced onto political and historical arenas he became suspicious and acted paranoid. He responded to his perception of external danger as would a frightened child; this resulted in his utilization of rather primitive methods to protect himself. At such times he had to pump up his threatened grandiose self by every means he could imagine, including those which were politically damaging and irrational. This was Nixon's third face, that of his paranoid self.

Many individuals in the press have referred to Nixon as having had a double personality. According to our psychoanalytic understanding of him, here we speak of his three faces. By no means do we suggest that he had a multiple personality problem. We simply refer to opposing aspects within one personality and his efforts in welding them together. Now let us start with the reflections in his policymaking of his grandiose self.

Centralization of Power

Determined to avoid what John Ehrlichman called "the dreary rut of politics,"[2] and to align himself with bold historic initiatives, Nixon designed two innovative strategies—the establishment of a new political party to attract voters from the middle and the right of the political spectrum, and a reorganization of the Executive Branch. We think that it was not "the dreary rut of politics" that caused Nixon to make such initiatives. It was the demands of his personality that directed him to form a new party that would be his own party, his extension, and a new organization of the Executive Branch that would bear his own mark. These internal demands, we believe, were dominant and at times they blurred reality for him.

Nixon persisted in these audacious proposals in spite of obvious practical political constraints, being very much aware of the "necessity of maximizing the positive public impression."[3] According to Ehrlichman, "with John Connally, his new economic adviser, Nixon speculated that he could get the new party started by calling a convention of the political leaders of the center and the right. Nixon and Connally would be elected President and Vice-President in 1972 by the new coalition party and could bring in with them a majority in both houses of Congress."[4] We see an early version of his wish to have his own new political party in his helping to found Whittier College's second men's society, The Orthogonian Club.

Ehrlichman reports that "these dreams were real," and he alludes to the difficulties they engendered. "There wasn't the time and they didn't have the resources so they basically . . . weren't the men to do it."[5] Paradoxically, whatever the feasibility was of establishing a new, viable political party, the revelation of Nixon's admittedly bold dream counters his popular image as a prudent and practical politician.

When interviewed, Ehrlichman attributed Nixon's interest in the reorganization of the Executive Branch to his "profound discontent with the way [it] was set up." Jurisdictional disputes between its units complicated and reduced its effectiveness, so a plan based on the recommendations of the Ash Advisory Council on Reorganization was devised to rectify the situation. Embedded in it was a proposal to restructure the Cabinet with four Secretaries as "counselors to the President."[6] Ehrlichman explained that this new structure, later referred to as the "Supercabinet," was comprised of "four Cabinet heads who could make decisions."[7] In addition to this Cabinet restructuring there were to be four men selected from the White House Staff who would "integrate and unify policies and operations throughout the Executive Branch."[8] In the third of a series of articles on Nixon's use of the powers of the presidency and its effect on the government and national life, John Herbers wrote: "The result [of the Supercabinet] is a highly centralized and homogeneous leadership in the executive branch that accelerates a long trend of concentrating more authority and decision-making under the White House umbrella.[9]

In his message to Congress on reorganization, Nixon said that "it is important that we move boldly to consolidate the major activities of the government."[10] One wonders why there was such a rush to change a system that had been implemented nearly two centuries earlier. Herbers concluded that Nixon's Supercabinet proposal was "an example of the President's method as he has gone further than any modern President in trying to shape the bureaucracy to conform to both the style and purposes of the President."[11] In reality, such a change would bring back a system that had been implemented nearly two centuries earlier, with a supercabinet of four persons directly advising the President: under George Washington the Secretaries of Treasury, State, War, and Attorney General conferred with the President or acted without the President when he was not there.

R.P. Nathan states that any President must choose between a strong cabinet that takes the lead in researching, delineating, and setting administration policy, and a strong White House staff armed with the authority to supersede cabinet officers and to determine policy.[12] Not surprisingly, Nixon chose to concentrate policymaking authority under the White House umbrella, so that the cabinet's role during the first six months of his administration atrophied. Nixon's rearrangement of the cabinet in June 1970 was attributed to his desire to "run the mammoth, unwieldy machinery of the government from one place—the office of the President."[13] As discussed earlier, the supercabinet restructuring stemming from the recommendation of the Ash Council suited the style and needs of Richard Nixon. Moreover, within the general White House umbrella there was further centralization, with only a few choice aides having direct access to and influence upon the President.

The decisionmaking processes Nixon exhibited in the realm of foreign policy paralleled his behavior in the domestic sphere. According to General Brent Scowcroft, "Policy-making itself tended to move more to the White House and away from the [State] departments. Nixon really wanted to move foreign policy-making into the White House, so that gave added emphasis to the National Security Council."[14]

Within the White House itself, Nixon and Kissinger installed a system that further centralized the flow of paper into the Oval Office. Alexander George wrote in *Presidential Decisionmaking in Foreign Policy*, "The foreign policy system that Kissinger . . . developed during the first year of the administration is generally regarded as by far the most centralized and highly structured model yet employed by any president."[15] When juxtaposed with President Johnson's "Tuesday lunch" crowd (so dubbed because of the unstructured and informal nature of the weekly gatherings at which national security measures were discussed), the focus on centralization and control in the Nixon-Kissinger reorganization plan seems more pronounced. According to Scowcroft "if one looks for a model of how the system operated best, that is it, the formal options model."[16] As Nixon watcher John Osborne so aptly reported, this emphasis on centralization and control reflected, on the surface, the President's "continuing struggle for neatness . . . [17] Fred Greenstein suggested that "if Nixon had been exposed to a wider range of advisors . . . it is likely that he would not have persevered in such a self defeating course of conduct."[18] Centralization of the decisionmaking process may have made the government run more efficiently but in the long run, in Nixon's case, this was not beneficial.

An Example of Boldness in Domestic Policy

Nixon wrote in his 1978 memoirs, "I was determined to be an activist president in domestic affairs."[19] This statement and others like it are the typical rhetoric of politicians, although they are heard less often from the mouths of conservative politicians who have conservative constituents. Richard Nixon surprised even his most fervent critics in the Congress and the press when he proposed major domestic reforms under an umbrella he called "The New Federalism." This included a revolutionary welfare reform program—the Family Assistance Plan—that was, by most standards, an "activist" one. Commenting on the plan, Richard Schweiker—former Republican Senator and later President Ronald Reagan's Housing and Social Services Secretary—said, "The Family Assistance Plan (FAP) pleased and surprised many people on the hill from both sides of the aisle. I think Nixon proposed a constructive, reasonable, and practical program to solve the welfare problem."[20] The following brief description of this welfare legislation illustrates Nixon's overwhelming concerns about establishing a legacy in domestic affairs, one that would be framed in bold outlines so as to dwarf other plans, such as Lyndon Johnson's "Great Society." Uncharacteristically "bold" and obviously anti-conservative, the FAP, as Nixon described it in a special message to Congress on September 11, 1970, provided for:

> . . . a basic national income supplement for all needy families with children. It abolishes the bankrupt welfare system of the past, which has so greatly contributed to our present crisis, and creates an altogether new system based upon work incentives . . . job training and provision, and directed primarily to creating self-sufficient independent families.[21]

This proposal was a top domestic priority for Nixon. He later recalled that Patrick Moynihan, his Urban Affairs Adviser, had "wanted to take a year to consolidate our domestic situation before proposing any domestic legislation. But a year was simply too long, so I pushed the Cabinet and the staff to develop a program of creative and innovative social legislation as soon as possible."[22]

Arthur Burns, Nixon's Chief Economic Adviser, later Chairman of the Federal Reserve, urged delay in proposing the FAP but Nixon forged ahead, preferring to rely upon the advice of the less conservative elements in his administration. Apparently the idea of immediately dismantling Johnson's "Great Society" and establishing his own revolutionary program for social relief, including the striking change from "welfare" to "workfare" appealed to him.

The FAP raised eyebrows, ruffled feathers, and sent a shock wave throughout Congress that was still reverberating during the Reagan administration. Burns commented, "It ran counter to everything I knew about Dick Nixon. . . . It seemed that he might do the unthinkable."[23] The President, over the objections of many on his staff, adhered to his pledge to be an activist president in domestic affairs, and he sent the legislation to Congress. According to Schweiker:

> It was a positive approach to the problem, but it was so much in the center of the road that both sides shot it down. As so often happens when you have a good program with good elements in it, both sides turn negative and eventually kill it. It was a classic case of getting squashed in the center of the spectrum.[24]

The House ultimately passed the FAP, but for three consecutive years the Senate Finance Committee bottled up the novel proposal and, as Nixon wrote in 1978, "FAP finally died."[25]

An Example of Boldness in Foreign Policy

Nixon was equally committed to the notion of a foreign policy that, when juxtaposed with Lyndon Johnson's, would be favorably regarded and considered a historical first—i.e., much more significant. Because of his preoccupation with the war in Vietnam, Johnson had allowed America's relations with its European allies to deteriorate. In his memoirs, Nixon expressed his desire to "show the world that the new American President was not completely obsessed with Vietnam, and . . . dramatize for Americans at home that . . . their President could still be received abroad with respect and enthusiasm."[26]

According to Ehrlichman, during the period of transition between the Johnson and Nixon administrations, "Nixon and Kissinger decided that they had to do something very quickly to symbolize a commitment to the North Atlantic Treaty Organization otherwise NATO was just going to fall apart."[27] Faced with the imminent demise of the alliance, and determined to make his mark as "number one" in foreign affairs, Nixon traveled to eight countries in as many days just one month after assuming the presidency. In order to ensure the success of this mission Ehrlichman, acting as tour director, assigned campaign advance men to each of the cities to be visited. He recalled, "We ran it like a political campaign, lots of visuals!"[28] Fitting Nixon's inner motivation to act boldly and forcefully, the European mission was transformed into a trip with more symbol than substance. Apparently, the trip was designed to send strong signals not only to European allies but also to the Soviets and to Americans at home. Nixon expounded on this theme when he wrote that the trip:

> showed the NATO leaders that a new and interested administration which respected their views had come to power in Washington. It served warning on the Soviets that they could no longer take for granted—nor take advantage of—Western disunity. And the TV and press coverage had a positive impact at home, instilling, however briefly, some much-needed life into our sagging national pride.[29]

Nixon was so immersed in the preparations for his mission that when Kissinger told him of a widespread attack in Vietnam, he refused even to see the Secretary of Defense and Chairman of the Joint Chiefs of Staff. Instead, he continued to prepare for his meetings in Europe.

Vietnamization

Vietnam became Nixon's grand focus; he was determined not to let it destroy him the way it had destroyed Lyndon Johnson. Before taking office, he instructed Kissinger to secretly contact the North Vietnamese in an effort to resume the stalled Paris peace talks. At the time Nixon was elected President, the Vietnam war continued to be a seemingly unhealable wound for the nation. Nixon's prescription was Vietnamization. Above and beyond many reality factors involved in this prescription, we suggest that the policy he adopted also reflected an inner voice that demanded self-sufficiency.

After Defense Secretary Melvin Laird returned from Vietnam and reported that the South Vietnamese would defend themselves if given sufficient material and economic support, Nixon approved a policy that was later dubbed "Vietnamization." Its central goal was to transfer combat responsibility from the United States to the South Vietnamese and to make them accountable for their own defense in the future. Nixon wrote in *The Real War*, "The most important aspect of Vietnamization was the development of South Vietnam's army into a strong *independent* fighting force capable of *holding its own* against the Communists."[30]

Nixon approved and continued to implement this policy of Vietnamization over the objections of Kissinger. In his lengthy "Memorandum for the President," dated September 10, 1969, Kissinger expressed his "concerns" with respect to the administration's policy. He was not optimistic about South Vietnam's capacity to assume additional military burdens, and he likened the withdrawal of U.S. troops from Vietnam to the way salted peanuts create an insatiable appetite for more: "the more U.S. troops come home, the more will be demanded."[31]

On the basis of Nixon's pre-Presidential adult years, there were clear indications of his emotional journey toward eventual support of Vietnamization. For many years he had claimed that the key to success in Vietnam lay with the local forces assuming control of the fighting with peripheral economic and military support, including training, from the United States. In a meeting of the National Security Council on January 8, 1954, which convened to discuss the crisis of the French position at Dien Bien Phu, then Vice President Nixon voiced his approval of the position that the local forces should be trained to support themselves:

Indigenous forces are the key to success or failure. While at the present plans call for the building up of the Vietnamese forces to a point where they can take over the defense of their own country, there was considerable question whether the French would really prove willing to allow us to assist them with their training program.[32]

The French hold on Dien Bien Phu was eventually lost. As Nixon wrote in 1978, "The French had failed primarily because they had not sufficiently trained, much less inspired, the Indochinese people to be able to defend themselves."[33] In 1967, Nixon as a private citizen was still convinced "that continuation of the Administration's policy of fighting a defensive war of attrition would inevitably lead to defeat . . . It had become America's war, and the South Vietnamese were not being adequately trained and equipped to defend themselves."[34]

Only Richard Nixon could end the war. He remarked to Haldeman, "I'm the one man in this country who can do it."[35] From Vietnamization came the Nixon Doctrine, announced at an informal press conference on the island of Guam in July 1969. Essentially, the Nixon Doctrine stated that the United States "would furnish only the material and the military and economic assistance to those nations willing to accept the responsibility of supplying the manpower to defend themselves."[36]

Perhaps Nixon was seeking to merge decisions in the area of foreign policy with an internal motivation that would force all nations to become their own internal regulators. Here, again, we can see an echo of the intertwining of real world issues, such as national security, with emotional issues, such as the need for both self-sufficiency and control. We learned from Haldeman's diaries that, in order to prevent problems in the 1972 election year, pulling out from Vietnam was postponed.[37] Nixon's determination to keep his number one status and title overrode other considerations to end the war sooner.

9

Reflections of the Peacemaker

In order to maintain the split between his grandiose self and his unwanted devalued self, besides collecting titles and historical firsts, Nixon undertook bold projects that supported his unique internal needs. We believe Nixon's presidency was successful during the periods when there was a "fit" between reality and his motivations to perform superior deeds. Nixon also functioned well when his political thinking and activities reflected his attempts to integrate his internally split parts.

In real-world politics "dividing and conquering" or making new alliances are routine occurrences and the end results of political calculations. For example, Nixon's attempt to exploit differences between the Chinese and the Soviets required logical thinking and careful political planning. We know that the condition of a person with a narcissistic personality organization who attempts to control both his own splits and splits in his environment is paradoxical. There are internal motivations not only to integrate split parts, but also to keep them apart. The urge to maintain the split and the urge to integrate the split portions are two sides of the same coin. The integration "normally" takes place during childhood. If it does not take place, and we have seen how in the young Richard's case it did not do so, an internal urgency to integrate and complete the psychological development stage remains strong.

When the coin referred to above is tossed in the air, the side that usually comes up is that which reflects maintaining the split, where the individual with a narcissistic personality holds onto his grandiosity and hides his devalued aspects, keeping them separate. At times, however, the coin's other side appears, showing an effort toward integration—in Nixon's case his repeated attempts to bring together his own opposing sides as well as those of others. Attempts at integration occurred when Nixon showed his second face, that of his peacemaker self, in his bridging or linking policies and conciliation activities in the historical arena. Nixon's conscious decisions toward peacemaking could occur under conditions where his grandiose self was not threatened, or, in the opposite case, when his bridging activities served to support his grandiose self, since integration would potentially tame the danger coming from the unwanted aspects of his external, real-world environment and his internal world.

Nixon's Peacemaker Self

Even before he entered the political arena, Nixon exhibited reflections of his inner attempts to mend his own splits and the splits in his environment. Nixon's brother Donald had no trouble recalling that "Dick was the peacemaker. When we had fights with the neighbor boys, he would step in and talk us out of it."[1] As a young lawyer assigned to handle his firm's divorce cases, Nixon consistently urged reconciliations, sometimes at the expense of his firm's or his client's interests. This cost his firm no small amount in legal fees.[2]

While Nixon's tendency to strive for peace was hardly an asset to him in his law practice, at times, it seemed helpful to him in his political life. During the Alger Hiss controversy, for example, Nixon did not actually seek peace between Hiss and Whittaker Chambers, but apparently it was important to him that they at least confront each other. He insisted on this and eight days before the public hearing they did so. Nixon thereby became a bridge between them. He later wrote that "The hearing came to an end with the feeling that a great hurdle had been surmounted; the two men had confronted one another and their pasts have been *linked*."[3]

Nixon's vice-presidential years are replete with other examples of his efforts to link people, issues, and events; to play the peacemaker in order to thwart divisiveness; and to mediate during times of crisis. When Senator Joseph McCarthy's anti-Communist crusade threatened to divide the Republican Party, Nixon intervened at the urging of Eisenhower. He acted as "a go-between for McCarthy and the administration,"[4] thus brokering the feud. Nixon, the fierce anti-Communist

пunter of the Hiss era, found himself in a peculiar position: he was pla-
cating the anti-Communist movement of which he had once been in the
fore, and its notorious leader, Joe McCarthy.[5] Of course, this reversal may
have been easy for him because of the existence of the two-sided coin in
his own internal world. In a separate but related incident, Nixon once
intervened during a fist fight between Senator McCarthy and journalist
Drew Pearson. Nixon, the ubiquitous peacemaker, entered the fray,
yelling, "Let a Quaker stop this fight." He later remarked, "If I hadn't
pulled McCarthy away, he might have killed Pearson."[6] Nixon's presidency offers numerous examples of his positioning himself to be the link
between opposing forces. This, in turn, affected his domestic and foreign
policies.

Mending Tactics in Domestic Policy

Acting as though he were Abraham Lincoln II, Nixon displayed a mending, peacemaking mentality early in his presidency. A sense of "trying to
make the country whole" (a phrase from Nixon's first inaugural address)
prevailed. He wanted to heal the wounds of the nation, as he stated after
attending Duke Law School, by "bringing the South back" into the
nation, and making it whole again.[7] As he vowed in his first Inaugural
Address, "Those who have been left out, we will try to bring in. Those left
behind, we will help to catch up." Dubbed the *Southern Strategy* by William
Safire,[8] it affected not only the administration's policy on school desegregation, but Nixon's nominations to the Supreme Court as well.

Balancing himself ever so delicately on the precipice of enforcing
school desegregation rulings, Nixon emphatically ordered Attorney
General John Mitchell and Secretary of Health, Education and Welfare,
Elliot Richardson, to comply with court orders, but "to do only what the
law required and not one thing more."[9] Later, Ehrlichman said, "The
President gave very specific instructions over and over again . . . His dic-
tum was that you will enforce court orders, but you will do it in such a way
that we won't poke a finger in the eye of the South; no rubbing their
noses in it."[10] Nixon, recapitulating his thinking on desegregation, wrote
in his Memoirs:

> I believed that with the right approach we could persuade people
> in the South and elsewhere not just to obey the law because it was
> the law, but gradually to bring them to an understanding and
> acceptance of the wisdom and humanity that lay behind it. In the
> meantime, I felt that as long as the law was not being deliberately
> disobeyed the federal government should be an instrument of per-

suasion rather than an engine of coercion; the President should be the conciliator rather than the divider.[11]

According to Ehrlichman, the "right approach" as far as Nixon was concerned was to have the administration act as the leader in helping to form local biracial, bipartisan citizen committees that would be responsible for delineating proper enforcement procedures for their respective school districts. In the end, Ehrlichman concluded, "We moved more school districts into compliance in the first four years than had been done in the whole history of the civil rights movement."[12]

Interested in implementing his integration plans and adhering to his pledge to "bring the South back," Nixon targeted the Supreme Court as an instrument through which he could begin to repair rifts, heal old wounds, and make the country whole again. Accordingly, when Associate Justice Abe Fortas was forced off the court because of charges of suspect financial dealings, so that a vacancy occurred on the Court, Nixon asked Attorney General Mitchell to locate an appropriately qualified Southern judge who shared Nixon's strict constructionist interpretation of the Constitution. Mitchell suggested Clement F. Haynsworth of South Carolina, who was then nominated by Nixon. Senate opposition swelled almost immediately after the nomination was announced. In addition, Labor considered him "anti-labor," while civil rights partisans questioned his position on racial matters. In addition, questions were raised about some of his decisions which may have benefited him financially. There was a heated Senate debate on issues involving racism and judicial impropriety relative to cases heard by Haynsworth against companies in which he held stock, and the nomination was rejected.

More determined than ever to place a Southerner on the Court, Nixon then nominated G. Harold Carswell of the Fifth Circuit Court of Appeals in Florida. Here, too, charges of racism were raised, based on comments made twenty years previously by Carswell. In addition, his mediocrity was obvious. Despite considerable bullying and lobbying by the White House, this nomination was rejected as well. According to former Senator Richard Schweiker, Nixon called Schweiker's financial contributors and asked them to pressure him into voting for the Carswell nomination.[13] Extremely upset by the administration's tactics, Schweiker (and a dozen other Republicans) voted against the nomination. Nixon was so angered and humiliated by their action that those who had opposed the nomination, Schweiker included, were blacklisted from all future social functions at the Nixon White House. (We will return to Nixon's anger and humiliation concerning these rejections in the next chapter.)

A Contemporary Lincoln

Related to his wish to bring the South back into the nation was Nixon's attempted identification with Abraham Lincoln. Nixon believed that he was the contemporary Lincoln, facing problems and crises similar to those of the Civil War years that required decisive Lincolnesque actions and measures. Nixon's comment made in the course of interviews with David Frost reflects this wish to identify with Lincoln. He said: "This nation was torn apart in an ideological way by the war in Vietnam as much as the Civil War tore apart the nation when Lincoln was President."[14] Indeed, Nixon made many of his important decisions while sitting in the White House's Lincoln Sitting Room.[15] One decision in particular is remembered not for its historical significance but for the profoundly revealing insights it yielded into a man troubled by seemingly endless student protests and continuing national divisiveness.

After a heated press conference in the East Room of the White House on the evening of May 8, 1970, Nixon was keyed up. Anti-war demonstrators were holding a candlelight vigil that night. Nixon could not sleep, which was unusual for him, but he was curiously relaxed and talkative. He made many phone calls, including one to speech writer William Safire, who had accompanied Vice President Spiro Agnew to Atlanta, where Agnew was to give a speech in Nixon's stead the following day. Nixon, who had taken part in writing the speech, commented to Safire: "In his speech I was trying to show how we are one people. I'm the goddamnest desegregationist there is, but it has to be done the right way. . . . This Southern Strategy stuff—all we're doing is treating the South with the same respect as the North."[16]

Following his spate of phone calls, Nixon retired for the night, but was still unable to sleep. He went to the Lincoln Sitting Room and proceeded to play some classical music on the phonograph. Hearing the music, his valet, Manolo Sanchez, looked in on him and asked if he wanted anything. Nixon inquired whether Sanchez had ever been to the Lincoln Memorial at night. When Sanchez replied that he had not Nixon said, "Get your clothes on, we'll go." It was close to four in the morning at this point.

At the Lincoln Memorial Nixon engaged several student demonstrators in conversation, and they were joined later by many more. An analysis of his conversation with them and his recollections of the affair illustrate his preoccupation with repairing the nation and healing the wounds caused by the Vietnam War. In a diary entry following this predawn expedition, Nixon made note of the inscription that is written over the Lincoln Memorial: "In this temple, as in the hearts of the people for whom he saved the Union, the memory of Abraham Lincoln is enshrined forever."

Egil ("Bud") Krogh, then a thirty-year-old Ehrlichman staff member, having overheard the President's request for a car on the intercom, followed Nixon in another car to the Lincoln Memorial. He drew up a memorandum on this "sunrise visit" for the President's file, and one of the subjects it touched on was the American Indian. In Nixon's words: "What we have done with the American Indian is in its way just as bad as what we imposed on the Negroes. We took a proud and independent race and virtually destroyed them. We have to find ways to bring them back into decent lives in this country."[17]

After speaking about the American Indians, Nixon went on to express concern about how blacks were separating themselves from whites on college campuses. He ended his speech by exhorting the students to "find a way to communicate with the blacks in your universities."[18]

Upon leaving the Memorial, Nixon was still euphoric. He wanted to show Sanchez the Capitol, which his valet had never visited. Inside, Nixon encountered a cleaning woman carrying a Bible. Apparently, the religious working woman reminded him of his mother. With a lump in his throat, Nixon referred to his mother as a "saint."[19] Forgotten for the moment were the old issues of Hannah's inability to mother him properly or to respond effectively to his crying.

Linkage in Nixon's Foreign Policy

By the end of 1970, Nixon and Kissinger had turned their attention to global strategy. Together they sought to reshape America's relationship with the Communist world. During the transition period, Nixon and Kissinger established a way of dealing with foreign policy that was called *linkage*. Nixon wrote that "Since U.S.-Soviet interests as the world's two competing nuclear superpowers were so widespread and overlapping, it was unrealistic to separate or compartmentalize areas of concern. Therefore we decided to link progress in such areas of Soviet concern as strategic arms limitation and increased trade with progress in areas that were important to us—Vietnam, the Mideast, and Berlin."[20]

Echoing this assessment, General Scowcroft said, "It was the notion of tying everything to everything else, on the theory that the U.S.-Soviet relationship was a unity and that one ought to improve that relationship."[21] Kissinger wrote in 1979 that "linkage is not a natural concept for Americans, who have traditionally perceived foreign policy as an episodic enterprise. . . . American pragmatism produces a penchant for examining issues separately."[22]

For Richard Nixon, however, linkage provided a framework within which he could also fulfill his unconscious wish to weld splits. It seems he enlisted Kissinger as an alter-ego to achieve these ends. In interviews conducted by Andrew Dod for this book with Richard Helms, Elliott Richardson, Kenneth Rush, and Brent Scowcroft, a portrait emerged of Nixon as the "composer" of foreign policy.[23] Kissinger, the one more comfortable with small talk and the fine, exacting art of diplomacy, appeared as the "conductor" of the foreign policy orchestra, which usually played a song called "linkage."

Nixon and Kissinger proved themselves exceptions to the notion that Americans do not practice foreign policy by design—they, themselves, were very conscious of world dynamics. By the summer of 1969 they had managed to work out a treaty with the Soviets in which for the first time in the history of the nuclear age the two superpowers agreed to limits in the use of nuclear weapons. They also began secret negotiations with China, fearing that it soon would be a country too powerful to ignore. And the first troops were coming home from Vietnam. Nixon was moving toward fulfilling his wish to become a peacemaker.

By facilitating a friendly U.S.-Soviet dialogue in various strategic areas through linkage, Nixon sought to prepare the world stage for repair, to alleviate tensions, and then to build a new world—but one conceived with an eye toward balance. Just as there was evidence of internal motivations to "repair" America and to make her "truly whole" on the domestic front, similar unconscious forces were played out in a sublimated way in the international arena. Nixon's obsession with repairing laid the foundations for *détente.*

Détente

In French, *détente* means calm, relaxation, ease. By calming, relaxing, and easing tensions between the United States and the Soviet Union, Richard Nixon hoped to mend and repair the divided world. To achieve this end, Nixon and Kissinger demanded that substantive negotiations on many topics begin.[24] The plan was to identify problem spots, open talks, and then engage the general policy of linkage, whereby progress in one area was linked to progress in another. Before becoming President, Nixon told an audience of politicians: "Diplomatically we should have discussions with the Soviet leaders at all levels to reduce the possibility of miscalculations and to explore the areas where bilateral agreements would reduce tensions. . . . I believe in building bridges but we should build only our end of the bridge."[25]

This image of linking, building, and shaping a new world for the future characterized Nixon's foreign policy. However, under the influence of his grandiose self even the linking and healing aspects had to be done in a grand fashion. Haldeman commented that "President Nixon saw himself as the world's foremost world statesman! He thought he was the world's final bridge because he had known Churchill, de Gaulle, Mao Tse-Tung, and Khrushchev . . . He loved it when Bill Rogers called him 'the world's youngest elder statesman.' That really caught his imagination."[26]

A Divided Berlin

Given his own internal contradictions, it is not surprising that a divided Berlin would capture Nixon's attention, above and beyond any realistic political concerns he might have had. John Donne might have described Berlin as "an island entire of itself." Situated 110 miles east of the West German border, an urban island surrounded by East Germany, Berlin had for years been the epicenter of crisis and tension in that region. The airlift of 1948 and the crisis of 1961, during which the infamous Berlin Wall separating the east and west sectors of the city was erected, exacerbated the already tenuous balance that existed. Recognizing that the reunification of Berlin was an impossibility during his presidency, Nixon urged formal negotiations to improve the predicament of the isolated West Berliners.[27] Two major issues had to be settled: first, the Western powers (Britain, France, and the United States) demanded a Soviet guarantee that access to West Berlin would be unimpeded; second, West Germany wanted the Soviets to accept the notion of "significant political ties" between West Germany and West Berlin.[28]

According to Ambassador Kenneth Rush, when the formal negotiations reached an impasse, Nixon suggested privately that Rush begin secret negotiations with the Soviet Ambassador to East Germany and his country's official representative to the formal talks, in an attempt to resolve the crisis. A Berlin settlement was absolutely essential to Nixon, who believed that because of his linkage approach, all other major areas of interest depended on a final agreement. Rush offered the following explanation: "President Nixon considered the Berlin Agreement not as a matter of linkage with détente, [but rather] it was a matter that you couldn't have détente with the Soviet Union unless you had the Berlin agreement. It all hinged there."[29]

In the course of the secret negotiations, Rush, a skilled negotiator in his own right, was able to obtain Soviet acceptance of each condition. In a hidden-channels cable to Kissinger he wrote, "A draft of the tentative agreement is enclosed, and it is still difficult for me to believe that it is as favorable as it is."[30] Signed on September 3, 1971, the final Berlin Agreement included the Soviet guarantees of "unhindered access to the Western sector of the Federal Republic to citizens of West Berlin."[31] In short, Nixon, through Rush, had achieved not only a major foreign policy victory, but a psychological one as well—a step toward reintegrating split aspects of a narcissistic personality organization.

We do not, of course, suggest that Nixon's interest and success in signing the Berlin Agreement can be reduced to an attempt to deal with his personality issues. The psychological force that was present simply induced unconscious motivations and supplied direction to the affairs at hand. What is important is what a person does with an unconscious force, and how much reality testing, thought, and reasoning are applied to express it. In Nixon's case his need to integrate splits within himself may have inclined him toward mending splits in the larger political world. Nixon's success, especially when he was showing his second face, that of the peacemaker, indicates his "ego strength" and his ability to work against the odds.[32]

It is useful to identify and understand a leader's reflection of his unconscious forces, however deeply they may be submerged. Only by understanding such forces can we know why certain patterns are repeated, and why the individual in question is internally directed toward certain behavior. While Nixon was achieving realistic as well as psychological success in respect to the Berlin Wall, he sought similar satisfaction elsewhere, in one of the world's most isolated sectors.

China

During a particularly sensitive moment in the Berlin negotiations Ambassador Rush received orders from Kissinger to delay completion of the talks. Unknown to Rush, President Nixon had been plotting a rapprochement with China in which any interference from Europe might have destroyed the China initiative. Nixon, when showing his second political face, was driven to repair and to mend. He had for many years urged steps toward normalization of relations with Communist China. In his 1967 *Foreign Affairs* article, Nixon wrote:

> Taking the long view, we simply cannot afford to leave China outside the family of nations, there to nurture its fantasies, cherish its hates, and threaten its neighbors. There is no place on this small

planet for a billion of its potentially most able people to live in angry isolation. For the short run, this means a policy of firm restraint, of no reward, of a creative counterpressure designed to persuade Peking that its interests can be served only by accepting the basic rules of international civility. For the long run, it means pulling China back into the world community.[33]

Nixon's desire for "pulling China back into the world community" and easing relations with that country led the State Department, at his request, to announce in March 1971 the termination of all passport restrictions for travel to China. In April, Nixon announced the termination of the 21-year trade embargo on the same day that China's Premier Zhou Enlai welcomed the United States Ping-pong team, saying, "You have opened a new page in the relations of the Chinese and American people."[34]

These symbolic signals indicated the possibility of a new era. On July 15, 1971, President Nixon announced before a national television audience that he had received an invitation from Premier Zhou to visit the People's Republic of China (PRC). No longer was it to be referred to as Communist China. He announced that he had accepted the invitation with pleasure, and that he would travel to China sometime before May 1972. Recognized as having made a bold effort to "build a lasting peace in the world," he said in his toast during the plenary session:

We have great differences today. What brings us together is that we have common interests which transcend those differences. As we discuss our differences, neither of us will compromise our principles. *But while we cannot close the gulf between us, we can try to bridge it so that we may be able to talk across it.*[35]

Unfortunately, Nixon could not tolerate success—and he could not maintain an integrated inner world. He had to show his third face.

10

The Final Face: Enemies Everywhere

With this chapter, our psychobiography of Richard Nixon comes to an end. In it we shall analyze the external destructive acts he committed and show how they were precipitated by destructiveness from within.

The plight of Richard Nixon began with his birth to parents who came from two different worlds. As we have shown, the child Richard was injured psychologically by physical and emotional separations from the mother. He suffered physically as well, in the form of life threatening accidents and physical beatings by an erratic father. He used his natural inner strength to grow up prematurely and to make himself so superior that he could rise above all the confusion, hurt, and grief in his environment. He excelled and aspired to be the leader of every organization that he came across—eventually becoming the leader of the most powerful nation in the world. He sought to achieve historical firsts, some of which were significant while others were, in fact, trivial. It did not matter to him; he treasured the trivial achievements as much as the superior ones, since all were needed to maintain his grandiose self, which had been erected originally to deny his dependency and his devalued, injured, hungry self.

When he was functioning at his best, Richard Nixon succeeded in actually accomplishing grand deeds or being a mender and a healer. Healing was a big factor in his motivations, as he wanted to heal the splits in his life—i.e., in his personality—between his grandiose self and his hungry self; in the conflicting representations of his mother, between the mother who perceived him as special and the mother who could not give him enough attention; in the representations of his father, between the father who was brutal and the idealized father he created in Abraham Lincoln and others. Unfortunately, he could not maintain his grandiose self and/or his healing activities for long and he could not allow himself to surpass his father, so he had to submit to an internal image of a brutal father, which caused him to punish himself. Furthermore, whenever he could not maintain his grandiosity, he felt threatened and humiliated by his devalued aspects and was unable to accept them. These devalued aspects he projected onto others (or other things) whom he then distrusted. He frantically attempted to control them and even destroy them. He regressed, and his responses to his regression included paranoid expectations that ultimately contributed to his downfall. This chapter examines Nixon's third face, that of his paranoid self. We will provide selected examples of events that illuminate the intertwining of his internal anxieties with external fears and his humiliation with his desire for revenge.

Destructiveness in Foreign Policy

While it was destructiveness in Nixon's domestic policy that led to his downfall, his decisionmaking skills in the sphere of foreign policy were also marred by his inability to maintain his grandiose self and accept success. Nixon was adept at international relations when he could plan, according to the dictates of his internal drives, to perform grand deeds and/or to heal. Thus, the same man who was capable of engineering a historic arms treaty with the Soviets and who opened the gates of China to the West could also sow the seeds of his own destruction in a war he did not create but could not permit himself to abandon. Nixon's decisionmaking in both the overthrow of the Allende regime in Chile and his secret war in Cambodia, we suggest, was contaminated with internal issues. As an example of his destructiveness in foreign policy, let us examine Nixon's decisions about Cambodia.

Blema Steinberg states that many scholars and journalists have raised unanswered questions regarding Nixon's order to secretly bomb North Vietnamese sanctuaries in Cambodia on March 17, 1969 and his committing American forces to Cambodia on April 30, 1970. In both of these decisions the role they served Nixon psychologically appears more significant than their role in any military strategy. In fact, his personal decision went against the counsel of some of his military advisers, and he twice rescinded orders to begin the secret bombing earlier in 1969, when his closest advisers convinced him the timing was wrong. Each time Nixon's "resentments and impatience increased" until finally he "wanted to do something."[1] After ordering the secret bombing in March 1969, he met with some of his advisers, giving them the impression that their input would be considered, although the order had already been given. He kept the bombing secret from the American public and preempted his advisers, telling Kissinger "State is to be notified only after the point of no return."[2]

The actual invasion of Cambodia occurred only a year later. Again, we see a psychological basis for his decision. Steinberg states that "While domestic political factors certainly played a significant role, they too cannot fully explain the nature of the responses that Nixon chose."[3] As she describes in detail, a series of historical and political events that began in 1969 threatened Nixon's grandiose self: on the domestic front, the Senate, as we have seen, had rejected the Haynsworth and Carswell nominations. This humiliated Nixon because it frustrated his efforts to appease the South and mend the North-South rift in the country. At the same time, the North Vietnamese were refusing to come to the bargaining table for peace talks. He had also had to cancel his plans to attend his daughter's graduation ceremonies at Smith College because of the potential for an angry confrontation with anti-war demonstrators. Nixon, who had won the election partially on his pledge to end the war, became frustrated. Steinberg writes: "The final straw was the aborted Apollo 13 moon trip on 13 April . . . Kissinger described Nixon as becoming increasingly testy and noted that Haldeman had joked that the President was in a 'charming mood'; in the course of covering one subject on the telephone, Nixon had hung up on him several times."

All these developments had left Nixon psychologically primed to replenish his narcissistic supplies by some action that would demonstrate his power in the face of the abasement that he had experienced. Invading Cambodia was to offer him just that opportunity.[4]

Regarding that invasion, James Barber underscored the linkage between humiliation and revenge when he wrote, concerning the 1970 invasion, that "Nixon moved from April and Carswell to May and Cambodia, from defeat to attack."[5] The combativeness of Nixon's April 30 speech announcing to the public his decision to invade Cambodia gives an indication of the personal, psychological importance of this attack; in it he says "we will not be humiliated. We will not be defeated," that America must not act like "a pitiful, helpless giant," and that "it is not our power but our will and character that is being tested tonight."[6] Nixon's actions would have a powerful ripple effect. Steinberg reminds us that May 1, 1970 marked the beginning of a full-fledged war that devastated

Cambodia. "In the process, a new civil war was set in motion between the Khmer Rouge and its opponents resulting in the country being turned into 'killing fields' with the death of more than a million people."[7]

At this point we will offer another illustration of how internal anxieties clearly affected Nixon's responses in the historical arena. Richard Nixon won the presidential election against Senator George McGovern in 1972 by a landslide. Looking back on it all now we know that for Nixon the campaign period had been contaminated with his internal anxieties. The political polls indicated that Nixon would win the election despite the shadow of Watergate, which continued to plague him even though its details were not yet fully available to the public. The landslide victory really made Richard Nixon "number one" in the external world. All indications are, however, that Nixon could not enjoy his success. He withdrew to Camp David and most likely was depressed. He may have felt that his grandiose self, which was so exposed at this point, might be envied by his internalized representation of a brutal father, and his own hungry self and, perhaps, by everyone else. The shadow of Watergate also threatened his grandiosity. He stayed at Camp David for two months following the election.

Depression includes turning aggression against oneself; Nixon's way of lifting himself out of a depression was to turn aggression outward. As President, the turning of aggression outward meant making a foreign policy/military decision. Nixon ordered a heightened bombing of North Vietnam in December, called "The Christmas Bombing," the intensity of which surprised even the military experts. Success, combined with the threat of humiliation, had made the President anxious, so he emerged fighting and killing.

As we discussed in the previous chapter, Nixon when showing his second face had an inclination to be a peacemaker. The Vietnam war was a source of tremendous frustration for him, but because of his exaggerated narcissism he was determined not to be the first American President to lose a war: the longer the war dragged on the more desperate he became to end it. Ironically Nixon had the same objective as had the anti-war demonstrators who opposed him—to bring the war to an end—but he wanted to do so in a fashion that would not jeopardize his status as President.[8] However, his delay in ordering the withdrawal of American troops and his massive demonstration of American military strength through intensified bombing of Hanoi served to destroy the country, rather than to achieve the peace he craved externally and internally.

Nixon's anxieties mounted further. As the anti-war demonstrations increased, he started blaming his critics in Congress and the press for failing to support their President's efforts. He called the demonstrators thugs and hoodlums and claimed he still had the support of the Silent Majority. But they too were becoming disillusioned because of rising inflation, rising unemployment, and the never-ending war. Nixon was becoming a president under siege.

By the summer of 1972 the "Pentagon Papers" had been printed and the name Daniel Ellsberg was a household word. Because of the secret negotiations he was conducting with the Chinese, the Soviets, and the North Vietnamese, Nixon was worried. Although the initial installment of the "Pentagon Papers" referred only to the first three decades of growing U.S. involvement in Vietnam, not to the Nixon administration's role specifically, the President and Kissinger still considered them a threat to national security and to their secret diplomacy. When papers concerning Nixon's foreign policy decisions and his arms control negotiations with the Soviets were later released, Nixon became furious. This served to confirm his worst suspicions about the press. Slowly the house of cards came tumbling down. He gave the orders that led to Watergate and ultimately to his own demise. In the meantime, the "Christmas Bombings" in the winter of 1972 resulted in a reactivation of the Paris peace talks. Nixon had remained stolidly silent during the twelve days of bombing. His critics said he could have ended the war months earlier if he had not been so stubborn, but that did not concern him. His popularity soared when the troops came home. By then, however, the wheels had already been put in motion for his destruction.

Nixon's penchant for strategic games helped him achieve glorious accomplishments, but it also created trouble. While he was busy negotiating secretly with the Soviets he was also communicating with the Chinese. Astute in his foreign policy posturing, he wanted to exploit the growing divisiveness in the Communist world. This gave him leverage with the Soviets and made them more amenable to an arms control agreement. When Nixon had ordered the major counteroffensive against the North Vietnamese in the spring of 1972, he had felt it necessary in order not to lose ground with the Soviets. He feared he would appear weak if he did not protect the American troops, and he gambled that his actions would not destroy his chances for a summit, that the Soviets, in fact, would respect him more for the tough line he took. This toughness led him to become the first president to step inside the Kremlin and to visit China. This same man would also be the first president to resign from office. Throughout this period Nixon felt he was being tested continuously. Some of his aides were resigning in protest against his military tactics, so he installed a taping system to protect himself in case those who supported him later said they had disagreed with him concerning the war. Eventually the taping system trapped Nixon, not the aides.

The same Nixon who had hoped to be loved as a Lincolnesque figure was capable of inspiring scorn and hatred. When calm, Nixon's foreign policy decisions exemplified his unconscious motivation to combine diversified bodies, to seek wholes. His inability to resolve his internal war intruded, however, and he permitted his internal battles to spill over into his external world. The same reflection of anxieties and aggression that characterized Nixon's foreign policy, dominated his domestic policy as well.

Suspicion in Domestic Policy

Some leaders externalize the image of a grieving or depressed mother or that of a troubled father onto a whole nation, and then go about repairing the nation/parent.[9] Those leaders who succeed in this endeavor are of the type known as *reparative*.[10] Nixon wanted to make the nation "whole" and as an extension of his Lincoln fantasy, he wanted to finish mending the North and the South.

But Nixon was not always able to succeed in his reparative efforts, as we have seen. He had to spy on his siblings, or their symbolic stand-ins, and those he identified as rivals. He unconsciously wanted to be sure that his "hungry" self would be cared for at all times and that his grandiose self would always stay in power. Thus, he had a tendency to be alert, suspicious, and at times paranoid, in addition to being shrewd: his need to assure his status is another reason he resorted to schemes such as the wiretaps.

In addition to the electronic surveillance of various figures in Washington, Nixon ordered Ehrlichman to ask the Central Intelligence Agency to follow his brother Donald who, he thought, was subject to business indiscretions. Presumably, this was done to protect the President from embarrassment, and to ensure that Donald Nixon did not attract attention. In this act we see the intertwining of personal and political issues in Nixon's mind, as though his internal needs and the demands of the external world had been put into one pot! However, the CIA charter specifically forbids agency involvement in domestic surveillance, so the CIA had to turn down Ehrlichman's request. The Secret Service, which had once kept President Johnson's brother under watch, was assigned the task instead, and eventually asked for permission to tap Donald's phone. According to Ehrlichman, Nixon approved this request himself.[11] One of the underlying reasons for this surveillance, incidentally, was Donald Nixon's former connection to Howard Hughes, who had once loaned him more than $200,000. (As will be evident in the Watergate section of this chapter, the President had a significant interest in any dealings in which Howard Hughes was involved.) It seems clear that Nixon's hunger for information, like the "best laid schemes of mice and men," went astray in this case. His political adversaries, his enemies, and simply those competing for the nation's (mother's) love were all subject to fallout from his suspiciousness and paranoid preoccupations.

Daniel Ellsberg was one such enemy. Nixon, enraged over Ellsberg's deliberate leak of the Pentagon Papers, demanded that he be punished. The FBI was not quick to respond, and Nixon, by urging swift White House intervention, set a tone for his administration that resulted in the break-in at Ellsberg's psychiatrist's office. Evidence provided by a conversation Nixon had with Haldeman and information obtained from Ehrlichman,[12] points to the President as having either ordered directly, or having approved, the break-in. At the very least he surely had prior knowledge about it.

According to Haldeman, Nixon spoke with him in November 1976, ostensibly "to probe" his memory about "the plumbers" and the Ellsberg break-in. Haldeman wrote, "The more Nixon spoke, the more I realized something strange. Nixon was worried that he had personally ordered the Ellsberg break-in."[13] Nixon confessed to Haldeman, "I was so damned mad at Ellsberg in those days . . . I've been thinking maybe I ordered that break-in."[14]

In writing a review of Haldeman's book, John Ehrlichman—who, at the time, was serving a prison sentence for a crime he believes Nixon himself committed—called several Nixon associates asking for substantive comments or contributions to prove that Nixon had ordered the break-in himself.[15] After publication of the review Ehrlichman found two former associates who confirmed Haldeman's impression. One said that Nixon had previous knowledge of and actually encouraged the Ellsberg break-in, and the other said that it was Nixon who put the break-in "into motion."[16] In effect, the break-in satisfied Nixon's need to monitor the positions of his enemies (siblings, oedipal father, etc.). As we shall see, Nixon's unconscious need to be a collector and accumulate information may also have precipitated the Watergate crisis. We think that the historical truth about whether or not Nixon actually ordered the break-in is not so significant as the understanding that his "psychic truth" had created an atmosphere in which it could take place.

Watergate

Nixon was inordinately concerned with Howard Hughes. His interest in the reclusive financier bordered on the obsessional. Hughes had collected vast amounts of money and was not only a threat to Nixon's hungry self, but also paradoxically a potential source for Nixon's narcissism.

Since the Hughes connection had been bandied about as being implicated in Nixon's defeat in both his presidential bid in 1960 and his gubernatorial loss in 1962, Hughes seemed a potential source of trouble when
Nixon at last became President. This explains, to some extent, Nixon's
outrage when he received information regarding Larry O'Brien. Then
Chairman of the Democratic National Committee, O'Brien was receiving
a lobbyist retainer fee of $180,000 from the billionaire Hughes. Here was
an opportunity for Nixon to get out from under the Hughes spotlight,
which had been cast on him originally through Hughes's loan to Donald
Nixon. Something as simple as a retainer fee to O'Brien, or a loan to his
brother Donald, could be experienced as a threat to his hungry self.
Nixon deliberately leaked the Hughes-O'Brien connection to the press,
inciting a major scandal. Several Nixon associates have testified and written about Nixon's preoccupation with Hughes as well as his desperate
desire to tie O'Brien to Hughes.[17] Nixon confided to Haldeman "We're
going to nail O'Brien on this, one way or the other."[18] Later, Haldeman
added:

> [Nixon] pushed hard for information tying Larry O'Brien to
> Howard Hughes and I could see where that desire could be pushed
> into trying to find out something through the DNC [Democratic
> National Committee]. . . . Nixon caused the [Watergate] break-in.
> . . . He indirectly caused it by setting the tone and by putting some-
> what relentless demands on me and [Charles] Colson, and maybe
> through other sources on the campaign . . . to get information on
> Hughes' connection with O'Brien. I would not be surprised to find
> somewhere Nixon saying [on the tapes] "I want information on
> Hughes and I want you to get it. I don't want excuses. I want the
> information."[19]

The burglars who broke into O'Brien's office on June 17, 1972, were
caught with electronic equipment. One burglar, Frank Sturgis, admitted
they had been ordered to look for "anything about Hughes."[20] Apparently, Nixon's unconscious psychological motivations made irrational
decisions seem logical: breaking the law became a minor issue in the
grand scheme of obtaining desired information, which was necessary in
order to ease his internal anxieties.[21]

Compulsivity

As is evident from his preoccupation with the Hughes-O'Brien connection, Nixon sometimes acted compulsively. Haldeman agreed, saying,

"Nixon would get caught up in something and get frustrated by the fact that someone else didn't deal with it in some way that solved the problem, so he would jump on it, hang on it, and pound on it."[22] Even when everything seemed just perfect, Nixon had the illusion that conflicts, especially derivatives of his unconscious childhood conflicts, were not under control. Ehrlichman provided two examples of Nixon's compulsive inability "to leave things alone":

> This was a fellow with a number of compulsions. He could not leave some things alone. About a year before J. Edgar Hoover died, Nixon, Mitchell, and I, had dinner at Hoover's house. When Hoover started talking about planting bugs in the new Soviet Embassy, Nixon moved right to the edge of his chair. He wanted to know all about it; he wanted to help with that; he wanted to do whatever he could because that was exciting. . . .
>
> When Watergate came up, we had a conversation in which he agreed to stay out of it. We were going to leave it to the Committee to Re-elect. . . . When Haldeman came in on 23 June 1972 [he] told him that Dean and Mitchell think that "you should get the CIA to tell the FBI to stop." I wasn't there, but I can just imagine that he moved right to the edge of his chair, that was too delicious. Instead of saying, "Look, we agreed to keep this away from me, the worst thing you can do for me, Haldeman, is to bring this to my desk. . . . You have to keep it away from the Presidency." Instead of that, he clutched it to his bosom and wouldn't let it go . . . He couldn't leave it alone.
>
> About two or three weeks after that we were walking on the beach in San Clemente. That was all he could talk about, he wanted to promise clemency to [Howard] Hunt. I told him "you cannot touch this thing, because once you touch it, it's like the tar baby; it'll be on you forever and you have got to stay away from it." "Yes, yes, you're right, you're right." The next thing you hear on the tapes is Nixon talking with Colson about clemency for Hunt. He couldn't leave it alone.[23]

The CIA Trap Theory

Another theory about the Watergate break-in that has gained attention but that remains controversial has been called "The CIA Trap Theory." Its adherents claim that Nixon's desire to bring the CIA under White House control, to coordinate and centralize the intelligence operations under the White House umbrella, deeply disturbed members of the agency. James McCord, a former CIA agent and one of the Watergate burglars, submitted a memorandum to the Senate Watergate Investigating Committee which outlined the CIA's concerns about the White House maneuvers to assume control. He wrote:

> It appeared to me that the White House had for some time been trying to get political control over CIA assessments and estimates, in order to make them conform to "White House Policy" . . . When linked with what I saw happening to the FBI under [new director] Pat Gray—political control by the White House—it appeared then that the two government agencies which should be able to conduct their business with complete integrity in the national interest, were no longer going to be able to do so.[24]

According to the proponents of the CIA Trap Theory, the Watergate break-in, in which several former and contemporary CIA agents were directly involved, was deliberately botched in an attempt to countermand this drive toward centralization and loss of political autonomy. A secondary purpose was to create political problems for Nixon. Eugenio Martinez, one of the burglars, was on the CIA payroll on June 17, 1972. Since normal agency procedures would have required Martinez to report to his case officer the projects in which he was involved, one may surmise along with Haldeman that the CIA had, at least, advance knowledge of the intended break-in.[25]

Whether one believes this theory or not, it is clear that the Nixon administration had tried to coordinate and control the intelligence community. Such a desire reflects Nixon's unconscious wish to bring together diverse bodies into one centralized and controllable whole while spying on them, and to control them by having "intellectual" awareness of what they were doing. This may explain the formation of the Inter-Agency Group on Domestic Intelligence, and its suggestions, which were labeled "The Huston Plan."

The Huston Plan

As Haldeman testified before the Senate Watergate Committee, "In 1970, the domestic security problem reached critical proportions as a wave of bombings and explosions, rioting and violence, demonstrations, arson, gun battles and other disruptive activities took place across the country."[26] In an effort to control this proliferating domestic violence, the President called upon the directors of the CIA, the FBI, the NSA (National Security Agency), the DIA (Defense Intelligence Agency), and White House staffer Tom Huston, in June 1970 to form an Inter-Agency

:e Group "to work out a coordinated plan for dealing with
:eats."[27] Haldeman confirmed this: "The concept was to try to
.. the intelligence gathering facilities . . . We were trying to tie
them in."[28] Intelligence collecting would be conducted under the White
House umbrella, as a means of dealing with the domestic violence that
was plaguing the country.

Undeniably, domestic violence and internal division were on a sharp
rise during this period, but it is questionable whether the Huston Plan,
which called for opening pieces of mail, installing unwarranted telephone taps, and conducting surreptitious entries, did not go beyond the
constitutional powers accorded the President. It is crucial, however, to
understand Nixon's thinking as he approved the Huston Plan. In the
Frost interviews he said, "When a President does it, that means that it is
not illegal."[29] Due to what he considered to be the revolutionary vicissitudes of the times, condensed with his grandiosity and a psychological
need to collect information, Nixon seems to have "believed" that the
Constitution granted him extraordinary powers. He later wrote:

> It is difficult—perhaps impossible—to convey a sense of the pres-
> sures that were influencing my actions and reactions during this
> period, but it was this epidemic of unprecedented domestic terror-
> ism that prompted our efforts to discover the best means by which
> to deal with this new phenomenon of highly organized and highly
> skilled revolutionaries dedicated to the violent destruction of our
> democratic system.[30]

We suggest that what we are hearing at this point is an echo of Nixon's
early years, during which there were many traumas, instances of physical
abuse, threats, and death. All these aspects paralleled *domestic terrorism* in
Nixon's mind. The stressful political environment that existed must have
reactivated the stressful conditions of his childhood. Thus, his external
responses as an adult mirrored internal elements that contained memories, feelings, and expectations from the past, thereby causing him to
become frantic and use poor judgment. In the end one might say he met
his Watergate.

The End of the Presidency

During the stressful Watergate period Richard Nixon regressed. Under
regression we try to pump up what has been our best defense in other
troubled times. So Richard Nixon turned to pumping up his grandiose
self, although it was too late by then to fit the dictates of his grandiose

self to the realities of the situation, which, for the most part, had been created because of internal dangers that threatened his grandiose self.

On Tuesday, August 6, 1974, just three days before leaving the presidency, he told his cabinet and other close advisers, "I've analyzed the best I can, the best memory I can, buttressed by miles and miles of tape, and have not found an impeachable offense, and therefore resignation is not an acceptable course."[31] Even after meeting on the afternoon of August 7th with Barry Goldwater, Pennsylvania Republican Senator Hugh Scott, and House Republican Leader John Rhodes, who informed him that he could expect only fifteen supporting votes in the Senate, Nixon tempestuously forged ahead. That same day, Edward Cox, Nixon's son-in-law, "wasn't at all sure the President was going to resign."[32] Only later that evening did Nixon finally decide that to continue was hopeless and that to resign was the only course left him.

Nixon had never quit before. As he stated in his resignation speech on August 8, 1974, "I have never been a quitter. To leave office before my term is completed is opposed to every instinct in my body."[33] One may speculate that, as Ehrlichman said, "He couldn't resign until his sense of political reality told him that his right flank had crumbled and Goldwater was against him, and his bastion of political support had failed."[34]

PART FOUR

Afterword

Thus the dilemma of executive power remains. In protecting themselves—their reputations, choices, resources—what are chief executives guarding? If they constantly protect themselves, to what extent are they also guarding the *purpose* they are supposed ultimately to be serving? How do they draw the line between preserving power for themselves and expending it for broader goals?

—*Political scientist James MacGregor Burns, 1978*

11

The "Real" Richard Nixon and the
Resurrection of His Reputation

At the close of a 1987 conference on "Leadership in the Modern Presidency" at Princeton University, a session was devoted to a discussion of the requirements for being a good President. The participants listened to a presentation by Larry Berman on Lyndon B. Johnson that touched just briefly on his psychology. Professor John P. Roche of the Fletcher School at Tufts University belittled the use of psychohistory and attempts at psychobiography. Wilbur Cohen, a Franklin Delano Roosevelt appointee who had worked for every administration since, unhesitatingly responded, "To be President, you need to have a good mother. The father doesn't matter. You need a good mother."

The audience, which consisted largely of distinguished political scientists, historians, and former presidential advisers from the last nine administrations, erupted into laughter. The mere mention of the word *mother* seemed out of place at a conference on the presidency. Had Nixon been present at the gathering he might himself have joined in the laughter, having once written "I happen to think that most of the so-called new 'science' of psychobiography is pure baloney."[1] For almost everyone in the audience, the association of "motherhood" with "Presidential Leadership" was as outlandishly humorous as Charlie Chaplin pretending his shoelaces were spaghetti and eating them. Simply hinting at the idea that there might be a connection between a President's relationship with his mother and his actions and decisions in later life, especially during his presidency, was most amusing to that audience.

Psychoanalytic psychohistory and psychobiography, however, are disciplines that can offer a great deal of insight, especially in the field of presidential leadership studies. Leadership is, at least in part, a derivative of unconscious motivations. A person's actions, decisions, style, and speeches are all influenced by such aspects as unconscious drives and defenses against them, by personality organization, and by intelligence and physical condition. Social, legal, military, economic, and historical factors must, of course, be taken into account, in order to see how one's internal world intertwines with external realities. To dismiss the psychoanalytic approach in studying leadership is, as Sigmund Freud wrote, "to make what is disagreeable into what is untrue."[2] To be sure, all is not analyzable and, accordingly, "knowable" about a man who has never been on an analyst's couch, but what can be observed, analyzed, and known should be considered vital to an understanding of leadership. Curiosity has often led to substantial breakthroughs in knowledge about human behavior, which psychoanalytic psychohistory studies.

If the laughter ever stops, and if those who engage in writing psychoanalytic biography can recognize and control their own countertransferences to their subjects, the frontiers of presidential leadership studies may be expanded. Such an expansion might not only broaden our understanding of a particular President's repeated or irrational actions and decisions, but also contribute to our understanding of all leaders in general. To do so we must differentiate between serious psychoanalytic psychobiography from sensationalist writing that does not benefit from adequate scholarly research. Sophisticated psychoanalytic psychobiography may help us to compose, like the police artist who sketches a portrait from a handful of clues, the profile of individual who seeks out and is driven to attain the presidency. If a serious attempt is made in this vein, we do not believe that a single "type" will emerge. However, there may be certain "characteristics" common to all presidents that relate directly to their respective mothers (as well as to fathers and important others from their formative years). Ultimately, one may discover that Cohen's remarks, though heading in the right direction, were slightly off target. It may be that in order to be a great President, you need a good-enough mother. Or, alternatively, if you have a "good-enough" mother in the first place, your unconscious motivations and aspirations may be less intense: thus, you might be less inclined (unconsciously driven) to attain, or even to run for, the presidency. Not having had a "good enough" mother most likely contributed to Nixon's need to resurrect himself from the disgrace and humiliation of his resignation from the presidency.

The Comeback

One of the areas of Nixon's life that nags at us and demands an explanation is his remarkable comeback after the humiliation of Watergate and his resignation. Of course, not all Americans consider Nixon a great man or forgive him for his transgressions. But rather than fading from the public view after his disgrace, he so successfully made a comeback that many people began to consider him a "senior statesman" and many active politicians who had avoided him in fear of contamination from associating with an undesirable began to seek his counsel. To understand this remarkable phenomenon, we must take into consideration both Nixon's inner motivations and Americans' shared perception of a fallen "hero."

Throughout this volume we have reported on the various reactions of persons with exaggerated self-love to frustrating and humiliating events. Explosive rage, for example, is a possible reaction, one that helps to explain Nixon's involvement in the secret bombing of Cambodia. When a narcissistic person is intelligent—as Nixon certainly was—and capable of finding or creating a "fit" in the environment to match his internal demands, that person may respond to frustration and humiliation by collecting new sources to support his grandiose self, and engineering a comeback.

Exile in San Clemente, even with all its external attractions of golf, the ocean, and fine food, meant life without a title, without being "number one," and without having a purpose—and that was a life Nixon could never survive psychologically. We conceive of those intelligent narcissistic persons who can effectively manipulate their environment to fit their internal demands as "button pushers." They push an invisible button to fill up the empty self with new glorified thoughts and deeds just as a bartender pushes a tap to fill an empty glass with bubbling beer. We are reminded of a young, beautiful, and intelligent woman who needed to collect adoration to satisfy her intense narcissistic needs. She would dress "to kill" and go to a certain country club in the late afternoon when club members would gather in a large room with a fireplace. She would stand in this room for about an hour, leaning on the mantelpiece. People, of course, would notice her, and she knew they found her attractive; she was "number one." She was filling up her cup with adoration! In a sense her action resembled Nixon's collection of presidencies.

One late afternoon, as she was standing next to the mantle like Aphrodite reborn, she noticed another beautiful woman, dressed almost identically, entering the room. Now she would have to share the adoration. For her, what she was receiving was like a pie, and now a piece of it would go to her "rival." At first she was enraged, wanting to throw things at her rival or push her into the fireplace and burn her. But she reorganized herself internally when she discovered that the other woman had thicker ankles than she had. She would remain "number one" after all. Her sense of humiliation and her upsurging rage over having to share the limelight with another woman disappeared. Once more she was ready to fill up her cup with adoration; she pushed her internal button and denied the reality that another woman could rival her in beauty.

After his humiliating resignation, Nixon, like the young woman above, reorganized himself internally. We can imagine that he started plotting his comeback almost from the very moment the Marine 1 helicopter lifted off the White House lawn on August 9, 1974. At least, his narcissistic personality, once relieved from the paranoid panic of having been under the siege of the "domestic terrorism" that had led to his downfall, demanded to be "number one" again. He should be the "first" President who had suffered the humiliation of forced resignation from office to return as the world's greatest statesman!

He was genuinely proud of his accomplishments. The idea that his skill at making foreign policy exceeded that of any other American leader of his time, that he could forecast future international developments, and that he had the stamina to hold his ground against the formidable troublemakers of the world, became the cornerstones of his comeback project. Alongside retooling his political image, he subtly appealed to the masses as a hurt child. While exhibiting a tough mien, he recited again and again, in a symbolic fashion, his Checkers Speech. As noted earlier, Nixon was a master at asking the public (but not individuals) for support. While individuals could remain cynical about Nixon, and find him unlikable, the masses symbolized for him the concerned caregiver who would respond to his hurts and consider him a special being.

The American people, who had lost leaders such as John F. Kennedy and Martin Luther King during the time of Nixon's presence on the political scene, did not want to "kill" another leader. After the shock of disappointment in him, the reality and the myth of his uniqueness combined with an atmosphere of forgetfulness and forgiveness in which Nixon's attempt at redemption could flourish. His publications (including *1999*),[3] his appearance on national television programs, and his diplomatic travels were calculated aspects of the comeback of the immortal Richard Nixon. Now let us return to where we started in telling his story: his visit with Vladimir Zhirinovsky. An aging but indomitable Nixon was back fighting a "bad guy" as his internal world demanded and as his real-world political wisdom supported. It would be difficult for Americans to continue to resent someone who sought to protect them from persons like Zhirinovsky, a man perceived as an enemy to American democracy and the American way of life.

Nixon had no other internal choice but to attempt the resurrection of his reputation. Perhaps it was all foreshadowed in a gift given to him by his grandmother for his thirteenth birthday, a copy of Longfellow's "Psalm of Life":

> Lives of great men oft remind us
> We can make our lives sublime,
> and departing, leave behind us
> Footprints in the sands of time.

After his resignation it would seem that Richard Nixon had been driven not so much to attain some exalted high public office, but rather to ensure his proper place in the history books—to leave behind his "footprints in the sands of time."

The Real Nixon

The enigma that was Richard Nixon has caused many curious people to ask "Who was the Real Nixon?" In answer to this question, John Ehrlichman said:

> I imagine you will get as many answers as you ask questions. Everybody sees him differently, and that was one of the problems with working [with] him. He was a man who presented an aspect to each individual that he came in contact with, and it was different to some degree to the aspect that he presented to everyone else. I account for this by the fact that he was a person who genuinely disliked face-to-face controversy. He would find out what the visitors' interests were and get them talking about themselves and size up how to best get along without a clash. He was pretty much all things to all people, to the extent that he could be. If he had someone in there who was profane, then he was profane. If he had someone in there who was not profane, then he was not profane.[4]

Garry Wills made a similar observation: "There is only one Nixon though there seem to be new ones all the time—he will try to be what people want."[5] Bruce Mazlish saw the reflection of a hidden, hungry self in Nixon's desire to perform: "Role, in fact, substitutes for an insecurely held self. If one is not sure of what one is, one can at least be one's role. The role then tells us what to do and how to act."[6]

Without the unconscious need for applause engendered by his search for a nurturing mother image and his avoidance of facing frustrations by developing excessive narcissism, and with his "ego strengths" to respond to such needs, Nixon might not have made presidencies, including that of the United States, his goal. Roger Ailes aptly observed:

> His overriding motives were to do great things for the world, coupled with his own personal need for attention, acceptance, and praise, something that I think he was starved of during youth because I don't think that he came from a demonstrative family. His family never said, "Hey Dick, I think you're doing a great job, and we are proud of you." And like all of us, he needed those things, and so he sought them in the outside world. I think his personal needs and his sincere desire to render public service drove him.[7]

In the following statement by Elliot Richardson, Nixon's Attorney General, the possibility is raised that a more secure Nixon might have followed a different path:

> My own feeling has always been that if you had adjusted or if you somehow had been able to eliminate the sense of insecurity felt by Nixon toward his place in the world, you would have at the same time removed the very source of his drive. I don't think that he would even have been President at all . . . You cannot tinker with the psyche of someone without producing very different results.[8]

We have offered another answer to the question "Who is the real Richard Nixon?" by studying his "total life" story through the lens of psychoanalysis. Given the existence and nature of information about an individual's early years, we tried to re-create the unconscious forces in Nixon that developed then. After studying and analyzing Richard Nixon's entire life, talking among ourselves and taming our countertransferences, we have come to "know" him. Learning about his mother, his father, his hurts, his grief, his joys, his achievements, and his failures made him a "human being" just like ourselves. We felt kinship for him, we admired his "courage" to find solutions to his inner struggles, we "scorned" some of the ways in which he reacted to events, we had "sympathy" for his having a self-destructive side that in turn injured the nation. We came to the conclusion that some of his irrational actions could be explained by using our methodology to illuminate Nixon's inner world. The Watergate break-in, for example, can be better explained through an understanding of Nixon's "psychic truth" than through extensive analysis of the "real" truth.

In writing about Nixon we aimed to show the close relationship between his inner world and external reality.[9] Thus, we posit a close relationship between psychoanalysis and history. We add a closing thought: Richard Nixon could have enjoyed greatness without challenge, but he lost sight of his priorities because of internal pressures that, paradoxically, had pushed him to excel as a historical figure in the first place. Only with psychoanalytic insight can we grasp why a powerful president would destroy himself when there was no need to do so.

In trying to be greater than everyone else, Nixon stomped where he should have stepped. In aspiring to be the Lincolnesque "healer" of this century, he became its great divider. In seeking to do right, he did wrong. Like Cervantes' Don Quixote, he saw unfriendly windmills where none existed. He did not understand, or recognize, that he was his own worst windmill. This was the real tragedy of Richard Nixon. If there is any consolation for Theodore Roosevelt's "man in the arena" who fought so long and hard, "marred by dust and sweat and blood," it is that "his place shall never be with those cold and timid souls who know neither victory nor defeat." Richard Nixon knew both extremely well.

Notes

1. Why a Psychoanalytic Biography?

1. Nixon (1990) describes his combative nature in his memoirs: "As I look back to the time I made a decision to enter politics forty-three years ago, three goals motivated me: peace abroad, a better life for people at home, and the victory of freedom over tyranny throughout the world. I have taken some great risks and have fought many battles in attempting to serve those goals" (pp. 119–120).

2. Von Drehle (1994).

3. Kissinger (1994).

4. Nixon (1978), p. 1004.

5. Beschloss (1994).

6. Ambrose (1987, 1989, 1991).

7. Falk (1985) states that Sigmund Freud himself adopted diverse approaches to biographical studies, as evidenced by the differences between his Leonardo study (Freud, 1910) and his Moses study (Freud, 1939).

8. Bergman (1973).

9. Erikson (1950).

10. Bergman (1973).

11. Bergman (1973), p. 843.

12. Gedo (1972).

13. Falk (1985), p. 611.

14. This should include such factors as the strength of the instinctual drives, developmental arrests, infantile neurosis and adaptations, identity crises in ado-

lescence, internal responses to external traumas, midlife issues, psychic transformations, and reactions to old age and approaching death.

15. Volkan and Itzkowitz (1984).

16. The four types of dangers described in this paragraph were first identified by Freud (1926).

17. In order to declare a process psychoanalytic it has to be examined through transference neurosis (Rappaport, 1960), since this procedure illuminates and authenticates the meaning of one's inner world.

18. Volkan (1984) has documented an actual psychoanalytic case from its beginning to its end, in order to show in detail what happens during this form of treatment. Those readers who are interested in transference stories may wish to consult this book for further information on the subject. The following, albeit brief, example may enable the reader to better understand what is meant by transference neurosis. In this example, a man in his late twenties sought analysis because he could not hold on to a job and seemed to fear success. His history included the death of his father when he was four years old. The analysand's free associations and repeated behavioral patterns suggested, in conjunction with the content of some of his dreams, that he could not permit himself to become successful and risk "surpassing" his father because he unconsciously thought that he was responsible for his father's death. Therefore, he felt he had to punish himself by failing. This understanding, however, could be authenticated only in his transference neurosis.

During the second year of his analysis, this young man began to "kill" his analyst symbolically. If, on his way to his sessions, he heard of a fatal automobile accident on the radio he immediately thought that his analyst was the victim. This felt very real to him and he became anxious. Of course, when he arrived at his session he would "learn" that his analyst was still very much alive, but he treated and responded to his analyst as if the analyst were a ghost. Since he felt guilty about "killing" the analyst he would, at the same time, defensively try to save him; this allowed him to respond to his guilt feelings and consequently avoid punishment. He became compulsive about checking on the fire safety of the analyst's building, for example. Day after day his time on the psychoanalytic couch was spent first imagining that the analyst had contracted some fatal illness and then creating some possible cure for him. Defenses and punishments against such wishes and thoughts would also appear. The analysand would make "mistakes" and wear black trousers with a blue jacket. He would be "black and blue"—that is, symbolically beat up.

Through such emotionally laden transference stories the analysand and his analyst were able to develop a history of the analysand's inner world, which included his unconscious thought that he had killed his father and his unconscious expectation of punishment. In actuality, he never committed the crime of killing his father, but the unconscious thought still dominated his life in adulthood.

19. Volkan and Itzkowitz (1984) have described their countertransferences toward Kemal Atatürk during the time they wrote their psychobiography of him. In the following example provided by Volkan (1987), a patient we will call Pattie

is described as being self-destructive and abusive toward others: she formed difficult interpersonal relationships and followed an eccentric lifestyle that included
sleeping in the barn on the farm where she lived. She had an unhappy relationship
with her parents as a child, and this association continued into adulthood. In her
third year of analysis she began reporting that she was raising baby peacocks.
Pattie focused on her relationship to the peacocks and their dependency upon her
in her sessions with Volkan. She talked of their needs and of them as though they
were her children.

Through countertransference, Volkan was unconsciously drawn into the day-
dream of the peacocks as though they were his babies too. He did not verbalize
this response, but used it to understand Pattie and to determine that during her
sessions she was unconsciously making Volkan a father figure/lover. Pattie's preoccupation with the peacocks was her way of expressing a sense of progress in her
analysis. It meant that in her mind she was growing up and becoming a woman.
Volkan's countertransference served to verify her womanhood, just as when any
father experiences the delight of seeing his baby girl mature. Although Volkan
became absorbed in the story along with the patient, his countertransference was
neutralized in the clinical setting, and he was able to help Pattie comprehend the
meaning behind her fantasy of the peacocks.

20. See Bergman (1973); Greenacre (1955); Niederland (1965); Volkan and
Itzkowitz (1984). For example, Niederland (1965) studied archeologist Heinrich
Schliemann's writings, which Schliemann called "language exercises." They were
written with the intention of mastering a new language, but they resembled free
associations in that they revealed Schliemann's unconscious wishes.

21. Volkan and Itzkowitz (1984).

22. Akhtar (1992).

23. In a normal situation, as constantly as possible, a mother offers "good-
enough mothering" or a "holding environment" (Winnicott, 1964, 1965) for her
child in response to the child's needs. She does not stimulate the child excessively
to satisfy her own needs, and she absorbs the child's aggressive expressions. If a
mother is not "constant," due to psychic or physical reasons, and if a mother's
own needs become intrusive, the mothering is said to be not "good-enough."

24. See: Brazelton, Koslowski, and Main (1974); Emde (1991); Greenspan
(1989); Stern (1985). For example, studies have shown that infants respond to
pleasure and displeasure (Lipsitt, 1966); they can make visual discriminations and
form primitive bonds (Klaus and Kennell, 1976; Meltzoff and Moore, 1977);
and they have a rudimentary mental capacity to organize their experiences
(Greenspan, 1989). Studies on child development (Spitz, 1957) demonstrate that
at eight months of age infants can differentiate between their dominant love
objects—those who care for them daily—and strangers. This is why the infant will
smile at his mother, but the sight of a stranger's face may cause anxiety.

25. Margaret Mahler applied the term symbiosis rather than psychobiological
mutuality to this intrapsychic relationship, and it is used in this metaphorical
sense in psychoanalytic literature to describe "that sense of undifferentiation, of
fusion with mother, in which the 'I' is not yet differentiated from the 'not-I,' and

in which inside and outside are only gradually coming to be sensed as different" (Mahler, 1968, p. 9).

26. Modell (1976); Kernberg (1975, 1984); Volkan (1976, 1982); Volkan and Ast (1994)

27. Freud (1936).

28. Technically, we consider such an image to be part of the individual's super-ego.

29. Freud (1923).

30. Erikson (1963).

31. Blos (1967); A. Freud (1958).

32. Blos (1967).

33. As an example, let us refer to a man who seeks therapy because of excessive anxiety. He exhibits a symptom (a maladaptive one) in that he experiences frantic activity whenever there is a birthday, be it his own or a family member's or a friend's. He forms indiscriminate relationships with women at this time.

The man's history is such that when he was a young boy, his family had moved to a new house. He left behind a beloved unmarried aunt, so the move was experienced as a trauma. It so happened that shortly after the move his mother became pregnant. A great deal of fuss was made over her and the new baby, and the little boy felt even more lost and confused. Under analysis the man reconstructs an unconscious fantasy that if he were inside his mother again, he would be safe and the object of everyone's happiness. He recalls playing a game with his mother that gave him pleasure, where he would hide inside a big toy box (symbolically representing his mother's belly) and she would sit on it, trying to figure out where he was. The derivative of the boy's unconscious fantasy of replacing his baby sister in his mother's stomach begins in adult life under stress situations such as birthdays—which unconsciously remind him of his sister's birth. Thus, at birthday times he adopts a maladaptive behavior pattern and treats women like boxes, entering them like he entered his toy box under his mother's skirts. Eventually the man is able to sublimate his anger about babies and redirect this emotion away from his sibling. After analysis he decides to become a teacher of small children. The repressed material that influenced his behavior is now considered adaptive. For similar unconscious fantasies, see: Volkan and Ast (1996).

34. In the following example, Volkan and Masri (1989) describe the rescue fantasy of a female transsexual patient who, as an infant, had responded to the depression and sexual deprivation her mother experienced when her husband was away. This patient believed herself to be a man and the analysis of the situation confirmed this belief. Through her transsexualism, she unconsciously attempted to "rescue" her mother. Unmodified rescue fantasies may be dealt with by more adaptive means. When a child's internal needs do not dovetail with the external circumstances of life, he or she may cling to a rescue fantasy that, in spite of being unconscious, affects his or her adult behavior to the extent that it may even be a motivating factor in his or her life. For instance, the child of a depressed mother may become a psychoanalyst who specializes in the treatment of depressed people. Selfish aspects may remain, or they may be sublimated in altruistic behavior, perhaps by influencing a person to enter public service as a career later in life.

2. Nixon's Parents

1. Volkan (1988, 1992); Volkan and Itzkowitz (1994).
2. Bradford (1985); Davis (1969); Reed (1983).
3. Redford et al. (1965).
4. La Faber (1963).
5. Erikson (1963), p. 285.
6. Erikson (1963), p. 288.
7. Clearly, Richard Nixon was aware of his father's personality traits. He revealed to one biographer, Bela Kornitzer, that "Dad was very strict and expected to be obeyed under all circumstances. . . . He had a hot temper, and I learned early that the only way to deal with him was to abide by the rules he laid down" (Kornitzer, 1960, p. 79). Describing his father in his memoirs, Richard Nixon wrote of Frank's "Irish quickness and tempestuous arguments" (Nixon, 1978, p. 6). After much research, Brodie (1981) concluded in her biography of Richard Nixon that Frank Nixon was a "gruff, bad-tempered, and tight-fisted yelling man, a hollering man" (p. 38). She also noted that Frank's brother Ernest spoke of him as being "aggressive . . . slow to anger but a wild bull if things went wrong" (p. 37) and that Richard Nixon's younger brother Edward was in the habit of calling their father "the executioner." Frank has been characterized as "unruly and violent" (Abrahamsen, 1977, p. 29), a man "too abrupt, proud, independent for political life or business success . . . " (Wills, 1979, p. 171) so that whatever skills he possessed were "canceled by prickliness and touchy pride" (Wills, 1979, p. 169). He has been described as "a gloomy and argumentative black Irishman moving in a cloud with frequent lightnings out of it" (Wills, 1979, p. 162).
8. Ambrose (1987).
9. Blos (1967); A. Freud (1958).
10. Nixon (1978), p. 5.
11. Nixon (1978), p.6.
12. Ambrose (1987), p16.
13. Hannah's sister, Jane Milhous Beeson, alluded to her family's disapproval in a 1970 interview (Schulte, 1978). The writer Jessamyn West, who is Richard Nixon's cousin, has also attested to the family's disapproval of Frank (Brodie, 1983), p. 38.
14. Ambrose (1987), p. 9.
15. Julie Nixon Eisenhower (1986). Also see the following sources: Dorothy Beeson (Richard's cousin), described her Aunt Hannah as "a quiet Quaker, a concerned type of person" (CSF Oral History #810). She was "a woman of iron, annealed in a Quaker sense of duty" (de Toledano, 1969, p. 14), and she had "tremendous self control" (Wills, 1979, p. 103). At the same time, she was a very giving person: "She was always taking [in] every tramp that came along off the street," (Mazo and Hess, 1967, p. 16) and was perceived as having a special quality, of making people "want to be close to her" (Longford, 1980, p. 2).
16. Nixon (1978), p. 51.
17. Reported in Julie Nixon Eisenhower (1986), p. 62.

18. Spalding (1972), p. 22.
19. Brinton (1973), p. ix.
20. Mazlish (1972), p. 19.
21. Spalding (1972), p. 15.
22. Cavan (1979).
23. Wills (1979), p. 161.
24. Spalding (1972), p. 26.
25. Wills (1979).
26. Ambrose (1987); Also see: Hannah Nixon (1960).

3. Childhood and Adolescence

1. Ambrose (1987), p. 21.
2. Ambrose (1987), p. 22.
3. Ella Furness, Oral History #856, p. 4
4. At this time of life the child takes steps to assert himself more, in various ways; he learns to master control of his bowel movements, for example. In this phase the child displays healthy aggression and says no very often, as though practicing to set up a psychological border between himself and others. He becomes ambivalent toward his caregivers, wanting to separate from them, yet knowing that he still needs them.
5. Winnicott (1965).
6. Ambrose (1987); Brodie (1981); Paul Ryan, CSF Oral History #941, p. 7.
7. Ibid..
8. Brodie (1981), p. 73.
9. Edith Timberlake: CSF Oral History reported by Ambrose (1987), p. 22.
10. Ambrose (1987), p. 23.
11. Spalding (1972), p. 29.
12. Hoyt Corbit, CSF Oral History #838.
13. Virginia Shaw Critchfield, CSF Oral History #840.
14. Ambrose (1987), p. 23.
15. Brodie (1981), p. 40.
16. Ambrose (1987), p. 23.
17. Wills (1979).
18. Nixon (1962), p. 296
19. Ambrose (1987), p. 22.
20. Mary George Skidmore, CSF Oral History #952, p. 1.
21. Hoyt Corbit, CSF Oral History #838, p. 19.
22. Mazo and Hess (1967), p. 110.
23. Spalding (1972), p. 42.
24. Ambrose (1987), p. 27.
25. de Toledano (1969), p. 20.
26. Ambrose (1987), p. 38.
27. Mazo and Hess (1967), p. 11.
28. His letter of application, dated January 24, 1924, read as follows:

"Dear Sir:

"Please consider me for the position of office boy mentioned in the Times paper. I am eleven years of age and I am in the Sixth grade of the East Whittier grammar school.

"I am very willing to work and would like the money for a vacation trip. I am willing to come to your office at any time and I will accept any pay offered. My address is Whittier boulevard and Leffingwell road. The phone number is 5274. For reference you can see, Miss Flowers princaple [sic] of the East Whittier School. Hoping that you will accept me for service, I am

"Yours truly

"Richard M. Nixon"

(Spalding, 1972, p. 42)

In spite of an obvious misspelling Richard's letter indicates the level of his intelligence.

29. Mazo and Hess (1967), p. 11.
30. Jane Beeson, CSF Oral History #808.
31. Brodie (1981), p. 44.
32. Ambrose (1987), p. 41.
33. "The American Experience" television series, 10/15/1990.
34. Brodie (1981), p. 97.
35. Ambrose (1987), p. 51.
36. de Toledano (1969), p. 7.
37. Helen Letts, CSF Oral History #896.
38. Nixon (1978), p. 15.

4. Adulthood

1. Nixon (1978), p. 17.
2. Wills (1969), p. 154.
3. Costello (1960), p. 24.
4. Nixon (1978), p. 20.
5. Soon after Richard Nixon's death a group of Duke University students wanted a minute of silence to be observed at a University ceremony to honor his memory. Others objected by stating that Nixon had disgraced the presidency and, thus, also Duke University. The first group's request was denied.
6. Wills (1969), p. 156.
7. Wills (1969), p. 155.
8. Nixon (1978), p. 22.
9. Nixon (1978), p. 21.
10. Spalding (1972), pp. 111–112.
11. Spalding (1972), p. 112.
12. Spalding (1972), p. 113.
13. Ambrose (1987), p. 88.
14. Nixon (1978), p. 22.
15. Ambrose (1987), p. 88.

16. Nixon (1978), p. 22.

17. Wills (1970).

18. Mazo and Hess (1967), p. 26.

19. Mazo and Hess (1967), Ambrose (1987), p. 63.

20. Ola Welch Jobe interview, in Brodie. Fawn Brodie Collection, Salt Lake City, Utah: University of Utah, Marriott Library; reported in Steinberg: unpublished manuscript.

21. Mazlish (1972), p. 63; quoted in Steinberg (1996), p. 137.

22. Steinberg (1996), p. 137.

23. Reported by Steinberg: unpublished manuscript.

24. Steinberg (1996), p. 137.

25. Morris (1990), p. 169.

26. Ambrose (1987), p. 92.

27. Nixon (1978), p. 23.

28. Ambrose (1987), p. 93.

29. de Toledano (1969), p. 14.

30. Morris (1990), p. 219.

31. Steinberg: unpublished manuscript, p. 217.

32. Steinberg (1996), p. 140.

33. Ibid.

34. Ambrose (1987), p. 99.

35. Julie Nixon Eisenhower (1986), p. 59.

36. Julie Nixon Eisenhower (1986), p. 66.

37. Steinberg: unpublished manuscript.

38. Steinberg: unpublished manuscript.

39. Dixon interview, reported by Brodie. Fawn Brodie's Collection., Salt Lake City, Utah: University of Utah, Marriott Library; quoted in Steinberg (1996), p. 140.

40. Dorn interview, reported by Steinberg (1996), p. 140–41.

41. Sherwood, George interview, reported by Brodie. Fawn Brodie's Collection., Salt Lake City, Utah: University of Utah, Marriott Library; quoted in Steinberg, p. 141.

42. Dixon interview, reported by Brodie. Fawn Brodie's Collection., Salt Lake City, Utah: University of Utah, Marriott Library; quoted in unpublished manuscript by Steinberg.

43. Brodie (1981), p. 257, and Ambrose (1987), p. 265.

44. Brodie (1981), p. 235.

45. Brodie (1981), p. 237.

46. Nixon (1978), p. 240.

47. Public papers (March 11, 1974), p. 632.

48. Steinberg: unpublished manuscript.

49. Dixon, interview, reported by Brodie. Fawn Brodie's Collection., Salt Lake City, Utah: University of Utah, Marriott Library; see also: Steinberg, unpublished manuscript.

50. Steinberg: unpublished manuscript.

51. Nixon (1978), p. 27.

52. "The American Experience" television program, October 15, 1990.

5. Nixon as a National Figure

1. Spalding (1972), p. 180.
2. Nixon (1962).
3. Nixon (1978), p. 55.
4. Nixon (1978), p. 69.
5. "The American Experience" television program, October 15, 1990.
6. "The American Experience" television program, October 15, 1990.
7. "The American Experience" television program, October 15, 1990.
8. Nixon (1978), p. 106.
9. Parmet (1990) and Ambrose (1987).
10. Glad and Link (1996).
11. Glad and Link (1996).
12. Hoff (1994).

6. A Bird's Eye View

1. Psychoanalysts call this the process of "feeding" ego identification. (Hendrick, 1951). During this process the child slowly assimilates ego functions. He learns how things can be done by copying the mother and by identifying with her. Thus, it is not just for reasons of providing nourishment that the mother holds the spoon while the baby is being fed. In the course of this activity, through repetition, the child eventually "learns" to hold the spoon himself. What happens in his mind involves more than just mastering the ability to feed himself, however. He comes to identify with certain functions that were performed by others earlier, and this identification contributes to his growing inner independence. If the mother insists on holding the spoon beyond the child's need for her assistance, or if she cuts the child's food in pieces because of her own anxiety that without her intervention the child will choke on his food, the mother is really interfering with the development of the child's mind. A mother's anxiety, depression, physical absences, etc., influence the crucial mother-child relationship. Of course, whether or not there is permanent damage depends on many factors, e.g., subsequent attempts to "correct" the trauma, the availability of substitute mothers, and the child's psychic and physical constitution. (see also: Volkan 1982a).
2. Erlichman interview with Andrew Dod, (1986).
3. Marvick (unpublished manuscript).
4. Nixon (1978), p. 683–4.
5. Winnicott (1957), p.57.
6. Abrahamsen (1977), p. 59.
7. Elizabeth Glover, CSF Oral History #864, p. 4.
8. Yoneko Dobaski Iwatsura, CSF Oral History #884, pp. 3–4.
9. Alsop (1960), pp. 184–185.
10. Abrahamsen (1977), p. 68.
11. James Grieves, CSF Oral History #868, p. 4; [Italics added].
12. Sheldon Beeson, CSF Oral History #809, pp.4–6.
13. Schulte (1977), p. 204.

14. Wayne Long, CSF Oral History #899, p. 4.

15. Alsop (1960), p. 214.

16. Alsop (1960), p. 215.

17. Psychoanalysts theorize that an infant is born with certain instinctual drives, mental representations of motivations, that are embedded in human nature. These drives are divided into two categories: libidinal (sexual) and aggressive. Henry Parens (1979), a child psychoanalyst, observed that at nine months of age an infant tries to express more aggression, as if he wants to learn how to assert himself.

18. Etheredge (1979).

19. Post (1983).

20. Volkan and Itzkowitz (1984).

21. See: Hannah Nixon (1960) regarding Richard's special room in Whittier; see also: Post (1993) who has written of parental dreams of glory that influence future leaders.

22. Wicker (1991).

23. Steinberg: unpublished manuscript.

24. de Toledano (1969), p. 87.

25. Ibid.

26. Ibid.

27. Ehrlichman interview with Andrew Dod (1987).

28. Nixon (1978), p. 13.

29. Nixon's search is similar to the one undertaken by the Turkish leader Mustafa Kemal Atatürk (Volkan and Itzkowitz, 1984). In the end, he took the name Atatürk, which means "Father Turk," when he felt that he had created the idealized father image within himself. In turn, his followers saw him as idealized, as the father.

30. Abrahamsen (1977), p. 16.

31. Mahler (1968) coined the term separation-individuation to refer to the child's intrapsychic struggle to separate himself from the mental representation of mother or the caregiver in an effort to establish his own individuality. Recent findings from neonatal research may cause us to modify Mahler's description of the earliest part of the process, but the notion that the child experiences "psychological birth" from being an undifferentiated psychological unit with the mother still remains valid. At about two years of age the child matures to the point where he is able to maintain an image of the mother or caregiver in his own mind. In other words, the child develops a psychic double (a mental representation) of the mother or caregiver in accordance with his real experiences and fantasized wishes, and his defenses against them. The more the child is able to crystallize and maintain this psychic double, the longer he can tolerate staying alone without needing to refuel the image of the mother or caregiver. The inner struggle toward individuation starts in the latter part of the first year of life and continues throughout the third year of life. At the end of this process the child is able to differentiate between who is "I" and who is "not I." Nixon had to pay a psychological price for his struggle with separation-individuation.

32. Nixon (1978), p. 117.

33. Volkan (1981).

34. Ehrlichman (1982).
35. Ehrlichman, interview with Andrew Dod (1986).
36. Ibid.
37. Frost (1978).
38. Wills (1969), p. 169.
39. Brodie (1981), p. 44.
40. Safire (1975), p. 92; [Italics added].
41. Schell, J. (1975), p. 342; [Italics added].
42. Frost (1978); [Italics added].
43. Frost (1978); [Italics added].
44. Haldeman interview with Andrew Dod (1987).
45. Frost (1978); [Italics added].
46. Freud (1923).
47. Olinick (1980).
48. Woodward and Bernstein (1976).
49. Akhtar, personal communication with Vamık Volkan (1988).

7. Nixon's Personality

1. Weigert (1967).
2. Volkan and Rogers (1988) and Volkan and Ast (1994).
3. Rangell (1980), p. 23.
4. Volkan and Ast (1994) describe the following types of narcissism: "normal" narcissism; masochistic narcissism; (this happens when the individual becomes a collector of suffering); exaggerated narcissism (this is seen in individuals who have narcissistic personality organizations); successful narcissism (this happens when a leader succeeds in being number one and is perceived as such by his followers while the leader performs actions adaptive to reality); and malignant narcissism (this occurs when the person destroys others in order to maintain his grandiosity). see also: Akhtar (1992) and Kernberg (1989).
5. Stone (1989).
6. Post (1993).
7. This term was coined by Heinz Kohut (1971). In terms of metapsychology, the content of the grandiose self "reflects a pathological condensation of some aspects of the real self (the 'specialness' of the child reinforced by early experience), the ideal self (the fantasies and self images of power, wealth, omniscience, and beauty which compensated the small child for the experiences of severe oral frustrations, rage and envy) and the ideal object (the fantasy of an ever-giving, ever-loving and accepting parent), in contrast to the child's experience in reality (a replacement of the devalued real parental object)" (Kernberg 1975, pp. 265–266).
8. Volkan and Itzkowitz (1984); Volkan and Ast (1994).
9. Kernberg (1975).
10. Volkan and Ast (1994). Persons with a narcissistic personality organization may seek psychoanalytic help after having their extraordinary demands thwarted by the realities of the external world, even while maintaining the facade of being above it all.

11. In psychoanalysis there is some controversy over the way a narcissistic personality organization develops. Psychoanalysts such as Kernberg (1975) and Volkan (1976, 1982b), have provided numerous examples of clinical experiences that demonstrate how repeated frustrations in the oral phase (the first year of life) that are accompanied by the mother's perception of something special in the child, can lead to the development of a narcissistic personality. Narcissistic concerns from the child's later years become condensed with oral narcissistic concerns as the child matures. Here our emphasis is on the beginning of the narcissistic personality organization due to oral level problems. To put this in psychoanalytic terms, such children are said to possess "oral rage and envy." The grandiose self has to be maintained at all costs as a defensive adaptation against early frustrations and to avoid experiencing the oral rage and envy.

12. Mazo and Hess (1967), p. 30.

13. See Nixon's own explanation of his return to the political scene in Nixon (1990).

14. Etheredge (1979). The term "idealizing transference" was first described by Kohut (1971).

15. Brodie (1981), p. 109.

16. Richardson interview with Andrew Dod (1987).

17. Ailes interview with Andrew Dod (1987).

18. Nixon (1978), p. 686.

19. Haldeman (1978), p. 124.

20. Isaacson (1992) In his journalist account of Kissinger's rise and fall Isaacson misses these points and does not even mention Kissinger's winning the Nobel Peace Prize. Schulzinger (1989) also fails to recognize these issues.

21. Haldeman interview with Andrew Dod (1987).

22. Nixon (1982a), p. 26.

23. Ehrlichman (1982), p. 23, footnote.

24. Brodie (1981), p. 25.

25. Brodie (1981), p. 507.

26. Loewenberg (1986), p. 30. By "ego strength" Loewenberg refers to Nixon's skill and cleverness in dealing with reality. However, we must add that under certain circumstances Nixon would blur reality, as we explained in the text. The main aim was to maintain his grandiose self. To do so he could enhance his reality testing or he could blur it.

27. Volkan (1976).

28. Haldeman interview with Andrew Dod (1987).

29. Ibid.

30. Anson (1972), p. 230.

31. Ehrlichman interview with Andrew Dod (1986).

32. Transformation in Adolf Hitler is described by Langer (1972), who, as far as we know, was the first author who described such transformations. Volkan and Itzkowitz (1984) reported Atatürk changed his name each time he thought he had solidified a new sense of self.

33. Ehrlichman interview with Andrew Dod (1986).

34. Volkan (1979). Also see Volkan and Ast, (1994). Modell (1976) speaks of the self-imposed enclosure as a cocoon, but Volkan's description of a "glass bubble" seems more accurate because it creates a sense of having both inviolable privacy and the ability to look outside scornfully, thereby enhancing one's sense of importance and self-sufficiency.

35. White (1969), p. 53.

36. Harold Saunders conversation with Vamık Volkan, (1987).

37. Ailes interview with Andrew Dod (1987).

38. Helms interview with Andrew Dod (1987).

39. Richardson interview with Andrew Dod (1987).

40. Nixon (1978), p. 841; [Italics added].

41. Barber (1977), p. 368; [Italics added].

42. Ailes interview with Andrew Dod (1987).

43. Barber (1977), p. 387.

44. Richardson interview with Andrew Dod (1987).

45. Ailes interview with Andrew Dod (1987).

46. Haldeman interview with Andrew Dod (1987).

47. Price (1977), p. 366.

48. Nixon (1978), p. 513.

49. Nixon (1978), p. 513.

50. Haldeman (1978), p. 161.

51. Ehrlichman interview with Andrew Dod (1986).

52. Haldeman (1978), p. 144.

53. Volkan and Itzkowitz (1984).

54. Crispell and Gomez (1988).

55. Kohut (1971) theorized about the mental fragmentation of body-mind-self when a narcissistic person regresses after being disappointed by those who reflected and supported his grandiosity. He stated that when the regression goes unchecked, it appears as hypochondriacal concern over physical and mental health. We suggest that psychosomatic conditions occur as well. The Finnish psychoanalyst Veikko Tähkä (1984), who had established a psychosomatic unit at Kuopio's Medical Center and served as its director for many years, states that "The so-called psychosomatic diseases are usually the outcome of a combination of biological predispositions, comparatively early disturbance in personality development and a triggering factor represented by a life crisis" (p. 140).

A survey of psychoanalytic literature reveals that hypochondriasis is an expression of threats to one's narcissism and varying degrees or stages of self-fragmentation. These threats are caused by infantile fears pertaining to separations and losses, castration, self-destructive impulses, feelings of persecution, or talionic punishments.

Wilson and Mintz (1988) have shown in a very convincing way, with clinical illustrations, that besides taking care of acute physical needs, the most essential treatment for those suffering from psychosomatic illnesses such as asthma, ulcerative colitis, and anorexia nervosa is the psychoanalytic treatment of the underlying personality organization.

56. For a summary of these theories, see Taylor (1987).

57. According to Spitz (1953), the beginning of rage can be discerned in the child of two or three months, and is expressed by screaming.

58. Jacobson (1964).

59. Taylor (1987).

60. Alexander (1950), p. 132. For decades psychoanalysts have appreciated the role that emotions play in the occurrence of asthmatic attacks (Alexander (1950); Dunbar (1938); French et al. (1941); Wilson and Mintz (1989), and in the triggering of tuberculosis (Benjamin et al., 1948). People who have psychosomatic illnesses have been shown to experience severe narcissistic regression Jacobson (1964); Schur (1955).

61. Clinical observations by Benedek (1973) are especially relevant in Nixon's case. She emphasized that in infancy crying is normally a signal to the mother: when there is frustration in adult life, a partial regression takes place, which threatens what is left of the ego, especially in compulsive personalities that are characterized by affect-isolation defenses, where massive defenses against feelings of helplessness and rage are employed. Her findings show that this situation brings about discharge via the autonomic nervous system.

62. Brodie (1981), p. 63.

63. Pollock (1989). Also see Volkan and Zintl (1993).

64. Nixon (1978), p. 898.

65. Anson (1984), footnote on p. 75.

66. Freud (1926).

67. Brodie (1981), p. 69.

68. Mazo and Hess (1967), p. 13.

69. Anson (1984), p. 61.

70. Scowcroft interview with Andrew Dod (1987).

71. Reported by Anson (1984), p. 68.

72. Anson (1984), p. 84.

73. Nixon (1978), p., 189.

74. Brodie (1981), p. 101.

75. Haldeman interview with Andrew Dod (1987).

76. Nixon (1978), p. 228.

77. Nixon (1978), p. 667.

78. Nixon (1982a).

8. Reflections of Grandiosity

1. Nixon (1962), p. 18.

2. Ehrlichman interview with Andrew Dod (1986).

3. Haldeman interview with Andrew Dod (1987).

4. Ehrlichman (1982), p. 259.

5. Ehrlichman interview with Andrew Dod (1986).

6. Nathan (1975), p. 68.

7. Ehrlichman interview with Andrew Dod (1986).

8. Nathan (1975), p. 69.

9. Herbers (1973), p. 1.
10. Nixon (1972), p. 412.
11. Herbers (1973), p. 1
12. Nathan (1975).
13. *U.S. News and World Report* (June 22, 1970), p. 17.
14. Scowcroft interview with Andrew Dod (1987).
15. George (1980), p. 155.
16. Scowcroft interview with Andrew Dod (1987).
17. Osborne (1970), p. 96.
18. Greenstein (1977), p. 78.
19. Nixon (1978), p. 414.
20. Schweiker interview with Andrew Dod (1987).
21. Nixon (1972), p. 526.
22. Nixon (1978), p. 425.
23. Reported by Burke (1974), p. 68.
24. Schweiker interview with Andrew Dod (1987).
25. Nixon (1978), p. 428.
26. Nixon (1978), p. 370.
27. Ehrlichman interview with Andrew Dod (1986).
28. Ibid.
29. Nixon (1978), p. 375.
30. Nixon (1980), p. 107; [Italics added].
31. Kissinger (1979), pp. 1480–1481.
32. Nixon (1982b).
33. Nixon (1978), p. 125.
34. Nixon (1967), p. 121.
35. Haldeman (1978), p. 121.
36. Nixon (1978), p. 395.
37. Haldeman (1994).

9. *Reflections of the Peacemaker*

1. Wills (1979), p. 171.
2. Spalding (1972), p. 115.
3. Nixon (1962), p. 36; [Italics added].
4. Nixon (1978), p. 139.
5. Greenstein (1982) and, to a lesser degree, Oshinsky (1983) portray Nixon as the bridge connecting the two opposing factions of his political party.
6. Oshinsky (1983), p. 180–181.
7. Nixon (1978), p. 21.
8. Safire (1975).
9. Ehrlichman (1982), p. 233.
10. Ehrlichman interview with Andrew Dod (1986).
11. Nixon (1978), p. 440.
12. Ehrlichman interview with Andrew Dod (1986).
13. Schweiker interview with Andrew Dod (1987).

14. Frost television interview of Richard Nixon (1977). Also see Frost (1978).
15. van der Linden, F. (1972), p. 23.
16. Safire (1975), p. 203.
17. Safire (1975), p. 206.
18. Safire (1975), p. 207.
19. Safire (1975), p. 206.
20. Nixon (1978), p. 346.
21. Scowcroft interview with Andrew Dod (1987).
22. Kissinger (1979), pp. 129–30.
23. Helms (1986), Richardson (1986), Rush (1986) and Scowcroft (1987), interviews with Andrew Dod.
24. Gaddis (1982).
25. Nixon (1978), p. 284.
26. Haldeman interview with Andrew Dod (1987).
27. van der Linden (1972), pp. 107–108.
28. Kissinger (1979), p. 824.
29. Rush interview with Andrew Dod (1986).
30. Reported in Kissinger (1979), p. 830.
31. Kissinger (1979), p. 830
32. Loewenberg (1986).
33. Nixon (1967), p. 121.
34. van der Linden (1972), p. 143.
35. Nixon (1978), p. 565; [Italics added].

10. The Final Face: Enemies Everywhere

1. Kissinger (1979), p. 245.
2. Ambrose (1989), p. 258.
3. Steinberg: unpublished manuscript.
4. Steinberg (1996), p. 185.
5. Barber (1977), p. 429.
6. Ambrose (1989), p. 345.
7. Steinberg (1996), p. 206.
8. Haldeman (1994).
9. Volkan (1980), and Volkan and Itzkowitz (1984), and Volkan and Ast (1994).
10. Volkan (1980).
11. Ehrlichman (1982), p. 175.
12. Ehrlichman (1982), pp. 399–401.
13. Haldeman (1978), p. 114.
14. Anson (1972), p. 204.
15. Ehrlichman interview with Andrew Dod (1986); and The Larry King Show, December (1987).
16. Ehrlichman (1982), p. 402.
17. See, Dean (1976); Haldeman (1978); Ehrlichman (1982).
18. Haldeman (1978), p. 155.

19. Haldeman interview with Andrew Dod (1987).

20. Haldeman (1978), p. 156.

21. Kutler (1990) on pp. 200–210 offers an overview theories explaining Watergate, but he does not include the psychological aspects we describe here.

22. Haldeman interview with Andrew Dod (1987).

23. Ehrlichman interview with Andrew Dod (1986).

24. Haldeman (1978), p. 144.

25. Haldeman (1978), pp. 133–134.

26. Haldeman testimony before the Senate Watergate Committee (July 30, 1973).

27. Schell (1975), p. 111.

28. Haldeman interview with Andrew Dod (1987).

29. Nixon television interview with David Frost (1977).

30. Nixon (1978), p. 471.

31. Woodward and Bernstein (1976), p. 387.

32. Woodward and Bernstein (1976), p. 466.

33. Bremer (1975), p. 232.

34. Ehrlichman interview with Andrew Dod (1987).

11. Conclusion

1. Nixon (1982a), p. 14.

2. Freud (1917), p. 23.

3. Nixon (1988).

4. Ehrlichman interview with Andrew Dod (1987).

5. Wills (1979), p. 371.

6. Mazlish (1972), p. 74.

7. Ailes interview with Andrew Dod (1987).

8. Richardson interview with Andrew Dod (1987).

9. According to Volkan (1988), "What makes psychoanalysis an appropriate tool of investigation is not its claim that all human beings have similar unconscious drives and advance on similar psychosexual paths, but its recognition that each individual or group has complex and idiosyncratic ways of dealing with the demands of the inner world and that external events and their mental representations must be taken into account" (p. 10).

References

Abrahamsen, David. 1977. *Nixon vs. Nixon: An Emotional Tragedy*. New York: Farrar, Straus, and Giroux.

Akhtar, Salman. 1992. *Broken Structures: Severe Personality Disorders and Their Treatment*. Northvale, NJ: Jason Aronson.

Alexander, Franz. 1950. *Psychosomatic Medicine: Its Principles and Applications*. New York: W. W. Norton.

Alsop, Stewart. 1960. *Nixon and Rockefeller: A Double Portrait*. New York: Doubleday.

Ambrose, Stephen E. 1987. *Nixon: Education of a Politician, 1913–1962*. New York: Simon and Schuster.

Ambrose, Stephen E. 1989. *Nixon: The Triumph of a Politician, 1962–1972*. New York: Simon and Schuster.

Ambrose, Stephen E. 1991. *Nixon: Ruin and Recovery, 1973–1990*. New York: Simon and Schuster.

Anson, R. S. 1972. *McGovern: A Biography*. New York: Holt, Rinehart, and Winston.

Anson, R. S. 1984. *The Unquiet Oblivion of Richard M. Nixon*. New York: Simon and Schuster.

Barber, James D. 1977. *The Presidential Character: Predicting Performance in the White House*. (2nd ed.). Englewood Cliffs, NJ: Prentice-Hall.

Benedek, Therese. 1973. *Psychoanalytic Investigations*. New York: Quadrangle/The New York Times Books.

Benjamin, J. D., J. V. Coleman, and R. Hornbein. 1948. A study of personality in pulmonary tuberculosis. *American Journal of Orthopsychiatry* 18:704–707.

Bergman, Martin S. 1973. Limitations of method in psychoanalytic biography:

A historical inquiry. *Journal of the American Psychoanalytic Association* 21:833–850.

Beschloss, Michael R. 1994. Nixon's other secret plan. *Washington Post.* May 1, pp. C1, C2.

Blos, Peter. 1967. The second individuation process of adolescence. *The Psychoanalytic Study of the Child* 22:162–186.

Bradford, M. E. 1985. *Remembering Who We Are: Observations of a Southern Conservative.* Athens, GA: University of Georgia Press.

Brazelton, T., B. Koslowski, and N. Main. 1974. The origins of reciprocity: The early mother-infant interaction. In *The Effect of the Infant on its Caregiver.* ed. M. Lewis and L. Rosenblum, pp. 49–76. New York: John Wiley.

Bremer, H. F. (ed.). 1975. *Richard M. Nixon 1913- :Chronology-Documents-Bibliographical Aides.* New York: Oceana Publishers.

Brinton, H. H. 1973. *The Religious Philosophy of Quakerism.* Philadelphia: Pendle Hill.

Brodie, Fawn. 1981. *Richard Nixon: The Shaping of His Character.* Cambridge, MA: Harvard University Press.

Burke, V. J. 1974. *Nixon's Good Deed: Welfare Reform.* New York: Columbia University Press.

Cavan, S. 1979. *20th Century Gothic: America's Nixon.* San Francisco: Wigan Pier Press.

Costello, William. 1960. *The Facts about Nixon: An Unauthorized Biography.* New York: Viking Press.

Crispell, K., and Gomez, C. F. 1988. *Hidden Illness in the White House.* Durham, NC: Duke University Press.

Davis, D. B. 1969. *The Slave Power Conspiracy and the Paranoid Style.* Baton Rouge: Louisiana State University Press.

Dean, James III. 1976. *Blind Ambition: The White House Years.* New York: Pocket Books.

de Toledano, Ralph. 1969. *One Man Alone: Richard Nixon.* New York: Funk and Wagnalls.

Dunbar, F. 1983. Psychoanalytic notes relating to syndromes of asthma and hay fever. *Psychoanalytic Quarterly* 7:25.

Ehrlichman, John. 1982. *Witness to Power: The Nixon Years.* New York: Simon and Schuster.

Eisenhower, Julie Nixon. 1986. *Pat Nixon: The Untold Story.* New York: Simon and Schuster.

Emde, Robert N. 1991. Positive emotions for psychoanalytic theory: Surprises from infancy research and new directions. *Journal of the American Psychoanalytic Association.* (Supplement) 39:5–44.

Erikson, Erik H. 1950. *Identity and Life Cycle.* New York: International Universities Press.

Erikson, Erik H. 1963. *Childhood and Society.* New York: W. W. Norton.

Etheredge, Lloyd S. 1979. Hardball politics: A Model. *Political Psychology* 1:3–26.

Falk, Avner. 1985. Aspects of political psychobiography. *Political Psychology* 6:605–619.

French, Thomas M. et al. 1941. Psychogenic factors in bronchial asthma, parts I and II *Psychosomatic Medicine Monographs II and IV,*. Nos. I and II. Washington: National Research Council.

Freud, Anna. 1936. The ego and the mechanisms of defense. In *The Writings of Anna Freud*, vol. 2. New York: International Universities Press, 1966.

Freud, Anna. 1958. Adolescence. *The Psychoanalytic Study of the Child* 13:255–278.

Freud, Sigmund. 1910. Leonarda de Vinci. *Standard Edition* 11:57–137.

Freud, Sigmund. 1917. Introductory lectures on psychoanalysis. *Standard Edition* 16.

Freud, Sigmund. 1923. The ego and the id. *Standard Edition* 19:3–66.

Freud, Sigmund. 1926. Inhibitions, symptoms, and anxiety. *Standard Edition* 20:77–175.

Freud, Sigmund. 1939. Moses and monotheism. *Standard Edition* 23:7–137.

Frost, David. 1978. *I Gave them the Sword: Behind the Scenes of the Nixon Interviews.* New York: Ballantine Books.

Gaddis, J. L. 1982. *Strategies of Containment.* Oxford: Oxford University Press.

Gedo, John. 1972. The methodology of psychoanalytic biography. *Journal of the American Psychoanalytic Association* 20:638–649.

George, Alexander L. 1980. *Presidential Decisionmaking in Foreign Policy.* Boulder, CO: Westview Press.

Glad, Betty, and Michael Link (1996) President Nixon's inner circle of advisers. *Presidential Studies Quarterly* 26:12–40.

Greenacre, Phyllis. 1955. *Swift and Carroll: A Psychoanalytic Study of Two Lives.* New York: International Universities Press.

Greenspan, Stanley. 1989. *The Development of the Ego.* Madison, CT: International Universities Press.

Greenstein, Fred I. 1977. A President is forced to resign: Watergate, White House organization, and Nixon's personality. In *America in the Seventies,*. ed. Allan P. Sindler, pp. 50–101. Little, Brown

Greenstein, Fred I. 1982. *The Hidden-Hand Presidency: Eisenhower as Leader.* New York: Basic Books.

Haldeman, H. R., with Joseph DiMona. 1978. *The Ends of Power.* New York: Times Books.

Haldeman, H. R. 1994. *Haldeman Diaries: Inside The Nixon White House.* New York: G. P. Putnam and Sons.

Hendrick, Ives. 1951. Early development of the ego: identification in infancy. *The Psychoanalytic Quarterly* 20:44–101.

Herbers, J. 1973. Nixon's Presidency: Centralized Control. *New York Times* March 6, p. 1.

Hoff, Joan. 1994. *Nixon Reconsidered.* New York: Basic Books.

Isaacson, Walter. 1992. *Kissinger: A Biography.* New York: Simon and Schuster.

Jacobson, Edith. 1964. *The Self and the Object World.* New York: International Universities Press.

Kernberg, Otto F. 1975. *Borderline Conditions and Pathological Narcissism.* New York: Jason Aronson.

Kernberg, Otto F. 1984. *Severe Personality Disorders: Psychotherapeutic Strategies.* New Haven: Yale University Press.

Kissinger, Henry A. 1979. *White House Years.* Boston: Little, Brown.

Kissinger, Henry A. 1994. *Diplomacy.* New York: Simon and Schuster.

Klaus, M. and J. Kennell. 1976. *Maternal-Infant Bonding.* St. Louis: C. V. Mosby.

Kohut, H. 1971. *The Analysis of the Self: A Systematic Approach to the Psychoanalytic Treatment of Narcissistic Personality Disorders.* New York: International Universities Press.

Kornitzer, Bela. 1960. *The Real Nixon: An Intimate Biography.* Chicago: Rand McNally.

Kutler, Stanley I. 1990. *The Wars of Watergate.* New York: Alfred A. Knopf.

La Faber, W. 1963. *The New Empire: An Interpretation of American Expansion, 1860–1898.* New York: Cornell University Press.

Langer, Walter C. 1972. *The Mind of Adolf Hitler: The Secret Wartime Report.* New York: Basic Books.

Lipsitt, L. 1966. Learning processes of newborns. *Merrill-Palmer Quarterly* 12:45–71.

Loewenberg, Peter. 1986. Nixon, Hitler, and power: An ego psychological study. *Psychoanalytic Inquiry* 1:27–48.

Longford, L. 1980. *Nixon: A Study in Extremes of Fortune.* London: Weidenfeld and Nicolson.

Mahler, Margaret S. 1968. *On Human Symbiosis and the Vicissitudes of Individuation.* New York: International University Press.

Marvick, Elizabeth Wirth, unpublished manuscript.

Mazlish, Bruce. 1972. *In Search of Nixon: A Psychohistorical Inquiry.* New York: Basic Books.

Mazo, Earl, and Stephen Hess. 1967. *Nixon: A Political Portrait.* New York: Popular Library.

Meltzoff, A., and K. Moore. 1977. Imitation of facial and manual gestures by human neonates. *Science* 198:75–78.

Modell, Arnold H. 1976. The "holding environment" and the therapeutic action of psychoanalysis. *Journal of the American Psychoanalytic Association* 24:285–307.

Morris, Roger. 1990. *Richard Milhous Nixon: The Rise of an American Politician.* New York: Henry Holt.

Nathan, R. P. 1975. *The Plot that Failed: Nixon and the Administrative Presidency.* New York: John Wiley.

Niederland, William C. 1965. An analytic inquiry into the life and work of Henrich Schliemann. In *Drives, Affects, and Behaviors,.* vol. 2. ed. Max Schur. New York: International Universities Press.

Nixon, Hannah (as told to Flora Rheta Schreiber). 1960. Richard Nixon: A Mother's Story. *Good Housekeeping.* June, p. 212.

Nixon, Richard. 1962. *Six Crises.* Garden City, New York: Doubleday.

Nixon, Richard. 1967. Asia after Vietnam *Foreign Affairs* 46:111–125.

Nixon, Richard. 1972. *A New Road for America: President Richard M. Nixon, Major Policy Statements, March 1970 to October, 1971.* New York: Doubleday.

Nixon, Richard. 1978. *RN: The Memoirs of Richard Nixon*. New York: Grosset and Dunlap.

Nixon, Richard. 1980. *The Real War*. New York: Warner Books.

Nixon, Richard 1982a. *Leaders*. New York: Warner Books.

Nixon, Richard 1982b. *Foreign Relations of the United States, 1952–54* 13: 949–950. Washington, DC: Department of State.

Nixon, Richard 1988. *1999: Victory Without War*. New York: Simon and Schuster.

Nixon, Richard. 1990. *In the Arena: A Memoir of Victory, Defeat, and Renewal*. New York: Simon and Schuster.. .

Olinick, Stanley L. 1980. *The Psychotherapeutic Instrument*. New York: Jason Aronson.

Osborne, John. 1970. *The Nixon Watch*. New York : Liveright.

Oshinsky, D. M. 1983. *A Conspiracy So Immense: The World of Joe McCarthy*. New York: Free Press.

Parens, Henri. 1979. *The Development of Aggression in Early Childhood*. New York: Jason Aronson.

Parmet, Herbert S. 1990. *Richard Nixon and his America*. Boston: Little, Brown.

Pollock, George. 1989. *The Mourning-Liberation Process,*. vols. 1 & 2. Madison, CT: International Universities Press.

Post, Jerrold M. 1983. Woodrow Wilson re-examined: The mind-body controversy redox and other disputations *Political Psychology* 4:289–306.

Post, Jerrold M. 1993. The defining moment of Saddam's life: A political psychology perspective on the leadership and decision-making of Saddam Hussein during the Gulf Crisis. In *The Political Psychology of the Gulf War Leaders*. ed. Stanley A Renshon, pp. 49–66. Pittsburgh: University of Pittsburgh Press.

Price, Raymond. 1977. *With Nixon*. New York: Viking Press.

Rangell, Leo. 1980. *The Mind of Watergate*. New York: Norton.

Rappaport, David. 1960. The structure of psychoanalytic theory: A systematizing attempt. *Psychological Issues,*. vol. 2, monograph 6. New York: International Universities Press.

Redford, E. S., D. B. Truman, A. F. Westin, R. C. Wood. 1965. *Politics and Government in the United States*. New York: Harcourt, Brace, and World.

Reed, J. S. 1983. *Southerners, the Social Psychology of Sectionalism*. Chapel Hill, NC: University of North Carolina Press.

Safire, William. 1975. *Before the Fall: An Inside View of the Pre-Watergate White House*. New York: Da Capo Press.

Schell, Jonathan. 1975. *The Time of Illusion*. New York: Random House.

Schulte, R. K. 1978. *The Young Nixon: An Oral Inquiry*. Fullerton: California State University at Fullerton: Delta Lithograph.

Schulzinger, Robert D. 1989. *Henry Kissinger: Doctor of Diplomacy*. New York: Columbia University Press.

Schur, Max. 1955. Comments on the metapsychology of somatization. *The Psychoanalytic Study of the Child* 10:119–164.

Spalding, Henry D. 1972. *The Nixon Nobody Knows*. Middle Village, NY: Jonathan David.

Spitz, René. 1957. *No and Yes: On the Beginning of Human Communication*. International Universities Press.

Steinberg, Blema (unpublished manuscript). The first draft of *Shame and Humiliation: Presidential Decision-making on Vietnam.*

Steinberg, Blema. 1996. *Shame and Humiliation: Presidential Decision-making on Vietnam,.* McGill-Queen's University Press.

Stern, Daniel. 1985. *The Interpersonal World of the Child.* New York: Basic Books.

Stone, Michael H. 1989. Murder. In *Narcissistic Personality Disorder. The Psychiatric Clinics of North America,.* ed. Otto F. Kernberg, Vol. 12, no. 3, pp. 643–651. Philadelphia: W. B. Saunders.

Tähkä, Veikko. 1984. *The Patient-Doctor Relationship.* Sidney, Australia: ADIS Health Science Press.

Taylor, Graeme. 1987. *Psychosomatic Medicine and Contemporary Psychoanalysis.* Madison, CT: International Universities Press.

van der Linden, F. 1972. *Nixon's Quest for Peace.* New York: Robert B. Luce.

Volkan, Vamık D. 1976. *Primitive Internalized Object Relations.* New York: International Universities Press.

Volkan, Vamık D. 1979. The "glass bubble" of the narcissistic patient. In *Advances in Psychotherapy of the Borderline Patient.* eds. J. Le Boit and A. Capponi, pp. 405–431. New York: Jason Aronson.

Volkan, Vamık D. 1980. Narcissistic personality organization and "reparative" leadership. *International Journal of Group Psychotherapy* 30:131–152.

Volkan, Vamık D. 1981. *Linking Objects and Linking Phenomena: A Study of the Forms, Symptoms, Metapsychology, and Therapy of Complicated Mourning.* New York: International Universities Press.

Volkan, Vamık D. 1982a. Identification and related psychic events: Their appearance in therapy and their curative value. In *Curative Factors in Dynamic Psychotherapy.* ed. Samuel Slipp, pp. 153–176. New York: McGraw Hill.

Volkan, Vamık D. 1982b. Narcissistic personality disorder. In *Critical Problems in Psychiatry.* eds. J. O. Carvener and H. Keith Brodie, pp. 332–350. J. R. Lippincott.

Volkan, Vamık D. 1984. *What Do You Get When You Cross a Dandelion with a Rose? The True Story of a Psychoanalysis.* New York: Jason Aronson.

Volkan, Vamık D. 1987. *Six Steps in the Treatment of Borderline Personality Organization.* Northvale, NJ: Jason Aronson.

Volkan, Vamık D. 1988. *The Need to Have Enemies and Allies: From Clinical Practice to International Relationships.* Northvale, NJ: Jason Aronson.

Volkan, Vamık D. 1992. Ethnonationalistic rituals: An introduction. *Mind and Human Interaction* 4:3–19.

Volkan, Vamık, and Gabriele Ast. 1994. *Spektrum des Narziβmus.* Göttingen: Vandenhoeck & Ruprecht.

Volkan, Vamık D., and Gabriele Ast. 1997. *Siblings in the Unconscious and Psychopathology.* Madison, CT: International Universities Press.

Volkan, Vamık D., and Norman Itzkowitz. 1984. *The Immortal Atatürk: A Psychobiography.* Chicago: University of Chicago Press.

Volkan, Vamık D., and Norman Itzkowitz. 1994. *Turks and Greeks: Neighbours in Conflict.* Cambridgeshire, England: Eothen Press.

Volkan, Vamık D., and As'ad Masri. 1989. The development of female transsexualism. *American Journal of Psychotherapy* 43:92–107.

Volkan, Vamık D., and Terry C. Rodgers (eds.). 1988. *Attitudes of Entitlement.* Charlottesville: University Press of Virginia.

Volkan, Vamık D., and Elizabeth Zintl. 1993. *Life After Loss: The Lessons of Grief.* New York: Charles Scribner's Sons.

Von Drehle, David. 1994. Historians must weight contradictions. *Washington Post.* April 24, pp. A1–A11.

Weigert Edith. 1967. Narcissism: benign and malignant forms. In *Crosscurrents in Psychiatry and Psychoanalysis.* ed. Robert W. Gibson, pp. 222–238. Philadelphia: Lippincott.

White, Theodore H. 1969. *The Making of the President—1968.* New York: Pocket Books.

Wicker, Tom. 1991. *One of Us: Richard Nixon and the American Dream.* New York: Random House.

Wills, Garry. 1979. *Nixon Agonistes: The Crisis of the Self-made Man.* New York: Mentor Books.

Wilson, C. Phillip, and Ira L. Mintz 1989. *Psychosomatic Symptoms: Psychodynamic Treatment of the Underlying Personality Disorder.* Northvale, NJ: Jason Aronson.

Winnicott, Donald W. 1957. *Mother and Child.* New York: Basic Books.

Winnicott, Donald W. 1964. *The Child, the Family, and the Outside World.* New York: Penguin Books.

Winnicott, Donald W. 1965. *The Maturational Process and the Facilitating Environment.* New York: International Universities Press.

Woodward, Bob, and Carl Bernstein. 1976. *The Final Days.* New York: Avon Books.

Index

Abortion, 63
Abrahamsen, David, 81, 155*n*7
Adolescence, 6, 16–17, 26, 36–39, 80–81
Afghanistan, 94
African Americans, *see* Black Americans
Aggression: depression and, 131; in early childhood, 73, 74, 75, 153*n*23, 156*n*4; in infancy, 160*n*17; in latency period, 16; in malignant narcissism, 89–90
Agnew, Spiro, 60, 61, 122
Ailes, Roger, 93, 98–99, 100, 148
Air quality, 62
Aitken, Jonathan, 1
Akhtar, Salman, 87
Alexander, Franz, 102–3
Allende regime, 129
Altruism, 154*n*34
Ambrose, Stephen E., 5
American Indians, 123
Anaheim canal, 34

Anality, 77, 96, 101
Anal phase, 76
Anniversary reactions, 103, 104, 154*n*33
Anti-communist movement, 55–56, 64, 79, 119–20
Anti-war protesters, 122, 130, 131–32; *see also* Pacifism
Anxiety: birthdays and, 154*n*33; childhood sources of, 8–9; defenses against, 8; of food hoarder, 96; "good-enough mothering" and, 32–33; historical arena and, 131; hypochondriasis and, 163*n*55; illegality and, 135; mother loss and, 81–84; personality and, 11; respiration and, 102; *see also* Castration anxiety; Claustrophobia
Apollo 13 moon trip, 130
Applause, 92–93, 148
Appomattox Court House, 23
Arizona, 37–38, 81, 103
Arms control, 64, 124, 129, 132

Artesia, 46
Artistic creativity, 6, 11
Ash Advisory Council on Reorganization, 111, 112
Assassinations, 105–6
Ast, Gabriele, 161n4
Atatürk, Mustafa Kemal, 7; counter-transferences toward, 152n19; idealized father image of, 160n29; names of, 162n32; "oral examinations" by, 11; "rescue" fantasy of, 75
Autonomic nervous system, 164n61
Avoidance, 8

Barber, James David, 99, 130
Baseball, 35
Bassett, James, 49
Beeson, Dorothy, 155n15
Beeson, Jane Milhous, 36–37, 80, 81, 155n13
Beeson, Sheldon, 72
Benedek, Therese, 164n61
Ben-Gurion, David, 75
Berlin, 123, 125–26
Berlin Agreement, 125–26
Berlin Wall, 125
"Berlin Wall" (aides), 84, 98
Berman, Larry, 143
Bernstein, Carl, 86, 87
Bewley, Thomas, 43
Biological determination, 13
Birthdays, 154n33
Black Americans, 62, 123; see also Desegregation
Blackmun, Harry A., 63
Bodily harm, 9; see also Physical illnesses
Boeing Aircraft Company, 62
Breckinridge, John C., 57
Britain, 125
Brodie, Fawn, 95, 155n7
Brown, Pat, 59, 92
Buchanan, James, 57
Buchanan, Patrick, 60–61
Budget deficit, 62
Bull, Steve, 86–87
Bundy, Ted, 90

Burdg, Almira, see Milhous, Almira Burdg
Burger, Warren E., 63
Burns, Arthur, 62, 114
Burns, James MacGregor, 141
Bush, George, 94, 105
Busing [Bussing?], 62, 63
Butterfield, Alexander, 61

Cabinet, 83, 112, 114, 139
California: attractions of, 30; broadcasts from, 57; gubernatorial race in, 59, 92, 100, 135; Senate race in, 55- 56, 62; Teapot Dome scandal and, 36
California Bar Exam, 43, 79, 86
Cambodia: bombing of, 5, 18, 64, 87, 129–30, 145; civil war in, 130–31
Camp David, 131
Capitalism, 24
Capitol Building, 123
Carnegie Endowment for International Peace, 54
Carolinas, 26
Carswell, G. Harold, 63, 121, 130
Carter administration, 98
Castration anxiety, 15, 18, 84–85
Central Intelligence Agency, 133, 136–37
Centralized power, 111–13, 137
Cervantes Saavedra, Miguel de, 149
Chambers, Whittaker, 54, 79, 80, 119
Chaplin, Charlie, 143
Character, see Personality
"Checkers Speech" (1952), 57, 72, 80, 95, 146
Chester County (Pa.), 28
Children: aggression in, 73, 74, 75, 153n23, 156n4; approval mechanisms of, 35; dependency in, 14; event "interpretation" by, 7; fantasies of, 17–18; FAP and, 114; high regard for, 75, 76, 160n21; intellectual development of, 76–77; latency period of, 16, 26; life space of, 6; male, 14–16, 78; mental conflicts of, 8–9; relationships of, 10; self-reliance in, 13–14, 15, 33,

159n1; separation- individuation of, 81, 160n31; sibling births and, 34; superego development in, 73–74; *see also* Adolescence; "Dangerous" events; Mother-child relationship

Chile, 129

China, 60; Communist takeover of, 55; reconciliation with, 64, 126–27, 129; Soviet differences with, 118, 132

"Christmas Bombing," 131, 132

Churchill, Winston, 70, 71, 106, 125

"CIA Trap Theory," 136–37

Citizen committees, 121

Civil rights movement, *see* Desegregation

Civil War, 23–24, 25, 122

Claustrophobia, 18

Clawson, Ken, 105

Cleveland, Grover, 27

Clinton, Bill, 2

Clumsiness, 86–87

Cohen, Wilbur, 143, 144

Colic, 71

Collecting: of "first times," 2, 18, 77, 94; of information, 96–97, 134; of presidencies, 44, 92, 145

Colson, Charles, 60, 61, 101, 135, 136

Columbus Railway and Light Company, 27

Compulsivity, 136

Committee of 100, 51

Committee to Re-elect, 136

Communist bloc, *see* China; North Vietnam; Soviet Union

Communist party, 54; *see also* Anti-communist movement

Compulsive behavior, 135–36; *see also* Obsessional personality

Concentration, 98, 99

Conflicts: interpersonal, 11, 61, 82, 136, 147; mental, 8

Congress: blaming of, 131; "cutting" by, 85; desegregation and, 62; electoral campaigns for, 51–52, 55–56, 60; FAP and, 63, 114–15; proposed

coalition party and, 111; reorganization message to, 112

Congress. House Un-American Activities Committee, 53, 54, 55

Congress. Senate: Carswell nomination and, 130; electoral campaign for, 55–56; Finch candidacy for, 62; Haynsworth nomination and, 121, 130; resignation decision and, 139

—Finance Committee, 63, 115

—Watergate Committee, 3, 103, 136–37

Congress of Industrial Organizations, 52

Connally, John, 60, 61, 62, 70–71, 111

Conscience, 8, 73–74, 154n28

Conscious fantasies, *see* Fantasies

Conscription, 64

Constitution, 38, 63, 121, 138

Coolidge, Grace, 49

Counterphobia, 8

Countertransference, 10, 11, 153n19; by biographers, 144, 148, 152n19; by leaders, 109

Cox, Edward, 85, 139

Cox, Tricia Nixon, 48, 51, 57, 96

Creativity, 6, 7, 11

Crises, 109; *see also* "Dangerous" events; Traumas

Critchfield, Virginia Shaw, 34

Cromwell, Oliver, 28

Crying, 33, 71–72; applause and, 93–94; reasons for, 19; respiration and, 102–3; signaling by, 164n61

Cursing, 18, 77, 87, 147

Dancing, 41

"Dangerous" events, 8, 9, 11; *see also* Crises; Traumas

The Dark Tower (play), 46

Darwin, Charles, 24

Dean, John, 60, 61, 136

Death, 15, 26, 39, 103, 152n18; *see also* Immortality; Mourning

Death wishes, 8, 18, 152n18; *see also* Murderous fantasies

Debates: with JFK, 58, 73, 100; with
    Khrushchev, 1, 58, 76; with
    Voorhis, 52; at Whittier High
    School, 38, 72–73; *see also*
    Speeches
decisionmaking, 109, 111–13
Defense budget, 64
Defense Intelligence Agency, 137
De Gaulle, Charles, 125
Democratic government, 109, 138
Democratic Headquarters, 4
Democratic National Committee, 135
Democratic party: Douglas and, 55;
    Hiss/Chambers controversy and,
    54; 1968 campaign and, 59–60,
    105–6; F. Nixon and, 27, 30;
    Stevenson and, 56, 58; Voorhis
    and, 51
Dependency, 5; in children, 14;
    clumsiness and, 87; denial of, 75,
    91, 92–101; in healthy narcissism,
    89
Depression (economics), 38
Depression (psychology), 131,
    154n34
Desegregation, 62, 63, 120–21, 122
Détente, 64, 124, 125
de Toledano, Ralph, 56, 79, 155n15
Developmental biographical
    approach, 7
Dien Bien Phu, 116, 117
"Dirty" words, 18, 77, 87, 147
Diseases, *see* Physical illnesses
Dismissals, 61, 82–84, 87
Displacement (psychology), 74
Divorce cases, 44, 119
Dixon, Tom, 48–49
Dod, Andrew, 124
Domestic events, 130
Domestic policy, 88; destructiveness
    in, 129; in first term, 61–63, 113–
    15; grandiose self and, 110; mend-
    ing tactics in, 120–21; 1968 elec-
    tion and, 60; suspicion in, 133–34
Domestic violence, 137–38, 146
Donne, John, 125
Donovan, Leisure, Newton, and
    Lombard (firm), 43

Dorn, Evelyn, 49
Douglas, Helen Gahagan, 55–56
Draft (conscription), 64
Drama, 45–46, 93
Dreams, 9–10, 19, 93; *see also*
    Fantasies
Drives (psychology), 6; *see also*
    Motivation
Duke University, 157n5
Duke University Alumni Association
    of California, 44
Duke University School of Law, 41–42,
    43, 45, 120
Duke University Student Bar
    Association, 42

Eagleton, Terry, 106
East Germany, 125
Eating habits, 70–71, 159n1
Economic conditions, 24, 62, 132
Ecrasons l'infâme (song), 40
Education, 26; *see also* School desegre-
    gation
Ego development, 16
Ego identity, *see* Self-identity
"Ego strength," 126, 148, 162n26
Ehrlichman, John, 60; CIA and, 133;
    on compulsive behavior, 136; on
    desegregation, 120, 121; on firings,
    82–84; on "firsts," 94; on hunger,
    70; "inner circle" and, 61; Krogh
    and, 123; on NATO, 115;
    "plumbers" and, 101; on political
    innovations, 111; privacy provided
    by, 98; on "real" Nixon, 147; on
    resignation, 139; review by, 134
Eisenhower, Dwight D., 56, 57, 58, 99,
    119
Eisenhower, Julie Nixon: birth of, 48;
    on grandmother, 29; last instruc-
    tions to, 96; pet of, 57; at Smith,
    50, 130
Eisenhower, Mamie, 49
Elections: collegiate, 41, 45, 93;
    Congressional, 51–52, 55–56, 60;
    gubernatorial, 59, 92, 100, 135;
    high school, 38, 92; presidential
    (*see* Presidential elections)

Electronic media, *see* Radio broadcasts; Television broadcasts
Electronic surveillance, *see* Wiretapping
Ellsberg, Daniel: at Gorbachev Foundation, 2; "Pentagon Papers" and, 65, 100, 132, 134; psychiatrist of, 101, 134
Embargo, 127
Employee firings, 61, 82–84, 87
England, 28
Environment (psychology): adolescence and, 17; individual difference and, 7; mental conflicts and, 8; personality and, 11, 12; self-identity and, 13
Environmental regulations, 62
Envy, 94, 162*n*11
Erikson, Erik, 6, 16, 24–25
Espionage, 55; *see also* Wiretapping
Etheredge, Lloyd, 75, 92
Europe, 56, 115–16, 126
Executive Branch, 111–13, 141; *see also* Presidential office

Falk, Avner, 6–7, 151*n*7
Family Assistance Plan, 63, 113–15
Fantasies, 17–18; of castration, 15, 18, 84–85; of grandiose self, 161*n*7; of independence, 98; narcissistic, 90; about parents, 9; about pregnant mothers, 18, 154*n*33; "rescuing," 18, 37, 75, 154*n*34; *see also* Death wishes; Dreams
Father figures: approval by, 35; Atatürk as, 160*n*29; death of, 15, 152*n*18; envy by, 131; Lincoln as, 80, 129; revised perceptions of, 9
Fear, *see* Anxiety
Federal Bureau of Investigation: application to, 42; CIA and, 136; "Pentagon Papers" and, 100–101, 134; "White House Policy" and, 137; wiretapping by, 61
Federal Republic of Germany, 125, 126
Finch, Robert, 62
Firings, 61, 82–84, 87

First Ladies, 2, 49–50, 94–95
"Firsts," *see* "Historical firsts"
Food, 70–71, 96, 159*n*1
Football, 35, 38, 42, 79, 86
Ford, Gerald, 94, 104, 105
Foreign Affairs (periodical), 126–27
Foreign aid, 53
Foreign policy, 88; centralized decisionmaking in, 113; destructiveness in, 129–33; discussion of, 61, 99; in first term, 63–65, 115–17; grandiose self and, 110; linkage in, 123–24; 1968 election and, 60; in pre-1968 period, 59; pride in, 146
Forensics, *see* Debates
Fortas, Abe, 121
France, 116, 117, 125
Franklin Society, 40
Freud, Sigmund: biographical studies by, 151*n*7; dangers identified by, 152*n*16; on father-child relationship, 15; on leadership studies, 144; on negative therapeutic reaction, 85; on symbols, 6
Frost, David, 84, 85, 122, 138
Fullerton High School, 38
Fund Crisis (1952), 56–57, 95, 99

Gambling, 51
Genetic determination, 13
George, Alexander, 113
Gettysburg Address, 23–24
Gladstone, William, 84
"Glass bubble" syndrome, 98–99, 163*n*34
Glover, Elizabeth, 72
Gold prices, 62
Goldwater, Barry, 139
"Good-enough mothering," 32–33, 70, 153*n*23
Gorbachev Foundation, 2
Gospel of John, 29
Grandiose self, 90, 109–17, 161*n*7; applause and, 93; Cambodian invasion and, 130; childhood losses and, 81; comebacks by, 145; constitutional powers and, 138; envy of, 131; firing and, 83; "firsts"

Grandiose self, . . . (*continued*)
  and, 94; integration of, 110,
  118–19, 126, 128–29, 133; linking
  policy and, 125; maintenance of,
  92- 101, 102, 133, 162nn11, 26;
  maternal grief and, 91; Oedipal
  complex and, 78; parental regard
  and, 76; political boldness and,
  118; protection of, 80; resignation
  and, 104, 138–39; Watergate tapes
  and, 96
Grand Old Opry (Nashville), 49
Grant, Ulysses S., 23
Gray, Pat, 137
Great Society, 114
Greenstein, Fred I., 113, 165n5
Grief, 23, 82, 91, 103
Grieves, James, 72
Gubernatorial election (1962), 59, 92,
  100, 135
Guilt, 80, 85, 104, 105

Habeas corpus, 3
Haig, Alexander, 60
Haldeman, H. Robert: Butterfield
  and, 61; on "charming mood," 130;
  on compulsive behavior, 135–36;
  on domestic violence, 137; on
  Ellsberg break-in, 134; firing of,
  84; on information gathering, 97,
  138; on "The Man in the Arena,"
  100; privacy provided by, 98;
  responsibilities of, 60; on states-
  man role, 125; on Vietnam War,
  117
Hanoi, 131
Harrison, Elizabeth Milhous, 32
Harrison, Russell, Jr., 32, 70, 81, 93
Harvard Law School, 54
Harvard University, 38, 62
Hawaii, 94
Haynsworth, Clement F., 63, 121, 130
Helms, Richard, 99, 124
Hendrick, Ives, 159n1
Herbers, John, 112
Hess, Stephen, 155n15
Hickel, Walter, 83
Hiss, Alger, 54–55, 76, 79, 119

"Historical firsts," 11, 18, 94–95, 128;
  comeback as, 146; in foreign pol-
  icy, 115; at funeral, 2; in Supreme
  Court, 63
Hitler, Adolf, 90, 162n32
Hitt, Pat, 83
Hoarding, 96; *see also* Collecting;
  Miserliness
Hoff, Joan, 61
Holmes, Oliver Wendell, 54
Hoover, Herbert, 55
Hoover, J. Edgar, 42, 61, 101, 136
Horack, H. Claude, 43, 79
Hughes, Howard, 133, 134–35
Humphrey, Hubert, 59, 60
Hunger, 70; *see also* Food
"Hungry self," 78, 90; accumulated
  titles and, 92; care for, 133; in
  childhood, 70; denial of, 91, 101;
  envy of, 131; Hughes and, 134–35;
  information and, 96–97; integra-
  tion of, 110, 118–19, 126, 128–29,
  133; paranoia and, 80, 110; politi-
  cal boldness and, 118
Hunt, Howard, 136
Hussein, Saddam, 90
Huston Plan, 137–38
Hypochondriasis, 102, 163n55

Idealizing transference, 92, 162n14
Identification with the aggressor, 15
Identity, *see* Self-identity
Illnesses, *see* Physical illnesses
Immortality, 104–6
Imports tax, 62
Independence, *see* Self-reliance
Individuation, 81, 160n31
Indochina, 117
Industrialism, 24
Infants, 6; frustrations of, 91; innate
  abilities of, 13, 153n24, 160n17;
  rage of, 102, 164n57; *see also*
  Crying; Mother-child relationship
Inflation (finance), 62, 132
Inner-light doctrine, 29
Instincts, *see* Drives
Integration (desegregation), 62, 63,
  120–21, 122

Integration (psychology), 110, 118–19, 126, 128–29, 133
Integrity (morality), 18, 87
Intellectual activities, 33, 34–35, 36, 76–77
Inter-Agency Group on Domestic Intelligence, 137–38
Internal affairs, *see* Domestic policy
Internal Revenue Service, 4
International relations, *see* Foreign policy
Interpersonal conflicts, 11, 61, 82, 136, 147
Interpersonal relationships, 11, 13, 14; *see also* Mother-child relationship
Ireland, 25, 28
Isaacson, Walter, 162n20
Itzkowitz, Norman, 7, 11, 152n19, 162n32
Iwatsura, Yoneko Dobashi, 72

Japan, 51
Jealousy, 94, 162n11
Jennings County (Ind.), 28
Jobe, Gail, 45
Johns Hopkins University, 54
Johnson, Lyndon B.: Berman on, 143; brother of, 133; Great Society and, 114; IRS and, 4; on public deficit, 62; "Tuesday lunch" crowd and, 113; Vietnam War and, 59, 60, 63, 95, 115, 116
Johnson, Paul, 4
Johnson administration, 65
Joint Council of Control (Whittier College), 41

Kaufman, George S., 46
Kennedy, John F.: assassination of, 59, 105, 146; contribution by, 55; debates with, 58, 73, 100; denial by, 95; IRS and, 4; loss to, 92, 106
Kennedy, Robert F., 59, 105–6
Kennedy administration, 65
Kernberg, Otto F., 162n11
Khmer Rouge, 131
Khrushchev, Nikita, 1, 58, 76, 82, 125

King, Martin Luther, Jr., 59, 146
Kissinger, Henry: Cambodian bombings and, 130; centralization by, 113; envied, 94; "inner circle" and, 61; Isaacson on, 162n20; linkage and, 123, 124; "Memorandum for the President," 116; NATO and, 115; North Vietnamese negotiations and, 64; "Pentagon Papers" and, 132; rational analysis and, 3; Rogers and, 60; Rush and, 126; on testiness, 130; wiretapping by, 101
Kiwanis Club, 44
Kohut, Heinz, 161n7, 162n14, 163n55
Kornitzer, Bela, 155n7
Kraft, Joseph, 101
Krogh, Egil ("Bud"), 60, 123
Kuopio Medical Center, 163n55
Kutler, Stanley I., 167n21

Labor movement, 51, 52, 62, 121
Laird, Melvin, 60, 116
Langer, Walter C., 162n32
Laos, 64
Latency period, 16, 26, 34–36, 80
Latent dream content, 93
Leaders: narcissistic, 89–90, 102, 161n4; parents of, 160n21; psychoanalytic studies of, 5, 144; transferences of, 11; *see also* Political leaders
"Leadership in the Modern Presidency" (conference), 143
Lee, Robert E., 23
Legal practice, 36, 43–44, 86, 119
Legal suits, 96
Libidinal drives, *see* Sexuality
Lincoln, Abraham: Gettysburg Address, 23–24; habeas corpus and, 3; idealized fatherhood of, 80, 129; identification with, 80, 84, 87, 122–23, 133; unifying role of, 59, 120, 149
Lincoln Memorial, 122–23
Lindsay, 36–37
Linkage (foreign policy), 123–24
Linking objects (psychology), 82

Little Theater (Whittier), 45–46
Loewenberg, Peter, 95, 162n26
Long, Wayne, 72
Longfellow, Henry Wadsworth, 147
Longford, L., 155n15
Los Angeles, 27, 41, 48
Los Angeles Times, 36, 156–57n28
Lying, 95; *see also* Perjury

McCarthy, Joseph, 55, 119–20
McCord, James, 136–37
McGovern, George, 19, 92, 97, 131
McGregor, Jennie B., 72
McKinley, William, 27
McNamara, Robert, 65
Magruder, Jeb, 61
Mahler, Margaret, 153–54n25,
    160n31
Male children, 14–16, 78
Male parents, *see* Father figures
Malignant narcissism, 89–90, 161n4
Manifest Destiny, 24
Manifest dream content, 93
"The Man in the Arena" (TV pro-
    gram), 100
Mao Tse-Tung, 125
Marshall Plan, 53, 56
Martinez, Eugenio, 137
Marvick, Elizabeth Wirth, 70
Masochism, *see* Self-punishment
Mass media, 2, 4, 99–100, 115; *see also*
    Press; Radio broadcasts; Television
    broadcasts
Masturbation, 87
Mazlish, Bruce, 147
Mazo, Earl, 155n15
Meet the Press (TV program), 94
Mental activities, 33, 34–35, 36,
    76–77
Mental concentration, 98, 99
Mental conflicts, 8
Methodism, 30
Microfilmed documents, 54–55
Middle East, 60, 103, 105, 123
Mid-life crises, 6
Milhous, Almira Burdg, 73; crying val-
    ued by, 33, 71, 74, 75; gift from,
    147; ideals of, 29; marriage of, 28

Milhous, Elizabeth, 32
Milhous, Franklin, 28–29, 30, 51
Milhous, Hannah, *see* Nixon, Hannah
    Milhous (mother)
Milhous, Jane, *see* Beeson, Jane
    Milhous
Milhous, Thomas, 28
Milhous family, 28, 29, 31, 43
"Military sufficiency," 64
Mintz, Ira L., 163n55
Miserliness, 76; *see also* Hoarding
Mitchell, John, 60, 63, 120, 121, 136
Modell, Arnold H., 163n34
Moral contradictions, 18, 87
Mother-child relationship, 12–13; in
    anal phase, 76; clumsiness and, 87;
    crying and, 71, 164n61; disrup-
    tions in, 159n1; grandiose person-
    ality development and, 91; psycho-
    somatic illness and, 102; superego
    formation and, 73; *see also* "Good-
    enough mothering"
Mother figures: death of, 26;
    depressed, 154n34; pregnant, 18,
    154n33; presidents and, 143–44;
    psychic double of, 160n31; separa-
    tion from, 8–9, 34, 81
Motivation, 7, 151n1
Mourning, 23, 82, 91, 103
Moynihan, Daniel Patrick, 60, 62,
    114
Murderous fantasies, 87; *see also* Death
    wish; Serial murderers
Music, 122; *see also* Piano playing;
    Violin playing

Narcissism, 5, 76, 89–106; childhood
    origins of, 14, 75, 91, 162n11; fir-
    ing and, 83; frustration of, 131,
    161n10; Hughes and, 135; negative
    therapeutic reaction and, 86; oedi-
    pal struggle and, 78, 88; paradoxi-
    cal splits in, 118–19; regression in,
    163n55, 164n60; replenishment of,
    130; resurgence of, 146; types of,
    161n4
Narcissistic rage, 100, 145
Nathan, R. P., 112

National debt, 62
The National Geographic, 35
National High School Oratorical Contest, 72
Nationalism, 24
National Security Agency, 137
National Security Council, 98, 113, 116
Native Americans, 123
Natural selection, 24
Naval service, 50–51
Negative therapeutic reaction, 85–86
Neutrality laws, 3
New Caledonia, 49
New Deal, 51, 55
New Federalism, 113
Newman, "Chief," 41, 61, 79
New York City, 42–43, 46, 59, 98
New York Times, 65
Niederland, William C., 153*n*20
The Night of January 16th (play), 45
Nixon, Arthur (brother): birth of, 34; death of, 37, 80, 104, 105; naming of, 32; sleeping arrangements for, 76
Nixon, Clara (sister-in-law), 97
Nixon, Donald (brother): with aunt, 37; birth of, 70; confidences to, 36; Hughes and, 133, 135; information on, 97, 133; mothering shared with, 81; naming of, 32; on peacemaking, 119; on reading, 35; rivalry with, 93; sleeping arrangements for, 76; on speaking, 72
Nixon, Edward (brother), 32, 38, 155*n*7
Nixon, Ernest (uncle), 155*n*7
Nixon, Frank (father): approval by, 35; in Arizona, 38; butchering by, 37, 80, 84; crying heard by, 33; death of, 103; early life of, 25–28; frustration of, 69; house built by, 32; land sold by, 37; lying to, 95; marriage of, 28, 30- 31; oedipal problems of, 78; personality of, 29, 155*n*7; punishment by, 34, 128; split images of, 79, 87–88, 129;

store opened by, 36; surpassing of, 86, 129; West on, 155*n*13
Nixon, George (great-great-grandfather), 25
Nixon, George III (great-grandfather), 25
Nixon, Hannah Milhous (mother), 48, 128; Bewley and, 43; birthday gift for, 39; childcare responsibilities of, 32, 93; confidences to, 36; convalescence of, 33; crying valued by, 71; death of, 82, 103, 105; denials by, 95; early years of, 28–30; emotional reserve of, 29, 44, 70, 96; first separation from, 32, 73, 74, 75, 80, 81; identity with, 77, 96; letter by, 82; maiden name of, 97– 98; marriage of, 30- 31; personality of, 155*n*15; privacy provided by, 76; Rez and, 35; second separation from, 36–37, 81; split images of, 78, 129; tender memories of, 74, 123; third separation from, 38, 81, 103; uprooting of, 69–70
Nixon, Harold (brother): childhood of, 34; confidences to, 36; death of, 38–39, 80, 104, 105; naming of, 32; in recitation contest, 72; sleeping arrangements for, 76; tuberculosis of, 37–38, 103
Nixon, James (great-great-great-grandfather), 25
Nixon, James Jr. (great-great-granduncle), 25
Nixon, Julie (daughter), *see* Eisenhower, Julie Nixon
Nixon, Pat Ryan (wife): burial site of, 2; coat of, 57; courtship of, 46–48, 74, 86; first pregnancy of, 51; at library opening, 94; lying about, 95; marriage of, 48–50; on presidencies, 92; in South America, 58; split images of, 78–79; Supreme Court nominations and, 63; in Wall Street period, 59
Nixon, Samuel (grandfather), 25
Nixon, Sarah Ann Wadsworth (grandmother), 25, 26

Nixon, Tricia (daughter), 48, 51, 57, 96
Nixon (film), 3
Nixon Doctrine, 64, 117
Nixon Library, 2, 94–95, 96
Nobel Peace Prize, 94, 162*n*20
North Atlantic Treaty Organization, 115
Northern states, 23, 122, 130, 133
North Vietnam: bombing suspended in, 60, 64; Cambodian sanctuaries of, 129; "Christmas Bombing" of, 131, 132; secret contacts with, 116, 132; talks refused by, 130
"Nothing but" fallacy, 7
Novelists, 11

O'Brien, Larry, 135
Obsessional personality, 14, 77, 78; *see also* Compulsive behavior
Oedipus complex, 13, 14–16, 18; clumsiness and, 87; negative therapeutic reaction and, 85; RN and, 78–80, 88
Office of Price Administration, 50
Ohio State Senate, 27
Olinick, Stanley, 85–86
Opinion polls, 57
"Oral examinations," 11
Orality, 77, 93, 96
Oral rage, 71, 162*n*11
Oral zone, 71
Orange County Association of Cities, 44
Oratory, *see* Debates; Speeches
Order of the Coif, 42
Organized labor, 51, 52, 62, 121
Orthogonian Society [Club?], 40, 41, 54, 86, 111
Osborne, John, 113
Oshinsky, D. M., 165*n*5
Outer world, *see* Environment (psychology)

Paar, Jack, 59
Pacific Electric Railway Company, 27
Pacifism, 50; *see also* Anti-war protesters

Painters, 11
Paranoia, 128–39; domestic terrorism and, 146; early trauma and, 74, 78; foreign negotiations and, 64–65; "hungry self" and, 80, 110; jealousy and, 94; wounded grandiosity and, 90
Pardons, 104
Parens, Henri, 160*n*17
Parent figures: high regard by, 75, 76, 160*n*21; identification with, 9; Oedipus complex and, 14–15, 18, 78, 84, 85; superego formation and, 73, 74
Parent-teacher association meetings, 72
Paris peace talks, 116, 132
Passport restrictions, 127
Peacemaker self, 110, 118–27, 131
Peacocks, 153*n*19
Pearl Harbor attack, 50
Pearson, Drew, 120
Penn, William, 28
"Pentagon Papers," 2, 65, 100–101, 132, 134
People's Republic of China, *see* China
Perjury, 54, 55
Perry, Herman, 51
Personal integrity, 18, 87
Personality, 11, 12, 16, 17, 90
Personal relationships, *see* Interpersonal relationships
Phi Beta Kappa, 42
Physical illnesses: knee injury, 58; phlebitis, 103, 104, 105; pneumonia, 33, 96, 103, 104, 105; scalp wound, 33, 104; sinus infections, 38, 103, 104; stroke, 2; undulant fever, 105; *see also* Psychosomatic illnesses
Piano playing: in childhood, 35, 37, 81; dexterity for, 86, 87; on Paar show, 59; for wife, 49
Ping-pong, 127
"Plumbers" (aides), 65, 100, 101, 134
Poker, 51
Political arena: boyhood interest in, 36; motivation in, 151*n*1; narcissis-

tic split in, 110; peacemaking in, 119–20; "resurrections" in, 92, 106, 145–47; speechmaking and, 93; strategies in, 118; talent for, 88; *see also* Elections

Political leaders, 109–10; eminent, 125; lying by, 95; media and, 99; mental symptoms of, 11–12; narcissistic, 75; reparative, 133; "rescuing" fantasy of, 18; rhetoric of, 113; *see also* Presidents

Post, Jerrold M., 160*n*21

Poverty legislation, 70

Powell, Lewis, Jr., 63

Pregnancy, 18, 154*n*33

Prescott, 38

Presidential elections: 1896: 27; 1952: 49, 56–57, 95, 99; 1956: 58; 1960: 58, 92, 100, 106, 135; 1968: 100, 106; 1972: 18–19, 92, 97, 117, 131

Presidential office, 112, 121, 138

Presidents: at funeral, 2; at library opening, 94; mothers of, 143–44; "past baggage" of, 5; Saunders and, 98; self- protection of, 141

Press: blaming of, 131; castration fears and, 85; on double personality, 111; early coverage by, 52; East Room conference with, 122; Fund Crisis and, 57; fury at, 132; Guam conference with, 117; Hughes-O'Brien connection and, 135; "last" conference with, 92; phlebitis and, 105; suspected leaks to, 61; on Teapot Dome scandal, 36; wiretapping of, 101; women members of, 50

Price, Ray, 100

Price Administration, Office of, 50

Price controls, 62

Privacy, 29, 76

Profanity, 18, 77, 87, 147

Projection (psychology), 74

"Psychic truth," 5, 19; transference neurosis and, 10; Watergate and, 4, 134, 148–49

Psychosomatic illnesses, 86, 90, 102–4;

immortality and, 105; studies of, 163*n*55, 164*n*60

Public approval, 92–93, 148

Public debt, 62

Public figures, *see* Leaders

Public opinion, 57

Public speaking, *see* Debates; Speeches

Public welfare, 62–63, 113–15

"Pumpkin Papers," 54–55

Punishment, *see* Self-punishment

Quakers, 51, 70; dancing and, 41; death doctrine of, 39, 103; gambling and, 51; inner-light doctrine of, 29; kissing by, 49; F. Nixon and, 30; pacifism of, 50; religious disciplines of, 35–36; separation from, 31; of Whittier, 27- 28

Racism, 121; *see also* Desegregation

Radio broadcasts, 57, 73, 85

Rage, 102, 164*n*57; *see also* Narcissistic rage; Oral rage

Railroad engineering, 36

Rand, Ayn, 45

Rangell, Leo, 1, 89

Rappaport, David, 152*n*17

Reading, 35

Reagan, Ronald, 94, 113

Reagan administration, 114

Rebozo, Charles G. ("Bebe"), 79–80

Reductionism, 6–7

Regression (psychology), 138, 163*n*55, 164*nn*60, 61

Regulatory legislation, 62

Rehnquist, William, 63

Reintegration, *see* Integration (psychology)

Reparative leaders, 133

Repression (psychology), 8

Republican party: "bridge" in, 165*n*5; Carswell nomination and, 121; economic policy of, 62; Eisenhower-Nixon campaigns and, 56–57, 58; McCarthy and, 119; 1968 campaign and, 59–60; F. Nixon and, 27, 30; postwar dominance of, 52, 53; resignation deci-

sion and, 139; Rockefeller and, 93; Whittier members of, 51
"Rescuing" fantasy, 18, 37, 75, 154*n*34
Respiration, 102–3
Revolutionary War, 25
Rez, Elizabeth Guptill, 35
Rhodes, John, 139
Richardson, Elliot, 93, 99–100, 120, 124, 148
Richard the Lion-Hearted, King, 32
Roche, John P., 143
Rockefeller, Nelson, 93
Roe v. Wade case, 63
Rogers, William, 60, 61
Roosevelt, Eleanor, 49
Roosevelt, Franklin D., 3, 54, 62, 143
Roosevelt, Theodore, xi, 2, 149
Rosenberg, Ethel and Julius, 55
Ruckelshaus, William, 62
Rush, Kenneth, 124, 125–26
Ryan, Pat, *see* Nixon, Pat Ryan (wife)

Safire, William, 85, 122
Sanchez, Mario, 122
San Clemente, 136, 145
Saunders, Harold, 98
Schliemann, Heinrich, 153*n*20
School desegregation, 62, 63, 120–21, 122
Schulzinger, Robert D., 162*n*20
Schweiker, Richard, 113, 114, 121
Scott, Hugh, 139
Scottish-Irish immigrants, 25
Scowcroft, Brent, 105, 113, 123, 124
Secret bombing, *see under* Cambodia
Secret microfilms, 54–55
Secret Service, 106, 133
Secret tapes, *see* White House tapes
Self-control, 29, 77, 82
Self-esteem: courtship rebuff and, 48; feared loss of, 9, 105; fluctuation in, 88; maintenance of, 91; presidencies and, 92; *see also* Narcissism
Self-identity, 6, 8, 13–14, 25, 75; *see also* Identification with the aggressor; Separation-individuation

Self-punishment: by children, 9, 15; by RN, 42, 86, 87, 104, 129; by young man, 152*n*18
Self-reliance: in children, 13–14, 15, 33, 159*n*1; in early adulthood, 44; "glass bubble" and, 163*n*34; immortality and, 104; media strategy and, 100; mirrored reflection of, 78; "Pentagon Papers" and, 101
Separation-individuation, 81, 160*n*31
Serial murderers, 89–90
Sexuality, 14, 16, 17–18, 19–20, 160*n*17; *see also* Masturbation; Transsexuality
Sherwood, Georgia, 49
Siblings, 34, 97, 133
Sighing, 102
Silent Majority, 31, 60, 132
Silverman, Samuel, 104
Sleeping arrangements, 76
Sleeping problems, 98
Smith College, 50, 130
Social Darwinism, 24
Society of Knights, 41
Solomon Islands, 50–51
South America, 58, 76
Southern states: desegregation in, 62, 120–21, 122; Northern dichotomy from, 23, 130, 133; Supreme Court nominees from, 63, 121
South Pacific, 50–51
South Vietnam, 64, 116, 117
Souvenirs, 87
Soviet Embassy, 136
Soviet Union, 60; Afghanistan and, 94; arms treaty with, 124, 129, 132; atomic bomb of, 55; Berlin Agreement with, 125-26; Chinese differences with, 118, 132; détente with, 64, 124, 125; European trip and, 115; linkage policy and, 123; visit to, 103, 105
Speeches: on Cambodia (1970), 5, 130; castration fears and, 84-85; "Checkers" (1952), 57, 72, 80, 95, 146; on China, 127; on FAP, 114; farewell (1974), 106; first inau-

gural (1969), 120; "firsts" claimed in, 94; for library opening (1990), 94–95; press handling of, 100; on reorganization, 112; on resignation, 139; on Soviets, 124; for vice-presidential renomination (1956), 93; *see also* Debates

Spencer, Herbert, 24

Spitz, René, 164*n*57

Stage performances, *see* Debates; Theater

Stanford University, 43

State Department, 54, 98, 113, 127, 130

Statesmen, *see* Political leaders

Steinberg, Blema, 48, 50, 130–31

Stevenson, Adlai, 56, 58

Stone, Oliver, 3

"Strict constructionists," 63, 121

Student Bar Association (Duke University), 42

Student protesters, *see* Anti-war protesters

Sturgis, Frank, 135

Success avoidance, *see* Self-punishment

Summit III, 103

Sunkist lemon packing house, 31

"Supercabinet," 112

Superego, 8, 73–74, 154*n*28

Supreme Court, 63, 121

Survivor guilt, 80, 105

Symbiotic phase, 13, 153–54*n*25

Symbolism, 6

Taft, Robert, 56

Taft-Hartley Act, 53

Tähkä, Veikko, 163*n*55

Tape recordings, *see* White House tapes

Teapot Dome scandal, 36

Telephone wiretapping, *see* Wiretapping

Television broadcasts: 146; 1952: 57; 1960: 58, 73, 100; 1963: 59; 1971: 127

Theater, 45–46, 93

Time (periodical), 52, 54, 104

Trade embargo, 127

Transference, 109; *see also* Idealizing transference

Transference neurosis, 9–11, 19, 152*n*17, 152*n*18

Transsexuality, 154*n*34

Traumas: in adolescence, 17; crisis management and, 110; in mother-child relationship, 159*n*1; of RN, 74, 138; of sibling birth, 34; *see also* Crises; "Dangerous" events

Trenton, Battle of, 25

Truman, Bess, 49, 50

Truman, Harry S., 54

"The Trysting Place" (play), 40

"20–30" Club, 44, 92

Unconscious fantasies, *see* Dreams; Fantasies

United Nations, 54

University of Southern California, 46, 48

Van Drehle, David, 3

Vice-presidential elections, *see* Presidential elections

Vietnamization, 64, 116, 117

Vietnam War: Civil War and, 122; economic impact of, 62, 132; European visit and, 115–16; in first term, 63–64, 116–17; LBJ and, 59, 60, 63, 95, 115, 116; linkage policy and, 123; 1970 speech on, 85; origins of, 65, 132; *see also* Anti-war protesters

Violin playing, 35

Volkan, Vam_k D., 98, 162*n*11, 163*n*34; *The Immortal Atatürk*, 7, 11, 152*n*19, 162*n*32; *Linking Objects and Linking Phenomena*, 82; *The Need to Have Enemies and Allies*, 167*n*9; *Six Steps in the Treatment of Borderline Personality Organization*, 152–53*n*19; *Spektrum des Narziβmus*, 161*n*4; *What Do You Get When You Cross a Dandelion with a Rose?*, 152*n*18

Voorhis, Jerry, 51–52, 55, 56

Wadsworth, Sarah Ann, 25, 26
Wage controls, 62
Wallace, George, 60, 106
War of Independence, 25
Warren, Earl, 63
Washington, George, 25, 112
Watergate Affair, 3, 4, 134–36; antecedents of, 65; castration fears and, 85; "CIA Trap Theory" on, 136–37; comeback from, 145; firings and, 84; Kutler on, 167n21; lying about, 95; main players in, 60–61; "negative therapeutic reaction" and, 86; 1972 election and, 131; "psychic truth" of, 4, 148–49; psychosomatic illness and, 103; Rangell on, 1; see also White House tapes
Weinberger, Casper, 83
Welch, Ola Florence, 45, 46, 48, 74
Welfare reform, 62–63, 113–15
West, Jessamyn, 155n13
West Berlin, 125, 126
Western powers, 115, 125, 129
West Germany, 125, 126
White, Theodore, 98
White House Lincoln Sitting Room, 122
White House Press Room, 85
White House tapes: Butterfield and, 61; installation of, 132; narcissism and, 95–96; retention of, 19, 77; Senate request for, 103
Whittier, John Greenleaf, 28–29
Whittier (Calif.): auto trips to, 48; family return to, 36; law practice in, 43–44; Quaker life in, 27–28; sleeping arrangements in, 76; theater in, 45–46, 93; Wills on, 30
Whittier College: football at, 42, 79, 86; H. Nixon at, 30; RN at, 38–

39, 40–42, 44–45, 93; trust fund at, 29, 38
Whittier College Alumni Association, 44
Whittier College Board of Trustees, 44, 51
Whittier College Joint Council of Control, 41
Whittier Union High School, 29–30, 38, 46, 72–73, 92
Wicker, Tom, 76
Will (testament), 96
Wills, Garry, 30, 147, 155nn7, 15
Wilson, C. Phillip, 163n55
Wingert and Bewley (firm), 43–44, 49, 119
Winnicott, Donald, 32, 71, 153n23
Wiretapping, 133; extension of, 101; foreign policy leaks and, 65; J. E. Hoover and, 61; Huston Plan on, 138; of O'Brien office, 135; of Soviet Embassy, 136
Women: indiscriminate relationships with, 154n33; rivalry between, 145–46; RN and, 20, 44–45, 49, 50, 74–75; see also First Ladies; Mother figures
Woodward, Bob, 86, 87
Woollcott, Alexander, 46
"Workfare," 114
World War II, 50–51
Wray, Herton, 72

Yale University, 38, 51
Yalta Conference, 54
Yeltsin, Boris, 1
Yorba Linda, 2, 31, 70, 76, 94

Zhirinovsky, Vladimir, 1, 82, 146–47
Zhou Enlai, 127